DEVELOPING EXPRESSION IN BRASS PERFORMANCE AND TEACHING

Developing Expression in Brass Performance and Teaching helps university music teachers, high school band directors, private teachers, and students develop a vibrant and flexible approach to brass teaching and performance that keeps musical expression central to the learning process. Strategies for teaching both group and applied lessons will help instructors develop more expressive use of articulation, flexibility in sound production, and how to play with better intonation.

The author shares strategies from today's best brass instrument performers and teachers for developing creativity and making musical expression central to practicing and performing. These concepts presented are taken from over thirty years of experience with musicians like Wynton Marsalis, Barbara Butler, Charles Geyer, Donald Hunsberger, Leonard Candelaria, John Haynie, Bryan Goff, members of the Chicago Symphony and New York Philharmonic and from leading music schools such as the Eastman School of Music, The University of North Texas and The Florida State University.

The combination of philosophy, pedagogy, and common sense methods for learning will ignite both musicians and budding musicians to inspired teaching and playing.

Gregory R. Jones is the Chair of the Department of Music at Indiana University–Purdue University Fort Wayne, following twenty-eight years as trumpet professor and conductor of the brass choir at Truman State University.

DEVELOPING EXPRESSION IN BRASS PERFORMANCE AND TEACHING

Gregory R. Jones

Chair, Department of Music, Indiana University–
Purdue University Fort Wayne (IPFW)

Routledge
Taylor & Francis Group

NEW YORK AND LONDON

First published 2016
by Routledge
711 Third Avenue, New York, NY 10017

and by Routledge
2 Park Square, Milton Park, Abingdon, Oxon, OX14 4RN

Routledge is an imprint of the Taylor & Francis Group, an informa business

Library of Congress Cataloging-in-Publication Data
Jones, Gregory R., author.
 Developing expression in brass performance and teaching / Gregory R. Jones.
   pages cm
 Includes bibliographical references and index.
 1. Brass instruments—Instruction and study.   I. Title.
 MT418.J66 2016
 788.9'143071—dc23
 2015035057

ISBN: 978-1-138-92900-5 (hbk)
ISBN: 978-1-138-92901-2 (pbk)
ISBN: 978-1-315-68145-0 (ebk)

Typeset in Baskerville
by Apex CoVantage, LLC

Senior Editor: Constance Ditzel
Senior Editorial Assistant: Aurora Montgomery
Production Editor: Sioned Jones
Marketing Manager: Amy Langlais
Copy Editor: Pam Schroeder
Proofreader: Amanda Wolfe
Cover Design: Mathew Willis

Printed by CPI on sustainably sourced paper

CONTENTS

FIGURES

PREFACE

Success as a performer and teacher starts with a love for music and a great desire to express your emotions using the instrument as your musical outlet. The ideas presented here are intended to provide you with some general concepts and philosophies as well as detailed techniques to improve both practice and inspired performances. Although music traditionally has been a master/apprentice endeavor, I hope that you will not abandon logic, common sense, and those thought processes that serve you so well in other aspects of life. To attain a high level of musicianship, you will need great discipline, organization, and communication skills to complement a passion for music and the desire to express the human condition.

The concepts presented here grow from the wisdom of my trumpet teachers: Barbara Butler and Charles Geyer at the Eastman School of Music, Leonard Candelaria and John Haynie at the University of North Texas, Bryan Goff at Florida State University, and Joe Murat in Orlando, Florida. These wonderful people, along with countless brass teachers and performers, ensemble directors, academic professors, and colleagues, all have contributed to these ideas. At times I will try to credit individuals for great ideas, but honestly, it becomes impossible to know exactly where all these concepts have originated. I do know that music, like all other learning, is certainly the cumulative exposure to the work of others, and my teaching, like others, is a unique interpretation of all I have experienced. I hope you can use some of these concepts to help your students enjoy the beauty of music and share it with others.

Dr. Gregory Jones
Fort Wayne, Indiana 2015

ACKNOWLEDGMENTS

I learned early in my music career that achieving success always requires the consistent help of teachers, friends, and family. My entire life was changed when a student teacher from Florida State University, Joseph Wise, urged my parents and me to consider the university rather than the army for my career. His dedication to my future put me, and others in a family whose culture had never included higher education, on a different path. It is important to remember how teachers of all types can be positive forces for change in the lives of their students.

My chances for a successful career, though, really started much earlier because my parents, Roy and Nancy Jones, instilled in me an appreciation for disciplined hard work, loyalty, and generosity. These ideals continue to guide me as I continue down my path in music, and I believe they are essential for all of us to constantly remember. I am very proud that our son, Derek P. Jones, was able to contribute the photographs and drawings found in this book. His dedication to his art is inspiring to me, and he, like so many of our students, gives me great confidence and optimism for our future as a society.

Thanks to those students who have taught me so much in my career. I appreciate Eian Zellner and Emily Killian for posing for these photos. I am truly thankful for all the wonderful collaborations with young people like them during my years in education. It is exciting to know there are many more adventures coming in the future! A special thanks to Truman State University in Kirksville, Missouri, which supported this written effort and also allowed me to serve its fine students for 28 years.

Finally, I am blessed with the love and patience of my wife, Margo, who has supported and, at times, endured my busy life in our art. Her steadfast patience and advice helps me keep grounded in this crazy and wonderful life.

Dr. Gregory Jones
Fort Wayne, Indiana 2015

1

THE CREATIVE TEACHER
AND STUDENT

"Keep away from people who try to belittle your ambi-
tions. Small people always do that, but the really great
make you feel that you, too, can become great."

Mark Twain

Music is truly a special art that offers us all the opportunity to express emotions with
infinite and individual combinations of sounds. From our earliest moments in life, we
hear and react to the feelings that different musical sounds can stir in us. Those of us
who devote our lives to teaching and playing music do so because we are called to it.
It is usually not only because we are good at it but also because we cannot imagine
our lives doing anything else. Keeping this love of the art foremost in our work is
vital to ensure our music is worth listening to and also to help the next generation of
musicians find their voices as well. Like all love affairs, the pursuit of music includes
a constant roller coaster ride of frustration and failure that brings along joy and
success. If we can keep the powerful connection between music and our emotions
central to our teaching and learning of the art, we can easily weather the challenges
and continue to grow as musicians. As teachers, we always must remind ourselves
of the emotional attachment that first drew all of us to the art as we share it with
our students.

A constant creative process is central to high-level music making; it must be developed from the earliest ages and always remain at the center of our playing and
teaching. Creative thinking involves problem solving and synthesis as each player
confronts and addresses technical challenges and physical conditions that can limit
his or her growth. It also involves the use of imaginative storytelling as we learn to
use our music as an expression of our lives and with their individual richness. Great
musicians find their path to success through these processes with the caring guidance
of others. Teaching music must strike the right balance between creating structured
work for technical mastery while also encouraging students to develop their own
expressive voices as players. If this balance is well maintained in our teaching, the
outcome will be a truly unique and special musician.

It is important for teachers to keep in mind that all students are different, and the triggers that will motivate them are also unique. Whereas we strive to develop similar capabilities in students, we always must remember that helping each student discover his or her inner artist is truly an individual path. Although teachers can do much to enrich the level of technical skill, the growth of the artistic storyteller is a fragile process that teachers can nurture but not control. In my years of teaching, I have seen too many skilled brass players whose personal artistry was very low or nonexistent. As most people tend to teach as they were taught, it soon became clear to me that these players missed out on the most important part of becoming a musician. Although they can negotiate the physical needs of playing a brass instrument and can use metronomes, tuners, and other devices to reach a high level of execution, the essential ingredient of expression is missing. For this reason, their performances are stale and somewhat lifeless compared to players whose use of technique is all guided by a higher order of musical imagery.

Although being systematic in teaching music is very inviting as we begin working with large numbers of students, we must be cautious of missing those moments that require more individualized treatment. Daniel Barenboim, the famous conductor and pianist, in his book *Music Quickens Time,* recalls the philosophy of Baruch Spinoza as he discusses the relationship between free and creative thinking with systematized behavior or ideology. He argues that *any* system for teaching or learning music applied equally to all students instantly begins to limit creative thought.[1] Although these concerns were first directed toward religious and philosophical systems, it is also valuable to remember them as we consider our approach to teaching music. In systematizing our teaching processes, we can certainly lose sight of how students learn differently and at varied paces. A teaching system that eliminates the need for constant questioning easily can become the enemy of creative thinking. Once we limit freedom of thought to a prescribed matrix, we already are ceding much of the great potential for the free expression of ideas.

Although the art of music can inspire amazing creativity and expression, it is important to identify and foster those behaviors that can best encourage this development throughout the learning process. Musial creativity in our field is most often referenced when describing composers as the creators of music rather than performers who reimagine their works. In this book I would like to offer some ideas for developing creative thought in teaching and performing as a specific, often overlooked process in music learning. Developing creative playing on brass instruments is, of course, dependent on the physical abilities of players and the characteristics of their instruments. Without a properly developed embouchure, expressive playing can be very limited if students cannot control the precise, athletic muscle movement required. Striking the right balance in developing the strength and agility to play these instruments, along with the inspiration for what playing expresses, requires that we continually connect technical development to musical expression. Forging this connection begins when students can establish expressive sounds in their imaginations through extensive listening that will serve as models to guide their growth.

In the master apprentice world of private teaching, there should be a progression from a mostly imitative learning environment to one that allows for greater individuality of expression. The hero worship that exists in music often blurs the development of individuality in young players as they are driven to copy their teachers and other models. Teachers always should work to broaden this narrow approach to playing, especially when considering interpretation and expressing music. Although the *hero teacher* may have a convincing musical rendition of a musical composition, he or she must share with students the possibilities and rationale for different interpretations as well.

As brass players, our early years are filled with ensemble playing in bands, orchestras, and jazz ensembles. These groups are rehearsed and led by conductors who hopefully express ideas through their body movements, facial expressions, and also with some verbal explanation that shares what feelings the music is supposed to convey. This shared expression of feelings is very impactful on ensemble players, and it is the reason most players decide to pursue music study after high school. Sometimes, however, players in these ensembles do not have enough motivation or opportunity to develop their own musical ideas and voices apart from this leadership. It is a big leap from playing what someone else wants musically and following directions to making our own decisions about what music means and how it should be played. To embrace this individuality, young players need to be offered and also accept the responsibility and freedom that comes with artistic expression. Teachers also need to accept new interpretations and musical ideas when plausible rather than simply asking their students to copy their approach. There always should be more than one way to play everything. If that is not the case, if musical individuality is not an essential part of playing an instrument, the motivation to play is changed fundamentally from an art to a lower level of simple copying.

Recognizing Personalities: Laborers and Professionals

To me there are basically two types of personalities I have found in my years of teaching and playing. These two personality types exist not just in music but also in all career fields and endeavors. The first personality type I will describe are the *laborers*. A laborer is person who really wants and needs to be told what to do, when to do it, and when it is done. Despite the title, they do not always engage in physical labor, and they can be present in all types of environments, including playing and teaching music. They might be hard workers, but they prefer to adopt a simplistic approach to their work. They are very oriented toward goals set by others and appreciate knowing from others when their work is *done,* so they can totally devote free time to other pursuits apart from their work. They tend to be most excited by nonwork activities, confident that others are attending the ever-present concerns of their workplace and profession.

The other personality type I refer to as *professionals.* These people prefer not to be told what to do and are more likely to decide on their own when to work, what work they should do, and when it is done satisfactorily, so they can move on to another project. They continue to consider their work outside prescribed work hours as they constantly strive toward their self-set goals and limitless boundaries. This personality type doesn't require much if any supervision and, if given support and freedom in the workplace, will normally accomplish great successes.

In the music profession, as in all professions, there are teachers and students of both personality types, though I find that most usually want to self-identify as a professional when asked. Despite placement in professional positions, I have observed many teachers and players who consistently operate as *laborers* because they always want to know what they *have* to do to fulfill the requirements of their job and how much time they need to devote to it. As teachers they prefer to avoid pondering about their students and musical ideas outside of teaching and tend also to target minimum, manageable requirements as they go about their work.

In orchestras I also see the laborer/professional dichotomy in *professional performers.* As labor unions have developed in the artistic workplace, their impact on professional music sometimes invites members of these organizations to adopt many of the behaviors of blue-collar *laborers* despite their elevated status in the arts world. Many labor-oriented orchestral musicians are most comfortable knowing what to play, when to play it, and exactly when the service is completed. They have conductors, music directors, and many recordings to tell them how to play, and for some, this allows for them to think only about the orchestra during prescribed rehearsals and performances. There are also true *professionals* in the orchestra who, on the other hand, are always concerned with the whole group and their role in making it a better ensemble. Like the music director, they think about their playing in relationship to others outside of required services and tend to be involved heavily with outside chamber, solo playing, and also teaching. It is not surprising that the best orchestras have a higher percentage of professionals to laborers than those groups that are less successful. As in all groups of workers, there are those who truly understand the value of self-direction and leadership and others who wish to follow and do the minimum.

These personality types develop early and can be seen in how students approach playing and practicing their instruments. Some students only play in ensemble rehearsal, and their individual practice is something that happens only when evaluations are looming and involves set technical goals. There are also students, however, who try to learn new musical works without being assigned and develop expressive ideas through their experiences listening and creating music outside of prescribed activities.

It is not surprising then that these two personality types influence how music is taught and learned. Laborers tend to seek out more prescribed practice directions as students and also offer less opportunity for individual creativity as teachers. Professionals stretch the boundaries even as students and work to allow their students more ownership over their learning when they are in the role of teacher. Professional-minded students are more likely to question and perhaps even challenge their teachers just as professional-minded teachers and performers are more apt to question and challenge administrators and conductors. A mind that questions the status quo is a key ingredient in a great musician, and as teachers we must be ready to entertain this mind-set rather than dismissing interpretive concerns or opposing musical ideas. Likewise, administrators and other leaders also need to welcome the questioning and challenges of their workers as characteristics of a *professional* mind-set, understanding the great potential these workers have for the future of the organization and the art.

Of course, it is worth remembering that most teachers tend to teach in the manner that they were taught. Most high-level teachers have achieved good success as players, and they feel that the path they took also can lead others to similar results. With some broad teaching experience though, they soon realize that students have vastly different needs from each other and also from the challenges the teacher experienced as a student. In my many years of teaching, I have learned much about myself through teaching students of many ages and ability levels. Requiring all of my students to do exactly what I did in the order and time line that I followed as a student is not practical or efficient for most of them.

The biggest fear I have as a teacher is that I will *underestimate* the abilities of my student. What if I have them follow my same path and time line that I did, but they actually could be a much better player than me? What if they could learn much faster than I did at their age? These thoughts compel me to offer them every opportunity to take more ownership over their playing and their expression of music. Of course, not all students are ready to take this bold step, but it is important for them to have the freedom and safe environment to express their individuality and ideas in their playing from an early age. This involves questioning and challenging, and we should welcome these behaviors as signs they are on the right path to taking ownership over what they are doing musically.

In fact, I even have found that students actually can teach their teachers something every single day. I constantly learn from my students in the private studio and ensemble rehearsal every time we get together. When students are encouraged to solve their own playing problems, they can come up with some truly revolutionary ideas. Especially when students struggle with a part of their playing that was not a struggle for their teacher, they can share their processes of finding solutions to these problems in a manner that informs others, including their teacher. In this way, they can enrich the understanding of the teacher, resulting in more strategies for future students who have similar challenges. If students really are aware of the sounds they wish to make but experience technical obstacles, the teacher always can offer ideas for working out these challenges and model them with playing demonstrations. It is the awareness of the student, however, that is the magic ingredient in their ability to improve their playing. The teacher telling the student what is wrong and what needs to change is only the first step in the process. The greatest learning occurs when students have a clear idea of their desired sound, and armed with that awareness, they will strive to discover what needs to be changed in their playing to realize it. The fostering of this awareness should be the most important goal in teaching.

Charlie Geyer often says that you only need two characteristics to be a great teacher. First, you must be *honest* with yourself and your students about all things. And second, you need to truly *care* for your students and their futures. Although this seems obvious and simple, teaching music well requires us to be the *professional* rather than the *laborer*. That applies to teaching ourselves as well as our teaching of others. Being truly honest about our own playing and the work of our students is often a challenge. It means sharing failures and weaknesses openly and often along with successes and strengths. In modeling this behavior, we can get the maximum benefit from the master/apprentice culture as our students will find the courage and self-direction to be honest about their work and also develop the motivation to strive for improvement. When musicians discover the potential for self-teaching and expression, they can achieve great artistic levels. It is important that teachers find the proper balance between systematized approaches and individual needs to create the best environment for these younger players. As we are also our own most important teacher, we must also find this balance as we manage our playing. You will find that it is a constant challenge to strike the right balance, and you certainly will change tactics as you evaluate your progress. This book is intended to offer you some ideas for changing tactics as you develop the duality of being an artist brass player balancing physical development and creative expression.

Exercises

- Take a moment to reflect on the first time that you remember feeling musically expressive while playing your instrument. What piece were you playing? Were you in an ensemble? Can you remember the emotions you were feeling? Be sure to relay this story to your students, and ask them about the feelings they have while playing. Perhaps it can result in a brief game of trying to express different emotions on the instrument as suggested by each other!

- Encourage your students, on their own, to find a new piece of music and prepare it for the next lesson. Tell them you want them to tell a story with their playing and relate that story to you. After the performance in the next lesson, ask them how it was different than preparing something that you had assigned them to learn and in the manner you chose it to be played. Discuss the differences between the professional and the laborer with them, and encourage them to take more ownership over their playing.

Note

1 Daniel Barenboim, *Music Quickens Time* (New York: Verso Books, 2008), 37–8.

2

THE ATHLETE AND THE ARTIST

"Music requires the most awesome techniques available to
bring out the emotion and beauty of each phrase."
Barbara Butler
Eastman School of Music

Barbara Butler, my major professor while at the Eastman School of Music, referred
to the two dimensions of a successful brass performer as the *poet* and the *athlete*. She
argues that without athletic ability, artistic ideas cannot be well expressed and also
that athletic prowess on a brass instrument without artistic direction is empty and
unfulfilling. In my teaching I also stress these two sides of playing with the labels of
athlete and *artist*. From beginning music study, it is vital that teaching and learning
include ideas for ensuring that both of these hemispheres are developed in players of
all ages. In this first section of the book, we will examine the building of athleticism
with basic technical development on brass instruments. In later chapters we will offer
ideas for developing the artistic side of playing through creative experimentation,
imagery, and musical planning.

Brass players have always felt a kinship with athletes because, really, our lives are
very similar. Even the most famous and accomplished athlete must continue to work
out regularly with organized goals to stay successful as they perform under pressure
in front of large audiences. When athletes lose their dedication to these ideals, their
performance levels drop, and they lose the chance to participate. The same is true
for musicians. To participate in musical ventures at the highest levels, we must understand that long-term commitment and tough discipline are vital. Oddly, I have found
that sometimes it is the more intelligent students who might feel that they can be successful without adhering to these principles. In other academic pursuits, especially
while in high school, they were able to achieve high grades easily without the rigor
of daily study due to a good memory and high-level cognitive ability. Unfortunately,
these gifts offer no shortcuts in developing physical playing ability through long-term
conditioning. Without such dedicated practice, these students often become non-
athletic artists. They can conceptualize great music but are unable to make it happen
on their instruments because they are unwilling to develop their physical abilities

in a consistent manner. Likewise, students who love simply to play high notes, fast notes, or loud passages outside an artistic framework are really nonartistic athletes. Although we may respect the athletic abilities of these players, without artistic direction, they will never reach more sophisticated levels of music making.

Athletic conditioning on brass instruments improves very gradually and over long periods of time. Great athletes build strength and ability in an organized and detailed manner, keeping track of their progress with information like the amount of weight and number of repetitions. Great brass players also need to have a routine that is organized similarly. Record keeping of some manner is needed to be the most successful. Some of this is done mentally, but keeping a log of abilities is much more productive than simply trying to remember the details of each practice session. Think about your playing in some very basic terms, and record where you are now in these areas of brass athleticism.

Mouthpiece range
Instrument range
Scales and technical ability in all keys
Ability to attack in various ranges and dynamics
Sustained single, double, and triple tonguing tempi
Endurance in terms of consistent tone production in long tones or lyrical passages
Endurance in terms of length of playing session
Speed of lip slurs in various ranges and also dynamics
Keys in which you can transpose well
Keys in which you can sight-read well

Knowing what you accomplished in a previous practice session or lesson in a detailed way helps you maximize your next session. Athletes and their coaches keep close records of their progress with performance scores. Each time they work, they try to increase efficiency, strength, and speed, often measured in small amounts of weight and time. Knowing as a musician that you increased your speed by just five clicks of the metronome or that you increased your range by one half step is actually a great achievement. If you can keep track of these small improvements, you can see your growth over time, and this will motivate further work and offer warranted feelings of accomplishment.

Often musicians are adverse to the concept of using numbers to evaluate achievement, but creating a numeric system within your own practice and teaching is an important way to both assess where you are in your playing and also chart a path for improvement. Numbers might translate to exact pitches in terms of range, tempi in terms of technical work, dynamic levels, or even time spent playing or holding onto a long tone. With my students, I ask them to keep a small notebook that will fit in their instrument case, so it is always with them for all practice and playing events.

THE ATHLETE AND THE ARTIST

Teachers must be creative in encouraging students to rate their playing and record it in some manner. With all the technological benefits we have at our disposal, such as smartphone apps and computer programs, this can be tailored to the age group and more appealing to the eyes and ears than simply keeping a notebook.

I also believe that practicing is a matter of percentages. Although it is unlikely that we can experience total efficiency in all aspects of playing every day, it comes down to the percentage of your playing that is efficient and honest each day. The higher the percentage of your overall playing that is soft, the more likely you will develop and maintain that skill. A higher percentage of high-register playing, done correctly, will lead to more skill and control in this range. I know this all sounds simplistic, but often players are not aware of how much time they actually spend in different areas of their playing. For example, in the case of high-register development in young players, we easily can see how this happens. All trumpet players want to increase their ranges in high school. It is one of the means by which they earn opportunity and praise. When you actually examine how they approach the upper register, however, you can easily see the obstacles to their improvement because they have not developed a logical course of range practice that plans for gaining in small increments over longer periods of time.

When asked about organized practice with controlled patterns like scales and arpeggios, most students admit that they usually do not practice regularly in the upper register, keeping track of their progress. Although they might be aware that excessive mouthpiece pressure is limiting the physical ability of their lips to gain the strength they need to play higher notes with control, they admit that they do not ensure less pressure by playing with the mouthpiece alone or in an efficient manner on the instrument. What we often find is that all the notes at or near the top of the range are played in only ensemble settings, with excessive mouthpiece pressure and overuse of air. As a result, their percentage of efficient practice in this area of playing is actually very low, and so is their growth. Developing the athletic side of playing requires us to be logical and organized in our approach, so keeping track of small increments of progress over long periods of time will be needed to maximize growth.

As we grow as players, our desires to be expressive musicians shape the athleticism we need to develop and maintain. The technical skill levels of brass players continue to grow because the demand of our music increases. Individual musicians must first know precisely what they can do, know what they want to be able to do, and finally chart their courses for getting there. There are really no limits to the athleticism you should strive to develop. The more you can do on your instrument, the more tools you have to express a wider variety of colors and sounds to your audience. With a vision for what you want to express and the tools to realize that vision, great music is usually the result.

10

Exercises

- Start your process of learning a new piece of music by contemplating it in terms of technique development and the music expression of telling a story. Consider how you can combine the process of practicing the music, even in small pieces, with this dual approach and unified goal.
- Make a list of five of the recorded musical performances that you like the most and that you listen to most often. Take a moment to consider why these exact renditions of these pieces have made such a strong impression. Try listening to other recordings of the same works by different performers. What is it that makes your *favorites* so uniquely attractive?

3

THE BRASS EMBOUCHURE

"Whose lips are these and what are they doing on my face?"
William Scharnberg, Horn Professor
The University of North Texas

A brass embouchure develops slowly over several years as muscles strengthen and gain memory of their role in creating a consistent formation of the lips paired with a reliable placement of the mouthpiece. This develops from the very first day of playing. It is, of course, very important that players are matched up with brass instruments that best suit the natural shape of their lips and teeth because a mismatch will ultimately limit the their progress. This is especially true with smaller mouthpiece brass instruments like the trumpet and horn. Because of the need for efficient lip movement within the confines of a smaller mouthpiece rim diameter, there is less room for error, and it is no surprise that these players have the biggest challenges in terms of embouchure formation and consistency.

My experience as an applied teacher and band director demonstrated over and over again the benefits from evaluating beginning musicians on several instruments to best pair their physical attributes with the demands of the instrument. During this process it is best to have students buzz their lips together to assess the alignment of the teeth and lips. Then give them the opportunity to buzz several mouthpieces to see if they can transfer the buzzing lips to the defined lip area governed by inner rim diameters. By taking the time to have students make sounds on mouthpieces and several instruments, it is likely that you will find the combination of instrument and embouchure that yields a productive sound immediately. Once this ideal is discovered, it is then up to the persuasive skill of the music teacher to convince the beginner and his or her parents of the wisdom in choosing that instrument. With the likelihood of greater, more rapid progress, these early negotiations can prevent bigger embouchure issues in the future that often lead to players quitting music because their physicality is limiting their progress.

In basic terms, the brass embouchure should first focus on the muscles at the corners of the embouchure. By keeping these corners firm throughout playing, beginners will establish a consistent and reliable setting that will yield a reliable tone and help build endurance and flexibility quickly. Concentrate on the consonant sound *mm* as they form their embouchures, and keep this physical formation consistently regardless of the register. If players lose these firm, muscular corners while playing, they still can develop manners of playing that can produce the notes in a beginning range but might limit more advanced development later. A less efficient smile formation is one example of a manner of playing that pulls the lips tighter and thus moves the embouchure corners upward. This will lead to a thin sound and less endurance because the lips are overly stretched horizontally at all times, leaving less muscle tissue to operate within the rim boundaries of the mouthpiece. Another less efficient embouchure involves over puckering the lips in the manner of a very firm kissing formation. This formation attempts to place too much lip muscle tissue inside the mouthpiece rim and results in low flexibility and a very hard and stiff sound. Both of these embouchures easily can be avoided with concentration on the *mm* formation as you cannot easily migrate to the smile or pucker formation while creating it.

Mouthpiece Placement

Everyone has differently shaped teeth lying beneath differently shaped lips. Brass mouthpieces need to establish three points of contact between the rim of the mouthpiece and the teeth underneath the lips to create stability and reduce the chance of the mouthpiece rocking back and forth on the embouchure. It has been my experience that students will first place the mouthpiece on their lips and teeth where is it most comfortable for them. Mouthpiece placement, along with minor adjustments in lip alignment, is, of course, impacted by formations in the underlying teeth. Generally, the three-legged positioning of the mouthpiece will find the exact places on the upper and lower teeth that allow comfort and consistency. If a student, for instance, has one front tooth that is crooked or protrudes forward from the others, it will have an impact on where that player places the mouthpiece.

Because the teeth are so important to the brass embouchure, it is important to keep in mind that young students generally lose their baby teeth, which are replaced by adult teeth in about the 10th to 12th year. If they start on an instrument prior to this age, be prepared for some setbacks and disruptions during this changeover process as the underlying size and formation of teeth change. The addition of braces also creates new contours underneath the embouchure and thus may pose many challenges to young players. Again, due to the smaller mouthpiece with more contact on the teeth and not the gums, trumpet and horn players will be impacted more by changing teeth and the presence of braces.

Another important component of an efficient embouchure is the control of the muscles that surround the formed embouchure and keeping the chin from bunching upward and the cheeks from puffing outward. A chin that bunches upward often can be a sign that the lower jaw needs to protrude a bit further forward to better line up the lips and teeth. If you see this in players, encourage them to eliminate this bunching effect by concentrating on a more pointed chin by pushing the lower jaw forward. Use a mirror to monitor this and other visible indicators of embouchure function. Puffing cheeks, another sign of weakness in embouchure corners, can be remedied easily by concentrating on the corners of the embouchure and the *mm* formation already mentioned. To be able to puff your cheeks, you need to relax some of the tension in these corners, and so seeing your cheeks puff is a sign that you need to focus on more corner tension.

Occasionally students will have weak facial muscles surrounding the embouchure, and this might allow air pockets to form between the teeth and gums and facial tissues while playing. This can limit productivity of the embouchure and impact tone production, so it is important also to identify and correct these weaknesses early in the development of young players. All of these embouchure variations can be identified both by differences in tone color and also through observation. For this reason, it is important to encourage some daily practice while looking in the mirror to reinforce the best playing habits because the ability to fully recognize poor formations by sound only takes many years to develop. For this reason, looking in a mirror can help players connect physical movements to resulting sounds. To maximize this observation, it helps if players can memorize some basic passages or patterns for use in mirror playing because it will allow them to train their total focus on playing and embouchure movement as they visually study themselves. Memorization of exercises is especially vital for young students as it allows them to focus on their tone productions aurally and visually as they develop the ability to hear and see when it is at its most efficient and also when it is not.

Upstream/Downstream and Pivoting

The alignment of the teeth when the mouth is closed, for most players, results in an overbite with the top teeth lying in front of the bottom row. Because of this natural placement of the teeth, the top lip also has a tendency to lie slightly in front of the bottom lip when the lips are placed together. If this relationship remains the same while playing a brass instrument, the result will be a downstream flow of the air resulting from the path created by the teeth and lips. For many of these players, a slight movement of the lower jaw forward will better align the teeth and lips, offering a more productive vibration between the lips and a more direct airstream into the mouthpiece. You can feel this redirection of the airstream if you place your hand in front of your embouchure and move your lower jaw forward and backward while blowing air (see Fig. 3.1). You will see that you can direct the air up into a straight trajectory and even upward if you extend the jaw as far forward as possible.

Figure 3.1 Hand to demonstrate airstream direction

For those players with an underbite when they close their mouths, the lower teeth and lips lie in front of the upper teeth and lip, and the air is directed upward due to this different pathway. These players tend to be upstream players, and they might consider pulling the lower jaw inward to facilitate a more direct path of the air and a more efficient vibration between the lips.

Helping beginners to understand these physical relationships can assist them in making the small adjustments in jaw position needed for success in earlier stages of playing. This will help them reinforce more productive teeth/lip alignment immediately, and they will be able to adopt the alignment easily and naturally after only a short time. Begin by having them blow the air into their hands as already mentioned, and also have them learn to buzz their lips together by finding the correct jaw position for their physical makeup.

Mouthpiece Placement

Placement of the mouthpiece is also directly related to the formation of lips and teeth and is most often initially in a spot where the player feels the greatest comfort. Again, smaller mouthpieces usually result in the most placement challenges because they have a smaller margin for error and demand greater lip strength and flexibility concentrated in a smaller physical area. There are generally accepted placement guidelines that were first introduced by Philip Farkas in *The Art of Brass Playing* that can help you consider the productivity of mouthpiece placement.[1]

Tuba, trombone, euphonium, and horn placement generally result in a two-thirds upper lip and one-third lower lip relationship inside the inner rim of the mouthpiece. Trumpet embouchures generally are suggested to be equal halves upper and lower lip. Trombone, euphonium, and tuba mouthpiece placement is a natural accommodation of the shape of the gums and teeth with the bigger mouthpiece size. Especially with smaller and younger beginners, this combination often determines placement and limits options. The smaller horn and trumpet mouthpiece, however, can be placed in a variety of spots even with young players, so it is not surprising that embouchure problems are also more often seen with players of these instruments.

It is important to understand that it is the upper lip that initiates the buzzing process, while the lower lip buzzes sympathetically to it. Because of this functional relationship, mouthpiece placement that is too low on the upper lip can unduly limit its ability to vibrate and result in a deader sound with reduced range, endurance, and flexibility. You can demonstrate how mouthpiece placement creates this limitation by rolling a pencil horizontally from the bottom of your nose downward while buzzing your lips. You will notice that as you reach the top boundary of the lip muscle and skin, the buzz will be less vigorous and then eventually stop (see Fig. 3.2). Like the

Figure 3.2 Using a pencil to define the boundary of top buzzing lip

pressure placed on the lip between the pencil and the teeth, the mouthpiece rim also will limit and even stop the vibration of the lip if it is placed too low on the top lip.

The best placement of the brass mouthpiece is one that allows for both lips to have an active role in the creation of sound vibration with unobstructed motion. For this reason, the inner rim of the mouthpiece should lie on the outside of the boundary line between the lip muscle and surrounding skin. It is also important to consider the immense variety of lip size and formation among the population. Larger, fuller lips and those with dramatic formations on the upper lip can pose problems for brass players, especially those on the smaller mouthpiece instruments. Examining potential for mouthpiece placement should be part of the evaluation of beginners already mentioned.

Lip Compression and Mouthpiece Pressure

As the lips change lip compression, or the strength with which the two lips push against each other to offer more resistance to the airflow, they do not simply press more or less firmly together but also pull inward slightly as compression increases and protrude forward slightly during decreases in this compression. Excessive mouthpiece pressure in any register can interfere with this back-and-forth movement of the lips and restrict both flexibility and the production of an efficient sound as we change register. Oftentimes mouthpiece pressure increases when playing higher and traps the lips in a more inward position. When the player attempts to return to lower parts of the range, the inability of the lips to move forward as they reduce compression causes interruptions in the quality of the tone and may even result in a loss of sound production. Similarly, players actually can use too much mouthpiece pressure in the lower register as well, especially at louder volumes. When this occurs, tone quality suffers when attempting to return to higher ranges because the lips are unable to move inward as they attempt to increase compression. In general, the use of too much mouthpiece pressure traps the lips in one fixed position and reduces their ability to make the small movements needed to ensure consistent tone quality when changing register.

Often when players trap their lips with too much mouthpiece pressure, they will seek more dramatic movement to ensure tone production, even though it is not efficient or consistent. The most common of these movements is the called the *pivot* as this movement of the angle of the mouthpiece on the embouchure allows for a slight repositioning of the lips and can assist in sounding tones in neighboring registers. Unfortunately, this also changes tone color and does not allow for consistency of sound. Another unfortunate remedy is to overuse the air to help overcome the inability of the lips to make their efficient movement inward or outward. This creates a larger aperture and a louder, harsher sound, though the note will likely speak if the blowing increases enough. As with all brass playing, it is focused listening to sound quality that reveals these secondary methods for achieving register changes, and it is important to identify their characteristic sounds to players, so they can focus practicing toward hearing sounds that accompany maximum efficiency in lip movement.

Moist and Dry Lips

It is logical that moist lips are able to make small and frequent movements more efficiently while in contact with each other and the mouthpiece when compared to lips that are dry. There are some players who propose that drier lips can assist in playing the extreme high register because the less slippery lips can be forced more easily to stay more firmly together inside the rim of the mouthpiece. Although there is certainly some truth to this concept, and there are many successful commercial dry lip proponents, the more gentle flexibility needed for most styles of music is enhanced with wetter, more slippery lips in the mouthpiece. Without enough moisture, the setting of the mouthpiece tends to stick wherever it is placed on the lips and, because this is not always in the exact spot required, dry lip players often reset several times before they locate the placement desired. Wet lip players can make small positioning adjustments once the mouthpiece is in contact with the lips and therefore do not need to reset to find exact placement.

Dry lip players also risk injury to the lips due to a lack of saliva and its lubricating qualities. They are more likely to create an abrasion on the surface of the lips or surrounding skin, and this can cause an interruption in the ability to play or even be a source of discomfort for the player. As in the case with chapped lips, dry lips and lips with abrasions have less sensitivity, and so players with them tend to have less control over their sensitive playing. In the highest levels of performance, it is the sophistication of this sensitivity and minute changes in lip compression and position that yield the wide myriad of colors sought by high-level players and audiences.

Ultimately, Focus on the Sound

There is such a wide variety in the formation of the human body, and experienced players and teachers learn that this yields many variations on successful embouchures and playing positions. Many players place their mouthpieces slightly off center or a bit higher or lower on the lips than most books recommend. Usually you can understand these variations on the proposed ideal embouchure by doing an examination of lip shapes and the tooth formations underneath. Many players also slightly adjust the positioning of their lips from side to side relative to each other in the process of forming an embouchure. Others may move their jaws from side to side as well. In all cases, if the player yields a quality sound and is not limited in his or her development of range, flexibility, and endurance, I encourage you not to seek big embouchure changes for them, even if it visually appears a bit different that the ideal.

My students have a slogan for this sound-centered approach that states *if it sounds good, do it!* It is always important to remember that music is an auditory delight, and so a pleasing sound should be our ultimate evaluator in terms of playing, even if it looks a bit unusual.

Embouchure Changes

I have worked with some players whose former teachers attempted to change their embouchures because they did not look correct without consideration of why students created their unique settings in the first place. Often these embouchure changes are unnecessary, and student achievement is limited until they return to their former embouchure, or worse, they quit playing. It is important to identify additional reasoning for changes based on tone production, range, flexibility, and endurance before asking students to disrupt their progress with embouchure changes.

Embouchure changes can be catastrophic for players and are largely unsuccessful, even in more experienced players. It is vital therefore that in the early stages of learning brass instruments, teachers identify limitations caused by the embouchure and make the necessary changes to the embouchure or switch instruments to set students up for the best possible future growth. In my experience, when changes need to be made but are not, it is often due to the stubbornness of the student or a lack of commitment in the teacher. In the latter case I even have known of band directors, for example, who avoided helping students make necessary embouchure or instrument changes to avoid downtime participating in their ensembles. Although these players in need of a change might continue to contribute to short-term successes on the marching field or in the concert hall, I encourage teachers also to consider the long-term possibilities for students and make choices that will best prepare them for their continued and long-term growth.

A Note for Instrumental Music Teachers

Even with the best evaluation, it is likely that some students will encounter limitations on their embouchures and progress, especially on the trumpet. For this reason, beginning teachers should start more students on trumpet than they think they will ever need for a balanced band. During the first two years, there likely will be students who you identify as less suited for trumpet due to embouchure considerations that will not be problematic on a larger mouthpiece brass instrument. It is not unusual to move these students to euphonium, tuba, and even horn. You will find that many players of these instruments who achieved great success actually started on the trumpet. In my university music department, for example, our current tuba professor, horn professor, saxophone professor, trumpet professor, and even two voice professors all actually started on the trumpet! The physicality of the trumpet continues to result in some students migrating to other instruments, especially after the beginning semester. To ensure that you have enough trumpet players in your advanced ensembles, therefore, you need to start at least twice as many trumpet players in each beginning class to accommodate for those who will change to other instruments.

Exercises

- Look into the mirror while buzzing on your mouthpiece. Begin with a fixed pitch in the middle register. Examine the corners of your embouchure for continuity as you gliss up and down to the extremes of your range. Be sure to hold the mouthpiece with only the thumb and one additional finger to minimize the use of excessive pressure.
- Create an embouchure, and then blow a steady stream of air while gradually extending your jaw forward and pulling it back in. Notice the changes in air direction by holding your hand, palm forward, about six inches in front of the embouchure. Try the same exercise while buzzing your lips, and notice the impact of jaw movement and teeth/lip alignment on the efficiency and consistency of the buzz.

Note

1 Philip Farkas, *The Art of Brass Playing* (Bloomington, IN: Brass Publications, 1962), pp. 25–34.

4

THE BRASS MOUTHPIECE

"Play the mouthpiece like you're a street musician and the mouthpiece is the only thing you have to compel passersby to drop money in your hat."

Jens Lindemann
Canadian Brass

The function of lip movement within the boundaries of the mouthpiece is by far the most important component in quality brass playing, so choosing the correct mouthpiece for a player is important at all stages of development. The process of finding the right mouthpiece can be somewhat confusing, however, because there are so many variations and brands available. Although it is easy to find a teacher or professional player who is touting a mouthpiece brand and size that will do amazing things for your playing and solve many of the challenges faced in controlling these instruments, we must always remember that variations in our physical features mean that a one-size-fits-all approach is not always appropriate. To navigate all of these messages, it is important to concentrate on some basic considerations when choosing a mouthpiece.

Rim diameter and cup depth are the most important measurements in a mouthpiece because they determine the amount of lip that will function inside the mouthpiece and how much air will be required to sustain a healthy tone. As you would expect, younger students generally begin on mouthpieces with smaller rim diameters and cup sizes due to their smaller physical size and lack of developed muscle strength and control. With so many quality mouthpieces offered now, it is important to understand how the rim size and cup depth compare among the various brands. Once this information is understood, it is easier to make changes when needed and recommend mouthpieces to students of varying levels of experience. For example, if a student has troubles with range and endurance, a mouthpiece with a smaller rim diameter and/ or a shallower cup depth might be needed to allow better efficiency because it creates more resistance. If students often overpower their playing with an overly bright tone and have good facility in range and endurance, they might be ready to move into bigger mouthpiece dimensions to achieve more colors in their tone due to less resistance to air and greater room for lip movements.

Throat and backbore dimensions also impact the resistance level a brass mouthpiece creates, with larger sizes offering less resistance and requiring a stronger embouchure and airstream to balance. Most mouthpieces come in standard sizes for these parts of the mouthpiece, with more experienced players gravitating toward larger sizes for a bigger and more robust sound. This is especially true in the orchestral brass section because of the demand for big sounds without reaching the point where the sound becomes *edgy* because, although this type of tone is brilliant and exciting, it is also a color that is less able to blend with other instruments in the ensemble.

I look for some basic abilities when suggesting mouthpieces that center on the relationship between the energy of the air and strength of the embouchure on one side and the resistance offered by the instrument and mouthpiece on the other (see Fig. 4.1). For a brass player to become proficient, he or she will need to find a mouthpiece and instrument that offer the proper amount of resistance to the input of air and use of embouchure to achieve a comfortable equilibrium. I call this *cruising altitude* because, although we might need to add more energy in the form of air and lip action at some points or less at other times, we need to be able to play comfortably most of the time. I often hear players who have to overuse their blowing process to create a consistent tone on a brass instrument and find that they are playing very large equipment. If they are not able to increase their physical ability to add this energy quickly, they will respond to the lack of a healthy equilibrium by developing bad habits in their embouchures and improper tension in their bodies due to the imbalance. Likewise I hear many players that exhibit overly bright tones and create obvious amounts of *backpressure* while they play. These players are trying to put

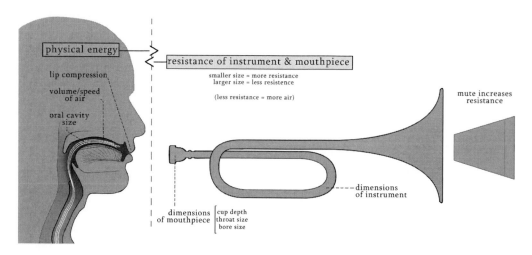

Figure 4.1 Physical energy/resistance of instrument and mouthpiece

too much energy into an instrument that is offering quite a high level of resistance. In the most extreme cases, I have seen players like this pass out from the enormous backpressure they create in trying to blow excessively against the resistance created by smaller horns and mouthpieces.

For beginners you can start the process of matching mouthpieces with players by trying standard beginning mouthpieces such as the Bach 7C for trumpet or cornet, the Bach 11 for horn, the Bach 12C for trombone, and the Bach 24 for tuba. Because achieving the desired equilibrium requires an efficient use of air, it is vital that students concentrate on relaxed breathing and blowing in a manner that will sustain the input side of the equation to balance the other side of instrument/mouthpiece resistance. After the first few months of embouchure development and learning how to blow the air correctly, some students may require a mouthpiece change, but generally, the sizes mentioned are appropriate for the majority of beginners in the 11-to-12 age group.

Mouthpiece Buzzing

I often tell students that the instrument is mostly a *megaphone* when it comes to the production of brass sound because 90 percent of our tone is created by the buzzing lips in the mouthpiece and the size and shape of the oral cavity behind this point of sound production. Because there is a direct relationship between buzzing and the resulting tone on the brass instrument, players and teachers increasingly have turned to mouthpiece buzzing as a normal part of practice and preparation. Because buzzing the mouthpiece requires the ability to match pitch, center the tone, and play in the extreme registers without undue pressure, it can serve all players well, starting with beginners and continuing throughout a playing career.

The mouthpiece is actually an independent musical instrument of its own, and we should think about its tone and expression in the same way we consider playing on our complete instrument. Canadian Brass member Jens Lindemann once told a student in a master class to play the mouthpiece "like you're a street musician and the mouthpiece is the only thing you have to compel passersby to drop money in your hat." I think this is a great way to approach playing the mouthpiece and believe that it should be a daily tool in improving our skills.

It is important when buzzing the mouthpiece to match fixed pitches as soon as it is possible to instill the correlation among hearing the note, buzzing it on the mouthpiece, and playing it on the instrument. Buzzing glisses and other non-precise tones are fine for getting the blood into the lips and working on basic lip function, but creating actual pitches will maximize mouthpiece practice and connect this process more closely with playing the instrument. Start with easy-to-hear patterns like arpeggios, scales, or simple tunes to help players make these connections. Stress the concept of a consistent tone on the mouthpiece and the ability to change volumes as well.

Examine the sound of articulation on the mouthpiece and its effect on this tone. The more focused you are in listening to your mouthpiece performance, the more it can help you improve overall as a brass performer.

Mouthpiece buzzing also should encompass the entire range of the player with special attention to holding the mouthpiece at the shank with the thumb and one finger to reduce the use of excessive pressure on the embouchure. All other fingers should be extended away from the shank to ensure that they will not be used to add such pressure against the lips (see Fig. 4.2). In the extreme low register, players may find it more challenging to sound the note on the mouthpiece compared to the instrument. This may have to do with less pivot movement without the instrument (a good thing) and also the need for more warm air in the process. Higher-register playing on the mouthpiece is especially challenging because, with the recommended holding position, players are unable to apply the type of mouthpiece pressure that is possible with both hands pushing the instrument toward the embouchure. By not allowing this excess pressure, mouthpiece practice actually positions the lips to do most of the work and gives these muscles the opportunity to increase in strength while doing so. Therefore if players practice only high notes on the instrument alone, the added pressure they are able to create with both hands actually can rob their lips from the opportunity to gain the very strength needed to improve in this part of the range.

Figure 4.2 Proper hand position while buzzing mouthpiece

Most players can reach about a third or fourth higher on the instrument than they can manage on the mouthpiece alone. This is mostly, if not all, due to the ability to use more mouthpiece pressure with the instrument, thus increasing lip compression through a secondary method. Although this extra *artificial* compression can achieve higher notes, it also reduces blood flow to the lip muscles, and this compromises endurance and flexibility. Generally, mouthpiece range measures the efficient range of a player, and it always should be a focal point in goal setting for range development. It is helpful to remind young players that as the mouthpiece range increases, so will the higher, artificial compression range. In other words, if they can learn to buzz higher notes, they also always will have the ability to push a bit more and achieve the additional third or fourth higher when playing the instrument. Another interesting fact is that the mouthpiece has its own harmonic system that does not mirror the instrument. This often means that buzzing higher actually might be easier in some parts of the high register than playing on the instrument, so it really can inspire players in terms of the notes they can attempt on the instrument.

Because playing the mouthpiece alone removes some of the sonority the brass instrument adds to the sound, it is more discriminating and revealing in some ways compared to playing the instrument. For this reason, many brass players avoid mouthpiece playing, so they do not have to confront more obvious issues in how they sound. Just because a playing issue is less noticeable on the instrument, however, does not mean it is absent. Because mouthpiece buzzing can better reveal deficiencies in our sound, it also can assist in diagnosing the strategies needed to overcome them. Confronting the need for this type of focused practice is vital to improving rapidly and gaining even more enjoyment from playing a brass instrument, so it is important to develop a keen awareness of mouthpiece tone quality through daily repetition.

It is also, however, possible to do too much mouthpiece buzzing, and I feel strongly that some of the most recent brass practice routines do just that. Although the benefits of buzzing are clear, it is also important to remember that it is a tool to playing well on the instrument. With less resistance and some other properties that are different from playing the instrument, players need to be aware that mouthpiece buzzing at its best is targeted to improve instrumental playing. One of the problems I have observed is in players who buzz for a very long period to start their playing day without playing the instrument. In an effort to achieve a full-sounding mouthpiece buzz, for example, they actually might play the equivalent of a *forte* dynamic on the instrument for this entire period, something they would recognize immediately as harmful in instrumental practice. As with all developmental practice, mouthpiece buzzing should never become part of an overly long routine that you feel is necessary to play the instrument well. Later I will discuss the philosophical differences between a *warm-up* and a *maintenance session* as you construct your daily practice. Buzzing the mouthpiece and other techniques are great daily drills to develop and maintain your skill on a brass instrument, but that process is wholly different from what you might need to do simply to warm up.

Using Mouthpiece Buzzing to Diagnose Poor Instrument Tone Quality

One easy way to diagnose poor tone quality in a brass player is to compare a note played on the instrument with the same pitch buzzed on the mouthpiece. In some cases, it is helpful to compare these directly by either removing the mouthpiece from the instrument while continuing the play the pitch or by first buzzing the pitch and then inserting the mouthpiece into the instrument receiver while continuing to play (see Fig. 4.3). I often do this to demonstrate the wide variety of tone qualities that can be produced by buzzing in the center of the pitch and also above or below it.

Although this comparison process might be a bit awkward for players, it gives immediate, high-quality feedback on your sound production. Even if you do not connect buzzing with playing in this manner, comparing the two processes quickly can be very revealing. Especially in the upper register, the buzzing of the mouthpiece, absent the ability to exert excessive pressure, can be compared quickly to playing the same pitches on the instrument. When doing so, you are more likely to replicate the

Figure 4.3 Buzzing and inserting mouthpiece into receiver

26

physical sensation of less pressure on the instrument due to the muscle memory that remains from buzzing.

An easy evaluation for our brass playing is to be able to buzz the sounding notes, articulations, and intonation of a passage we are playing on the instrument. If we are able to replicate the passage at pitch on the mouthpiece, this is an indication that we are hearing the passage well and also are efficiently using our embouchure in establishing centered notes. If we listen carefully, the vibrancy in our tone, including vibrato, also can be heard in our mouthpiece buzzing, and this will enhance the likelihood that our instrumental rendition is also vibrant.

Glisses

Although it is important to strive for quick and efficient movement between notes on the mouthpiece to develop centered note-to-note movement on the instrument, glisses on the mouthpiece can have a unique role in embouchure development. Especially when attempting larger intervals, players quickly can add excessive pressure, over pivot, change corner embouchure tension, or even overblow to compensate for other inefficiencies in embouchure function. Buzzing these intervals as slow glisses on the mouthpiece can help develop more efficient embouchure use and reduce excessive and unnecessary movement. I find that most players are challenged by larger intervals, especially those that are slurred in music. Although we eventually want the lips to make these movements quickly and with good muscle recognition, the initial work to develop that precise recognition can be enhanced with a slower, more gradual repositioning of the lips offered by glissing. Too often these larger intervals are managed with less precise use of the lips and air, compensating instead with the less efficient processes mentioned. If players do not use glisses and other methods to instill a more efficient use of the embouchure in these moments, this imprecision will continue until such a method is employed. By stretching the interval with glissing, the movement of the lip and the use of the air can be examined in a focused manner with less chance of interference from excessive pressure or physical movement. Just as a slow exercise of muscle movement is stressed in weight training to maximize efficiency, these glisses can strengthen the lips while also increasing flexibility and precision. I like to call this gymnastic strength to differentiate it from a more brute strength that relies on excessive pressure, pivot, or air rather than on more precise lip movement.

Exercises

- Play arpeggios alternately on the piano and then on the brass mouthpiece while listening carefully to match pitch. If possible, do both at the same time by playing the piano with one hand while buzzing the mouthpiece with the other. This will instill pitch focus and also help you keep track of how high and low you can buzz with clarity. Even if you do not have a piano, you can use your computer, iPad, or smartphone to do a similar exercise, and you can do that anywhere!

- Sound a fixed pitch on a tuner or other device, and play an arpeggio against this drone root. When a piano is not available, this method is also very helpful. Be sure to seek out an app on your phone that can assist you.

- Practice below the normal range of your instrument with the understanding that, on the mouthpiece, there is not the same limitation of harmonics as on the instrument. On the trumpet, for example, you should strive to play down to the fundamental pedal C. Although this is a pedal tone on the instrument and rarely used, the process of developing lip motion to effectively play it will clarify your lower register and also reinforce lip strength and movement that will positively impact your upper range as well.

- At the limits of your high and low ranges, use glissandos to help train your lips to feel the exact amount of lip compression needed to achieve a clear tone without overusing the air or adding excessive mouthpiece pressure.

5

TONE AS OUR VOICE

"When I started learning the cello, I fell in love with the
instrument because it seemed like a voice—my voice."
Mstislav Rostropovich
Cellist and Conductor

Everything we do on our instrument relates to sound production. In our lessons at
Eastman Charles, Geyer constantly used to ask me, "Is that your best sound?" It was
unnerving because he asked it often when I thought I was sounding great. The fact
is that technical ability means little if it is not accompanied with a beautifully expressive tone. "You sound is like your signature" is one of Barbara Butler's oft-uttered
mantras. Like our voice, our brass tone is very individualistic and makes us identifi-
able to others. This is because our tone starts in our imagination as a defined sound in
our heads. Brass technique development really should center on the process of figur-
ing out how to get the instrument to make that imaginary sound we already hear. If
the sound that resides in our imagination is not beautifully expressive, however, then
our mental image of a great sound must be modified through the influence of others.

Our concept of brass tone is the product of all the listening we do to quality musicians. Singers, violinists, and countless others have contributed to the trumpet tone
that resides in my mind. Even though there are many wonderful brass players, none
of them sound exactly alike because they are imagining the sum total of all their
experiences as a listener. You certainly can tell a lot about players' listening histories
and who influenced their sound by how they play their instrument! We all need to
work hard to input the best and richest variety of sounds into our imaginations,
and we will find that achieving a great tone is much easier and less mysterious. The
opportunity to experience an expressive, lyrical sound live, especially in close proximity, is extremely valuable to our growth as musicians, and so such moments should
be pursued regularly. As a player, I have been blessed to be onstage with amazing
musicians, hearing them and observing their habits in close proximity. As a teacher, I
work hard to offer my students similar chances for this stimulation by attracting guest
artists who offer the same meaningful closer interaction and playing with that best
personal sound that Charlie Geyer alluded to as often as possible.

What is a good tone anyway? Too often we urge players to achieve this without really defining it. Although it must start inside you, as already mentioned, there are certainly some technical aspects we can consider as well. In this way, we can do some athletic work to ensure that a flexible and expressive sound is available to realize our artistic goals.

One of the first positive tone descriptors I use is the term *pure*. A pure tone is free of unwanted distortion or disruption in the sound. Impurity can include airy sounds, double buzzes, and other varieties of inconsistencies. These disruptors limit the subtle expression we can achieve in the manipulation of our tone, and so they need to be eliminated as soon as possible. An airy tone is usually the result of air passing between the lips without being set into vibration. This often happens when we have done too much loud playing and not enough soft practice. Unfortunately, many players actually never develop purity in soft dynamics and simply compensate by playing everything louder than needed. When players find themselves in this situation, whether temporary or long term, the aperture that forms from the relationship between lip compression and airflow is too large for the air passing through it. As a result, a more gentle use of the air is not vigorous enough to set the lips efficiently into vibration, and the resulting sound is not pure. Even if you are an efficient player at loud volumes, you must remember to balance this with the requisite amount of soft work to develop and maintain efficiency at softer volumes. It is all about percentages really. If you devote too much of your playing time to loud tone production, it is likely that you will lose security in your tone when playing soft and sensitive passages. Likewise if you always play softly, you will not be able to control your sound when asked to play at the loudest volumes. Remember that you are the sum of all your playing. If your school band rehearses five times each week, and you are playing in the *f*-to-*ff* range for most of this time, you must balance this with much practice time dedicated to very soft tone production. If you fail to achieve this balance, you always will struggle to make the purest tone.

If you are able to make a *pure* tone without distortion, especially in the soft dynamic range, even in a limited range, you are on your way. All you have to do is use that clear tone production as a model as you expand into other ranges and volumes. The presence of at least one high-quality note you can model your sound on is vital. If that is not the case, then you must strive for that first great note to reach a level of purity you can then work to develop across all of your playing.

Once purity of tone is reliable, it is important to think of your sound like it is a living organism that is always moving even when at rest, as with breathing or even a pulse. The constant subtle undulation of our brass tone sends a very human message to listeners and makes connections to human emotions more natural. This means that our sound must be flexible enough to create expression by using vibrato or vibrancy. I make the distinction here between a vibrant sound and a non-vibrant or *hard* sound. Imagine for a moment the sound a tuner makes when it emits a pitch.

The sound wave emitted from such a device is amazingly consistent and also in tune. Unfortunately, if you could have that tuner play a melody for you, it would be annoying in its perfection and not attractive in terms of tone quality. How can this be so if the emitted pitches are right on pitch and consistent in their sound production? Isn't that the ideal many teachers tell us to strive for in our playing? Why then does it sound so cold and inhuman?

Oddly enough, it is actually the fluctuation of the pitch, imperfections if you prefer, in the sound that make it less cold and hard and more warm and resonant. Even when we are not playing a solo line, our sound should have some underlying motion to keep it from becoming hard because if this motion is absent, it is not only hard to listen to, but it is also hard to blend with others in an ensemble. The descriptor often used for such a desired and flexible sound is *vibrant*. The desired *imperfection* in this type of fluid tone is *shimmer* or *vibrancy* and denotes very small fluctuations in the sound controlled and manipulated by experienced players. This is not always a discernable vibrato but still contributes a warmth and liveliness to the sound. Many players also refer to this concept by thinking of a sound *spinning out* from the instrument. When we have this motion in our sound, it sounds alive and offers the best possible platform for creating expression in our playing. When it is missing from our sound, we must overly rely on other musical tools of expression, like changes in volume or attack, to create energy. Even when brass players are able to be expressive with these tools, it is not as successful because hard sounds without shimmer sound louder and blend less well, so simply increasing volume to increase excitement often creates only painful, raw, and unblended sounds for listeners. The emotional response to such playing is ugliness and repulsion due to the quality of the brass sound. To create a wider range of emotional responses, performers must develop warmth through vibrancy that can be heard in the brass sections of the world's best orchestras.

Of course, solo vibrato is created in the same physical manner as vibrancy by using small changes in lip compression to change the pitch slightly. Vibrato is a more noticeable part of our tone that should be developed so well that it responds directly to our emotional state. Different vibrato speeds and widths help distinguish musical style and also can create changes in expression that stimulate emotional responses in listeners.

We will discuss the development of vibrancy and vibrato in later chapters as well as their vital roles in playing expressively. For now we need to recognize that the fluidity it creates in tone production is an essential component for an expressive sound. Even instruments like the horn and tuba use vibrancy to create warmth and expression, although their characteristic vibrato is not as pronounced as the trumpet, euphonium, and trombone traditionally.

So our early definition of great sound involves three components—*purity*, *vibrancy*, and *consistency*—because your sound must maintain these qualities to be successful in creating musical expression for your audiences. To develop and maintain these characteristics in our sound, we must understand it involves a daily and lifelong undertaking. At the core is the awareness of what sound you want to create and what you must do to continue to strive for this model.

Remember to listen to your tone always for these features. It sounds simple, but often we are distracted from the focus we really need to detect and remedy tone issues in our practice. Especially with the revelations soft playing brings, we need to be vigilant not simply to play a bit louder to mask these inconsistencies. When buzzing the mouthpiece, you must also listen for purity and vibrancy in the tone, especially at softer dynamics. Any exercise that allows you to focus on the tone quality, including the playing of sustained notes with gradual movement into slurs and then articulation passages, will allow the focus on critical listening you should establish early in each playing day.

Exercises

- Play long tones with gradual crescendos and decrescendos from piano to forte at a slow tempo of 60 per quarter note.
- Do regular, slow, slurred expansion of register exercises that begin in the middle register and expand higher and lower.
- Perform slow, soft lip slurs that begin in the middle register and gradually expand in range and speed.
- Play through slow, lyrical melodies from Arban, Concone, and Rochut and other vocalizes concentrating on the purity, vibrancy, and consistency of your sound.
- Do slurred lip bends of one half and even two subsequent half steps below the pitch while maintaining a consistent flow of sound at a constant dynamic level.
- Use a measured vibrato to *exercise* the lips that lie within the rim of the mouthpiece to realize smaller and smaller sound fluctuations that define the differences between vibrato and vibrancy.
- Take time each day to challenge the soft boundaries of your playing with decrescendos in different registers that go until there is no sound production. Keep track of where you lose the ability to play softly, and work to extend the decrescendo into a true disappearing act.

6

UNDERSTANDING BRASS INTONATION

"The only time I'm miserable is when I can't keep an instrument in tune."

Steve Vai
Guitarist

It is important to realize that, for brass players, tone quality is directly related to and impacted by many other elements of playing. Intonation has an overwhelming effect on the sound quality of any note. Hearing in tune and being able to use the mechanism of the instrument efficiently are critical to creating the consistent, open, and expressive sound mentioned earlier. Even when a note might be *in tune*, oftentimes the sound quality reveals an underlying issue that is still pitch related.

For all brass players, there is a sophisticated relationship between matching pitch and the physical movements involved in doing so. Students who hear well can manipulate their bodies to match pitch from the very beginning yet often these physical movements can lead to problems in playing that impact tone production and even limit proper embouchure development. Too often, young students develop inefficient physical manipulations to sound notes and match pitch that can go unchecked during years of playing. Many of these students even win chairs in all-state bands and high marks on high school solo ensembles because they play all the correct notes and rhythms and are able to match the pitch of the piano and others around them. It is when they work to reach higher levels of playing, however, that they encounter imposing challenges as they must really *reinvent* their playing, or they cannot move forward. This realization usually occurs in the last year of high school and the beginning of university-level music study because they might, for the first time, have the opportunity to have focused, private study with an expert brass performer and teacher. It might also be the first time that they consider not simply the challenge of the moment, like an audition or a solo competition, but their long-range future career in music.

Intonation then is an indicator of many processes in brass playing that are interrelated. Hearing and matching pitch, proper embouchure development and air use, and knowledge of the characteristics of both the individual instrument and the individual player are all factors that help brass players play in tune with a great sound. There are many things that music teachers can do to firmly establish these keys to efficient playing. Selecting music with playing requirements that do match ability levels and offer opportunities to develop controlled playing is one good example. We must always remember that muscle strength grows slowly over many years and at different paces in different players. Intonation and how it impacts tone quality can be a major indicator that you have overprogrammed or that your players need a break in rehearsal. Remember that simply matching pitch should never be enough. You need to match pitch with an efficient sound quality. When this is happening, you are on the right track.

Mechanical Over Physical Pitch Adjustment

Students often ask the question, "If you can lip the note in tune, and that feels natural, isn't that the best way to match pitch?" The natural proclivity to find the center of the pitch in this way is a great attribute in players, but sometimes it works against the development of the best approach to playing in tune with a great sound. The answer to this question is complex but begins with the truth about *natural* or *just* tuning and the construction of brass instruments. The invention of valves in the early 19th century started a quest to design and manipulate valves in a manner to achieve the full range of chromatic notes to line up with the idealistic equal temperament system devised almost a century earlier. Unfortunately, even today, the laws of physics keep getting in the way of creating the perfect valve system that allows all chromatic tones and ensures easily finding the center of pitch in this equal-tempered world.

Although we all use tuners that set pitches in one place and also play with keyboard instruments that can only play pitches in one place, we actually still mostly play with *just intonation* when it is possible. This means lowered thirds in major chords and other departures from exact equal temperament as each key demands subtle changes in pitch levels to achieve the consonance in harmonic and melodic presentation. Brass players constantly are changing environments from just intonation to equal temperament in their daily ensemble playing and especially in their collaborations with pianists. Because equal temperament actually is not a natural system seen in overtones, brass instruments cannot be constructed to be totally comfortable in this environment. Even if we had the possibility for equal temperament brass instruments, our ears and the physicality of our lips would still gravitate toward just intonation whenever they could.

For example, in early three-valve systems, designers found that the length of valve tubing for valves played independently did not allow for tuning needs when played in combination. If we consider the simple concept of the slide on the trombone, we can illustrate this phenomenon. When you play and teach trombone, you realize that the distance between the slide positions is not equal but rather grows larger as you move the slide outward. This, by the way, works against the short arms of young players, who tend to move the slide less the further their hands move away from the trunks of their bodies (see Fig. 6.1). Likewise, as you increase the tube length with valves used in combination, the segments of tubing required to play each half step grows as well. Trying to make valve tubes that are one length will leave them way too short when used in combination (see Fig. 6.2). Because of this challenge of changing tube lengths, designers have devised many ways to accommodate the need for changing the length of the sounding instrument while playing. Adding extra valves as in the tuba and euphonium, the compensating system, the double horn, and of course the trombone slide are all mechanical additions intended to bridge this gap in tube length to allow for better tuning and pitch center.

The trombone, because it uses one large slide that affects the entire instrument, is the most capable of making the small changes in tube length needed to match pitch and maintain an efficient sound. Even with the unlimited number of options for slide placement this instrument offers, however, it is not assured that young players can

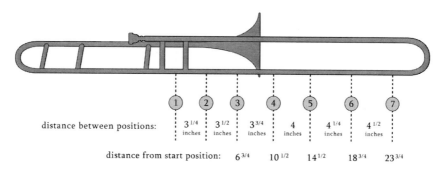

distance between positions: 3 1/4 inches | 3 1/2 inches | 3 3/4 inches | 4 inches | 4 1/4 inches | 4 1/2 inches

distance from start position: 6 3/4   10 1/2   14 1/2   18 3/4   23 3/4

Figure 6.1 Trombone slide positions

Compromise System of Valves (measurements in inches)					
Valve Used	Slide Length	Actual Total Length	Correct Total Length	Total Length Error	Tuning Discrepancy (semitone)
0	-	100	100	0	0
2	6.25	106.25	105.95	+0.30	-0.05
1	12.57	112.57	112.25	+0.32	-0.05
3	20.35	120.35	118.92	+1.43	-0.21
12	18.82	118.82	118.92	-0.10	+0.01
23	26.60	126.60	125.99	+0.61	-0.08
13	32.92	132.92	133.48	-0.56	+0.07
123	39.17	139.17	141.42	-2.25	+0.28

Figure 6.2 Compromise system of valves

avoid the overuse of physical lipping mentioned earlier. The options also increase when the player moves to an instrument with an F attachment to allow for more possibilities to aid technique and pitch, especially in the lower register. If the slide is not in the position most capable of allowing for a centered, efficient sound, the student can still manipulate the air and embouchure to match the pitch but with a poorer tone. Although the trombone is the closest brass to string instruments in terms of variables of pitch placement, string players cannot develop the same poor physical habits when trying to match pitch because their poor physical action also results in poorer pitch. On brass instruments, even the trombone, lipping instead of manipulating the physical instrument often can yield good pitch but also poorer tone quality.

The double horn, because of its construction, offers many options for mechanical manipulation of intonation; it combines two complete sets of valve slides and also the use of the hand in the bell as a pitch modifier. Again, like the trombone, all of these options do not ensure that a player will always find the best mechanical solution for pitch challenges because they may still rely on lipping and other physical movements to match pitch as they seem more *natural*, especially in early years of playing.

All valved brasses are designed using the *compromise system* as it is the best method available to match equal temperament with the overtone series created by tubing. This system creates a compromise in the length of valve tubes and adds valve slide manipulation or additional valves to assist the player in finding pitch and sound center. As you can see in Fig. 6.2, this requires the valve tubes to be constructed longer than needed for individual valves to accommodate the even longer tube lengths required for valves used in combination. The use of triggers on the first and third valve tubes allows trumpet players also to extend the tubing to facilitate tuning and achieve good sound quality. Likewise, euphoniums and tubas are constructed with extra valves, and the double horn offers mechanical solutions to intonation challenges created by the need for changes in tube length.

Charles Geyer often tells students that "the trumpet is the most out of tune of all the instruments," and there are compelling reasons for this view. Although there have been attempts to create a compensating trumpet and to add extra valves, the trumpet is the only valved brass instrument that attempts to match the tuning needs of all notes and equal temperament with only three valves. Especially noting the challenges above and along with the understanding that shorter tube lengths and smaller bore sizes aggravate tuning and limit solutions, the trumpet is easily the most challenging of the brass instruments to play consistently in tune and also with a centered sound.

All brass players, of course, can and do some lipping to impact pitch; however, this should be a last resort as it can affect tone color adversely. With the added design features of slide manipulation, alternate fingerings, and other mechanical options, brass players have several ways to change pitch and at the same time preserve a consistent tone quality (see Fig. 6.3). Using the lips to change the pitch, when compared

Mechanical Versus Physical Tuning

Mechanical: Using the instrument to adjust pitch while playing as honestly as possible

-Alternate valve combinations
-Alternate slide positions
-Adjusting valve slides using triggers
-Utilizing another side of the double horn
-Pulling valve slides on the tuba
-Adjusting main tuning slide for a particular passage
-Adding mutes or bell covers
-Loosening valve caps on piston valves
-Changing mouthpieces

Physical: Using physical bodily movement to adjust pitch

-Increasing or decreasing air speed
-Adjusting lip compression
-Increasing mouthpiece pressure on embouchure
-Changing angle of mouthpiece on embouchure (pivot)
-Blowing more vigorously with more volume

Figure 6.3 Mechanical versus physical tuning

to this mechanical manipulation, is actually less desired for several reasons. First, if the player is altering lip compression to a point beyond comfort, he or she will play less efficiently and thus negatively impact endurance. Lip compression and air use that do not match the physical properties of the instrument well also impact tone color and make it much more difficult to play with a more consistent tone color. Lipping also limits the small pitch changes that might be required in a performance because the increase or decrease of lip compression takes the lip formation out of the comfort range for maximum efficiency, and if additional changes in compression are suddenly needed, it might not be physically possible as the lips are now at the limit of their adaptability.

There are characteristics of tube length and bore size that are designed to facilitate a corresponding pitch level on a brass instrument. Tone quality is a by-product of matching the proper lip compression and airflow to create frequencies that work best with the physical dimensions of the pipe. Many players call the good matching of lip compression, airspeed, and the characteristics of the pipe *finding the sweet spot* as it yields the most relaxed and vibrant sound just like the right spot of the baseball bat and strength of swing maximize the power of hitting a baseball.

For example, let us consider for a moment the written key of F major on the Bb trumpet (see Fig. 6.4). When playing the F chord, the high A presents a challenge for the trumpeter. Because the A is the third of the chord, the natural tuning we hear leads us to lower this note for a more perfect harmony. Unfortunately, the A on the trumpet tends sharp because of its use of the first and second valves together. If no

*The A is the third of the major chord.
It must be lowered to achieve just intonation.
*This 12-valve combination is already sharp on the trumpet.
It can be lowered by both mechanical and physical means.

*Mechanical
Extend first valve slide to achieve desired pitch.
Use alternate third valve fingering to lower using longer valve slide length.

*Physical
Lip the note lower to achieve desired pitch.
(This method will negatively impact sound vibrancy.)

Figure 6.4 Tuning third of chord with valve slide

other mechanical adaptations are added, most players will simply lip this note down-ward if they are strong enough to do so. Because the action of the lips is now working counter to the length of the pipe, the result is a less open and less vibrant tone. Although the player can perform the note in tune with the chord, the sound quality is greatly diminished. If the player instead matches the pipe length to more closely relate to the desired pitch level by extending the first valve slide trigger or using the lower alternate fingering of the third valve, the mechanical instrument is now better suited to the required pitch level. When playing the note in this situation with this mechanical adjustment, the sound is more vibrant and relaxed, and the player exerts less lip work to play. The result is a more even and open sound and more endurance for the performer.

In many cases, the use of the lip to find the correct pitch without the use of mechan-ical intervention also often brings into play strategies like excessive mouthpiece pressure, changes in basic embouchure shape, and excessive pivoting of the mouth-piece on the embouchure. When players resort to these methods to produce notes or match pitch, tone production suffers greatly, and consistency becomes impossible.

The process of using mechanical pitch adjustment versus physical methods may seem like it would be easy, but in reality, it is more challenging due to the naturalness of lipping that is likely embedded in players from earlier years. It takes focused prac-tice to stop lipping and allow the player to try mechanical fixes with the instrument to allow its most efficient use in finding the desired pitch and sound quality. This process often starts with allowing yourself to play out of tune at first while experi-menting with methods of mechanical adaptation. Early on in this process, you can fill out charts with your pitch tendencies to begin realizing connections between tone openness and pitch level. It is important always to remember that although there are some commonalities among instruments and players in regard to pitch tendencies, there are also countless variables created by physical and mechanical factors. With so many sizes and abilities of players playing so many varieties of mouthpieces and instruments, it is always important to know your playing habits and the characteristics of your instrument above all.

Mouthpiece size and shape also impact the balance between mechanical and physical pitch matching. The choice of a larger mouthpiece allows for more tone colors and a greater dynamic range and also allows for more lip use within the internal rim diameter. Smaller mouthpieces generally offer less variety of tone color and dynamics and also less lip movement within these boundaries. As a result, lipping to achieve pitch on smaller mouthpieces is a bit less tiring, and the change in instrumental tone is less noticeable due to less differentiation inherent in the equipment. For this reason, players of these smaller mouthpieces, such as in the commercial playing world, often advocate more lipping and less reliance on mechanical pitch manipulation. Lead trumpet players and trombone players, for example, play both smaller mouthpieces and smaller bore instruments to assist them in creating the brightness and comfort in the extreme upper registers they are required to play. By using a high velocity of air along with small equipment, they can create an exciting sound that matches this style well. When compared to classical players, however, you can readily hear the limitations of tone color and dynamics in this style of playing. It is important as you teach brass players that they are aware of these different playing roles and what equipment and style of pitch manipulation is needed.

Honest Playing

I often repeat a term I learned from Barbara Butler when working with students on finding the best combination of mechanical and lip manipulation. Seeking maximum benefit from the instrument requires the player to play very correctly without employing the excessive lipping and other embouchure bad habits that may have been learned over several years. The term *playing honestly* directs us to use the air and embouchure as efficiently as possible while relying on maximum mechanical manipulation to find correct pitch. When first playing in this manner, you might find you have a vibrant, open sound, but it is out of tune on certain pitches. It is at this point that you should experiment with your instrument and its mechanical pitch manipulation to adjust the pitch while preserving the *correctness* of your playing. As you might imagine, this takes great awareness of your productivity, especially in terms of sound quality and intonation but also of your physicality.

If players cannot find this base level of efficient playing, the combination of physical and mechanical adjustment can be very difficult to control, and in the end, the sound, endurance, and expressive qualities in performance can be limited. Serious players need to find their honest playing in all keys, ranges, and techniques and on all the horns they play. Although this seems like too much to try and accomplish, it is the focus on your sound that will help you more than anything else. When you hear the sound as less open, less centered, or less flexible, it is a strong clue that you are not playing as honestly as you can and that there are likely some mechanical changes that can help you if you are willing to undertake the investigation to find them.

The Tuner and the Piano

A common sense of pitch is essential to the ability to collaborate with other musicians successfully. Currently, the established concert A at 440 Hz (or 442 Hz), along with the development of digital devices and recordings, has reinforced common pitch more than ever before in history. Although there is certainly some natural hearing ability that we bring with us as musicians, we all need to work constantly to establish good pitch center on a daily basis. Musicians, like everyone else, learn to be comfortable with what they are used to hearing. Many times I hear players who play consistently at pitch levels other than 440 and seem completely unaware. This is not because they cannot hear but rather because they have become comfortable relying on their playing alone to establish a sense of pitch without constant comparison to accepted norms. Many times I walk into my building early in the morning and hear some diligent practicing echoing in the hallway from an upstairs practice room. Too often, the player is basically in tune with themselves but 20 cents sharp to A = 440. Even when this player tunes prior to an ensemble rehearsal at 440, he or she will quickly revert to the sharper level as it has become his or her natural center. The only way to be successful in great ensembles is to work to make your natural pitch center 440 on a daily basis. The same is true in your hearing of natural tuning in each key. You easily can become comfortable playing pitches out of tune, especially considering the variety of pitch levels brass instruments allow. Sometimes I tell players, "You need to play your horn, not let the horn play you." There is always the possibility that you can become comfortable with notes placed where the instrument tends to put them, even if this is quite out of tune. Your mental image of pitch and tone quality constantly must be updated to avoid these pitfalls.

Each day, when you buzz your mouthpiece, use a well-tuned piano or pitch-emitting device to establish your pitch at 440. Make sure you remember that the key in which you are playing changes the exact placement of notes as to their place in the scale or chord. Unfortunately, matching every single pitch to the tuner or piano is not really how professionals play. This equal temperament is used only when natural tuning is impossible. Lowering the third of the major chord is something, for example, that all players do when possible. You should continue to do this in your practice with the understanding that there are times when the piano or some other fixed-pitch instrument might double this third of a chord, so you cannot lower it and still match. These instruments and the tuner are still useful to tune the root and fifth of a chord though, and you can use this to practice many passages and patterns. I suggest you hold out the chord root by pressing the sustain pedal on the piano or sounding a constant note on a tuner. You can then play scales and other patterns against a root sound. Remember that needle watching on the tuner is only minimally helpful and not the ultimate manner in which you develop your sense of hearing. You can use this method as a checkup on pitch tendencies in new instruments and musical passages, but remember that it is hearing and matching, not seeing, that develop the highest level of collaborative playing.

Challenging Conditions

Players need to monitor their intonation under differing circumstances, so they are aware of their personal habits and what challenges are posed to playing in tune with a consistent sound. When unable to warm up at all and loosen up the embouchure by bringing blood flow into the lips, check where your pitch tends. For many players, this yields sharp playing, though because we often compensate for lower lip control with increased airflow. It also might tend flat if you do not add enough support. Monitor your pitch security as you warm up and reach maximum lip response. When your pitch is centered and reliable, it is a strong message that you are now properly ready to play and do not need further loosening of the embouchure.

Playing in extreme volumes is also a facet of playing that needs attention with regard to intonation. Too often players check their pitch only in moderate ranges and volumes. If you will need to play it onstage, it is important to gauge your tendencies, so you are not distracted or surprised in the performance. At softer and louder volumes, pitch can rise or fall depending on the player, the use of air, and the development of embouchure. Although trends in the playing and teaching of others can be helpful in understanding what pitches need manipulation, it is vital that each player listens to his or her own playing and measures intonation against fixed-pitch instruments and tuners. Know what happens when you crescendo and diminuendo in all registers and dynamic levels. Once you hear the changes in tuning, you can experiment with the mechanical and physical techniques to remedy them.

As brass players tire, many things happen in their playing that impact intonation. When the lips lose focused strength to create greater lip compression needed for higher and softer playing, the response is usually to play a bit louder to accommodate the larger aperture. Another reaction is increased pressure as players push the instrument against their embouchure to *squeeze* the lips between the mouthpiece and the teeth to create more compression. This creates a secondary type of lip compression I call *artificial compression* as the lips are pushed together in reaction to the smaller space between the teeth and mouthpiece. These two reactions to fatigue are actually slight changes in embouchure function, and this impacts tone quality and pitch alike. For many, this raises the pitch noticeably for some time until the fatigue becomes overwhelming and the embouchure becomes so weak that keeping pitch up is impossible, and the result is very flat intonation.

Many times in orchestras and bands, I have measured the pitch tendencies and found that in the last, loud sections of the concert, the pitch rises very high. In one regional orchestra where I was principal trumpet, the majority of players were amateur, and they would tire quickly and engage the physical processes previously outlined. This raised the pitch dramatically and made the job of principal trumpet very difficult in those moments. Often in frustration I would set my tuner to emit the tonic final note and play it immediately following the release of the last note in the piece, so we could compare our rendition to the original tuning at 440. Sometimes we had raised the pitch an entire half step, and our final chord was indeed in a new key! With this awareness and more practice, the brass section was able to accommodate this issue with more conditioning and also mechanical manipulation of pulling slides and seeking other ways to keep pitch down. Once we had made these adjustments, playing principal trumpet was much less strenuous, and the orchestra also sounded richer and fuller as the woodwinds and strings did not have to struggle to raise their pitch as well. The process of playing in tune with a great sound always must begin with vivid awareness of your playing and how it matches those around you.

There are so many variables that impact intonation and sound quality that it is difficult to always know exactly where pitch will be at all times. The best we can do as players and teachers is to stress knowing our individual playing habits and how differing circumstances impact our ability to play in tune. The more we listen to and play with musicians who find pitch and quality sound consistently, the more likely we are to strive for and achieve this in our own playing. Do not fall into the false security that you just hear so well that you do not need to check up on your pitch. As mentioned previously, you can become comfortable with many different quality levels of sound and pitch based on repeated exposure. Just like the 20-cent sharp practice players referenced earlier, this comfort with out-of-tune playing will negatively impact your work with others. It takes time and consistent effort to play in tune just like it does to be comfortable playing out of tune. You will decide which player you will be based on your level of commitment and focus.

Exercises

- Be sure that you devote time to tuning with efficient tone quality from the beginning level upward. Ensure proper playing posture, air use, and tone quality when tuning, and notice players who have difficulty matching tuning notes with quality sounds. It is likely they need individual attention to correct embouchure, air, or instrument issues.
- First play an open note on the instrument where it responds with the richest tone; play as honestly as possible then check this pitch with the piano or tuning device.

Adjust the main tuning slide to find the desired pitch level without changing the manner of playing. After the open note is in tune while playing honestly, slur from open notes to those using slides and valves while continuing to play honestly. Use slides and alternate fingerings to find the maximum resonance of notes without using lipping or other physical changes.

- Begin the process of understanding intonation characteristics by first playing the root and fifth in each key against a tonic drone. Use your ears and the tuner to check that your roots, fifths, and octaves line up with the equal temperament of the tuner or piano. Make a chart of your tendencies in each key on these pitches, and investigate mechanical possibilities for meeting challenges. These will include alternate fingerings, alternate slide positions, and playing with different sides of the double horn or with trombone attachments.

- Listen carefully for consistent tone quality as you play each melodic line of your etude or solo. If you have a well-centered, vibrant tone for most but tend to have a harder, duller sound on some other notes, immediately investigate the possibility that you are lipping the note to the point of diminished tone quality. Again, seek out alternate fingerings and slide positions to achieve a more vibrant sound on these notes while playing as honestly as possible.

- Warm up with a well-tuned piano or drones emitted from a tuner to consistently reinforce a home base of A = 440. With a held sustain pedal on the piano or an electronic drone, play scales, arpeggios, and other patterns to listen for a vibrant, in-tune tone.

- Sing through your musical passages to check the intonation tendencies of your voice. Because the connection to hearing pitch on the instrument is similar to the connection with your singing voice, this can help you understand where you need work to establish a stronger mental hearing of pitch.

- Explore the web and resources for *just intonation* or *natural tuning* to increase your awareness of the differences between this concept and that of equal temperament.

7

A PHILOSOPHY FOR TECHNIQUE

"I always work from the music, not the instrument. . . .
We work based on products not methodologies."

Arnold Jacobs

Technique Defined

I prefer to think of a definition for brass technique as finding a way to get the instrument to make the sound that you already can hear in your head. Once you clearly can imagine the sound you want to make, then you have a great model to copy as you try to recreate it on your instrument. The procedures you use to successfully recreate this imaginary sound should become the very core of your technical practice. Often I find myself trying to teach students to play music and conclude that they have not yet developed models of the sound they want to make in their minds. The learning process therefore takes much longer because first they have to *feed their heads* with listening models that they can copy or spend some time singing and creating sound models first. Imagine for a moment trying to coach someone to imitate John Wayne, but he or she has never seen one of the actor's movies! The best way to begin the process would be to spend a lot of time viewing the actor on screen to imprint the sound of his characteristic voice. Without this imprint, the next-best teaching tool would be if the teacher could recreate the same voice in demonstrations for the student. Trying to share how John Wayne sounds with verbal description alone is very limited and inefficient compared to this aural method. The two most vital components for the development of technique are really the images of sound students already possess and the model sounds that a teacher and others can present in their time together.

The first phase of developing a mental model sound in players involves having them simply copy the sounds they hear coming from other players. This style of learning can be very successful, especially if it employs frequent rapid *call-and-response* sessions between the teacher and student. The teacher demonstrates the model sound, and then the student should immediately repeat it with as close of an imitation to the same sound as possible. Although this kind of applied lesson does not involve much dialogue between players, the aural imprinting process is very valuable as the student learns to manipulate his or her sound to match the model. In addition to the role a teacher plays in imprinting a sound concept, other listening to both live and recorded performances is also vital as students distill these influences into the individualized model sounds in their minds.

Sometimes when I am recovering from an illness or suffering from allergies, I begin to lose my voice. There was one day when I could not speak at all but still taught all of my brass lessons with only this call-and-response type of feedback. I handed the students a note stating that I could not use my voice and that the lesson would be spent with them repeating whatever I played right after me. It also told them that if I did not feel they had done an adequate job of copying the style of my sound, or if their renditions contained mistakes, I would continue to repeat the same passage until they had satisfied these criteria. It was very frustrating for some students as I kept repeating a passage without telling them what I thought they needed to change in their playing. They now had to rely solely on their hearing of my sound compared to their subsequent renditions to guide them. With great patience from both of us, students eventually focused their listening and adapted their sound appropriately. That day taught me not to be too quick to *tell* them what they need to change in their playing when what they really need for their long-term development is the ability to *hear* it for themselves.

This initial copying stage begins the process of creating our individual sound derived from the models we encounter. The wealth of up-close playing that I have been afforded impacts my imaginary sound every day. Hearing Wynton Marsalis do those cornet solos up close, duets with Phil Smith in my office, the incredible matching between Barbara Butler and Charles Geyer, and the jazz sound of Randy Brecker are among many images I still can hear plainly in my mind and constantly use as models to develop my own ultimate sound. We can be only the sum of what we hear when it comes to making great sounds. If you listen to great players on recordings, you will develop further than those who do not. If you also get to hear great sounds live and up close, your development will be even faster and more sophisticated.

For instance, if students have not listened to fast passages on recordings or in live performance, it is quite difficult for them when they attempt even a simple fingering at a very rapid tempo. It will be even more difficult for them to prepare a solo with such technical passages for performance. Hearing the sound of well-played rapid technique must be the beginning of this process. Some students, however, approach this in a backward manner as they try to create a model sound for this faster technique based only on their own playing attempts. When they approach music in this way, the model they are trying to copy is unfortunately only their own rudimentary level of playing. If they are not exposed to other models, this serves as their only guide and will severely limit their progress. If we can point them to great models in recordings and also give them aural images with our demonstrations, we can modify what they hear in their heads and shorten their development no matter what techniques are involved.

The real key to the development of great technique is therefore not about using the right method book or knowing what material to practice but rather what sounds you want the instrument to make. This philosophy must be central to our teaching and learning. We must always remember that music is first and foremost an aural tradition that is developed with focused listening to see if what is coming out of our horns matches what is playing in our heads. If you want to learn how to double tongue with a great sound, you must first hear what the end product sounds like and then seek out a teacher who shares that vision and can demonstrate how to make it on an instrument. With good guidance and great models, you can learn how to develop that sound, beginning with slow playing and consistent airflow. At each step in this learning process, the teacher needs to demonstrate how double tonguing sounds as it develops, so students can recognize the sound at various speeds, internalize it, and then learn to recreate it on their own. Although there is a place for description along with modeling, like teaching someone to imitate John Wayne, it alone is a very limited teaching tool, especially without the addition of aural stimulation.

Technique in a Box

When contemplating the whole of my technical abilities, I like to picture the limits of my capabilities and playing like the boundaries contained inside a large box. The inside of this *ability box* represents what I can do on the instrument currently in all areas of technique. The walls, ceiling, and floor of this imaginary box represent the boundaries of my abilities in different areas of playing. Each day, I want to move those boundaries further out, thus making the box bigger. The more room inside this imagined cube, the greater variety of sounds I can create, and this increases my ability to express musical ideas.

To continue to move these boundaries, you must keep track of your abilities in an organized manner. As in all focused evaluation, this will involve some numbers for measurement. Over many years working with musicians, I often have found a true avoidance of numbers and record keeping when self-evaluating, even though they are critical to establishing goals and maximizing progress in any endeavor. These numbers can measure tempo, range, endurance, and other abilities in a manner more precise than words or memories can. Because progress on brass instruments is slow, it is vital that we be able to measure even the smallest improvement to demonstrate growth. When students report that they do not feel they are progressing, I always uncover either a lack of practice time or a lack of keeping measurements of their playing. The truth is that everyone improves if they approach the instrument in this way. Being able to see the progress is vital to keeping students engaged and excited about their study.

Too many players also enter the practice room with no real plan for the practice session. Although they have literature to learn, they sometimes fail to focus on what they want to accomplish in their practice. Especially for brass players, who are limited in the amount of time they can play each day and in each session, it is vital to plan the time carefully, set manageable goals, and record results. In the athletic, initial practice session, you should always test your boundaries in range, speed, and other areas. If you are not sure where those boundaries are or are unwilling to assess them regularly, you are already limiting your forward progress. If you know them well, you will test these boundaries more quickly in your practice and allow the opportunity to move the confinements of your ability box further outward each day.

Understanding Levels of Repetition

With each passing year, the immediacy of information, and all forms of entertainment through technology, one of the fundamental understandings lost is often the simple concept of repetition. To learn any physical skill well and develop the necessary muscle memory takes many more repeated motions than most students usually feel should be necessary. Students at my institution are characterized as high academic achievers, and we have rigorous academic standards for admission to our programs. As a result, these students were all very successful in high school and do very well on standardized tests. They are intelligent and know it by the time they reach university study. What is difficult for many of them, however, is a true understanding of the difference between theory and practice in areas like music and physical conditioning. In music, knowing what something should sound like and how to approach it from a practicing standpoint are only the first steps in achieving your goals. Without the required repetitions in the practice room, even the smartest student cannot be successful in performance. I spend a lot of time reminding these quick learners about this process as they tend to get frustrated sooner and more deeply than those with less success in other academic areas. One of my teachers often professed that the best brass players are not the most intelligent thinkers because these thinkers would not want to spend so much time in the practice room doing the same thing over and over. This self-effacing humor is, of course, partly true. Many bright students do not practice with enough repetition because to them it is boring. In such situations it is important that teachers address these feelings by helping students increase their listening ability, so they may more easily hear the smallest differences in each repetition and also keep a record to help them follow their progress. It is also important to keep musical creativity at the center of their learning because if playing an instrument becomes only repetition without musical inspiration, it is much more likely that they will turn away from its study.

The brain is also still the world's best computer, and our growing knowledge of computer programming can therefore help students realize that the brain, like a computer, can recall patterns very easily once they are programmed with several identical repetitions. If we have a student trying to learn a harmonic minor scale, for example, it is interesting to describe this function of the brain to them early in the learning process. When programming the sequence of notes in the scale, the brain first identifies the notes as individual items in a sequence. If we play the scale several times with no mistakes, the identical sequences will soon be remembered, and the brain will then begin to group all the notes of that scale into one individual sequence. When this transfer happens, students find that they no longer need to think about each note individually because the entire scale is now one item as the brain completes the note sequence easily for them. Because of this process, students learning Ab melodic minor may find this scale a different thought process than the Bb major scale because the Bb scale is a sequence that has already advanced to single-item status, while the Ab melodic minor might still be in a note-to-note chain of sequences.

If students make mistakes on subsequent renditions of the new scale or pattern, however, the brain tries to sort each new combination of fingerings and notes into separate sequences. If the fingerings keep changing, more sequences are added with no sequence earning preeminence. This reduces the likelihood that the correct scale can advance its status. Slow repetitions without error are, therefore, the fastest means by which students can learn to play fast! If we can get students thinking in this manner, and keeping track of the exact tempo they are playing, their improvement will be fast and furious.

Young players often try to approach all note sequences in the same manner despite their status as individual items or members of a previously learned sequence. Once they have one pattern, like a scale, that has made the transfer to a one-item sequence recall, they try to play a new pattern immediately with the same approach and thought process. Unfortunately, the brain is not ready to recall the entire new sequence by thinking of the one-item trigger because the player has not yet successfully repeated the correct pitch order several times in a row. It is important that students comprehend where patterns are in this learning sequence and create a logical process of moving from note to note and then on to note groups. First, reading the correct pattern with focus on slow movement from note to note is necessary in all new sequences. Then as they increase the speed and begin to play without reading each note, the sequence eventually will transfer its status. Once they achieve this level of learning the pattern, they simply need to see the pattern as a whole, and the brain can recall and place all the individual notes in the sequence. When accomplished performers bring music onstage for a concert, it is usually only to remind them of these larger unit triggers. This learning process can lead to larger and larger units that the brain can recall, and in time, you can connect these recalled sequences to emotional states as well.

The biggest hurdle always is convincing students of the value of starting the process of learning new music with a slower, correct performance. Most young players also need help validating when their playing is accurate, along with an understanding of the benefits of a very slow tempo at the start of the learning process. One strategy music teachers could copy from online games and apps might be to develop a process so that when mistakes are made, like on these games, players automatically return to the most basic level, where they must start again. If we can relate the development of technique to this concept, it might be more appreciated and understood by the next generation of players.

Exercises

- As you start to practice on a new note sequence either in a scale or a passage from your music, begin by choosing a tempo slow enough to guarantee that you will play it absolutely without error. Once you do that once, immediately repeat it before speeding up the tempo but only to the next setting on your metronome. Make a plan from the slower starting speed to the desired performance speed, and divide the increase in the tempo number by the days you have to achieve top speed. You should find that with dedicated, slow practice, you will achieve your goal well in advance of even your initial plan.

- Create a chart of your basic techniques and the tempi at which you can comfortably play them. In each day of practice, start at this comfortable tempo, and then move the tempo up by one full metronome number per repetition. Keep track of your progress as you reestablish your comfort tempos each day.

- When learning new scales, turn on the metronome, and speak the notes of the scale in time while also fingering them on the instrument. Do not try to play them on your instrument until you find the tempo at which you can say the note names and finger them without mistakes. Once you can do that, play them on the instrument at the same tempo, this time thinking the note names as you play. If you have any errors, repeat the process.

- With a fellow musician, bring a bag of quarters into the practice room for scale practice. Set the rule that, for each scale, you will bet each other on the likelihood of a perfect performance. The performer can set any tempo but cannot change tempo for each scale. If any mistakes are made or the pace of the scale is interrupted, the listener collects 25 cents!

8

LIP FLEXIBILITY FOR
EXPRESSIVE TONE

"Most young players don't spend enough time developing
efficient tone production, articulation and lip flexibility
because they are in a hurry to play fast, loud and high."
Dr. Leonard Candelaria, Trumpet Professor
The University of North Texas

Lip flexibility is an essential component for maximizing tonal expressivity. The gentle athleticism needed for precise lip control requires consistent and focused training. Although lip slurs often are taught to increase range and for help in finding correct pitches, it is also important to note the role of flexibility in assuring the best and most productive tone production, especially in softer, gentler playing. The key ingredient for vibrancy in sound is lip flexibility because note-to-note movement that utilizes maximum lip control is less likely to involve excessive use of mouthpiece pressure, air volume, heavy articulation, and other disruptors to the easy flow of sound.

When establishing a lip slur practice regimen, it is important to stress slower tempi and softer dynamics to ensure the most lip control possible. Although there are many lip slur books available, the most important thing to remember is to identify routines that begin in the middle register with very slow movement between harmonics and gradually increase the range and speed. Lip slurs at softer dynamics take the most controlled lip movement as does the higher register. Be sure to include many softer lip exercises, especially in the upper register, to offer your embouchure the most refined development. As with all instrumental methods, there is no *magic book* of lip slurs. The magic will come from the player and his or her ability to focus on the quality of the playing and knowing goals for the next level of ability.

When moving from harmonic to harmonic, a player must be able to move without hesitation while keeping the volume and tone color even. For this reason, all lip slurs, even the slowest ones, should be done with a metronome to ensure there is no delay in the movement of the lips. Softer dynamics also are vital to maximize lip efficiency. Too often players and teachers are willing to accept imperfections in the timing or tone to achieve faster, higher, or larger slurs. When a lip slur does not involve efficient lip movement, it is always audible in the sound. Sometimes, for example, we hear an accent on the arrival of the note following the slurred interval. Such sounds reveal overreliance on a sudden increase in air to produce the movement. This type of blowing, often referred to as *huffing*, will interrupt sound flow and also inhibit faster lip slurs later due to its overreliance on this rapid increase in air. Likewise, listen for slurs that are not exactly in time. When this occurs, immediately slow the tempo down until movement is achieved precisely with the metronome. The movement from partial to partial should be immediate and without excessive effort. It's really like flipping a light switch: quick, effortless, and immediate.

Also when listening to lip slurs, focus on the tone quality and tuning as you move from note to note. Often when slurring up, you will hear a more closed sound on the upper note that also may be out of tune. This is usually an indicator that you are pressing the mouthpiece against your lips to create artificial lip compression rather than allowing the lips to create compression on their own. This behavior stems from lip slurs and other upward motion on brass instruments that are attempted in a manner that cannot yet be accommodated with controlled changes in lip compression. Instinctively, young players will learn to increase mouthpiece pressure and also increase the airflow dramatically to achieve slurs that are faster or higher than their embouchures are ready to do efficiently. When working to develop more strength and conditioning with lip slurs, especially those involving higher and faster movement, they should be practiced when the lips are fresh and at their most responsive. Practicing lip slurs when tired serves only to reinforce bad habits of pressing and overblowing, so be sure to plan this work when you have not played too much in the day.

The Pivot System

The action of *pivoting* the angle of the mouthpiece on the embouchure is also a part of playing that can be overused to achieve movement between harmonics. In smaller intervals with most players, the normal amount of pivot motion is imperceptible as any such motion is indeed very small. Even in larger movements such as octave slurs, the movement is perceptible but still usually small with less than an inch change in position of the bell. Players with a natural overbite normally will pivot down when ascending and up when descending intervals. Underbite or upstream players generally have the same range of pivot in their movement in opposite directions to upstream players. When playing higher, the bell rises slightly and lowers as they descend (see Fig. 8.1).

If the lips are not working efficiently in changing lip compression to achieve different harmonics, some players instinctively learn to over pivot to assist the movement from note to note in a lip slur. This process of over pivoting creates many obstacles in tone productivity, especially when the movement becomes faster. Also, once they use the bigger pivot to move from one harmonic to the next, further movement without resetting is inhibited because they already have maximized the impact of such movement. There is only so far you can move the angle of the mouthpiece relative to the

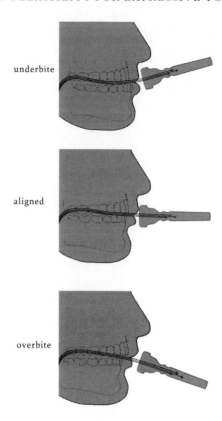

Figure 8.1 Upstream/downstream pivot

teeth, and if you use that entire range of motion for one interval, you have exhausted this potential for further motion in one direction. In rapid movement, the pivot needs to be minimized also to limit obstacles to an even tone production. In a rapid lip trill, for example, attempts to rely on over pivoting will result in a choppy sound, and this excessive movement will keep the player from the faster tempos and the smooth sound that efficient lip flexibility can create. As a matter of course, I prefer to ask students to try *not to pivot or move this angle at all* as they play between registers, especially in rapid passages. Although they will probably end up moving slightly, I find that this goal reduces the chance that they will become reliant on over pivoting and establish the most productive use of their lip flexibility possible.

As with all fine muscle training, it is vital to focus on absolute correctness at a slow tempo and in a controllable range initially, with progress dependent on meeting the previously listed criteria. Gravitating from the comfortable center of the range into upper and lower registers, along with moving from mezzo dynamics to softer and louder dynamics, will build controlled lip movement through modeling. This not only facilitates lip slurs and trills but also all intervallic motion, including that involving fingering changes or even the use of tongued articulation as the movement of the lips should be just as efficient in these situations.

Vibrato and Flexibility

Brass players physically create vibrato with changes in lip compression and also some slight jaw motion. The movement of the lips within the confines of the inner rim of the mouthpiece to create vibrato is a very small and controlled motion. It takes some time to develop the flexibility to create such movement, but players should work on this skill early in their training. The inability to create vibrato is usually a physical limitation in lip flexibility, often combined with a lack of awareness of how vibrato should sound and even if it should be used.

Vibrato on brass instruments requires a very flexible embouchure, and its use demonstrates a more sophisticated lip action in the player. Many times I hear high school players who have been studying a brass instrument for four years or more yet cannot create vibrato in their sound. I hear this often as an adjudicator for brass solos and bands when brass players serve in solo roles. Many of the players have strong embouchures and adequate endurance but lack the refined control to create the vibrato so necessary for musical expression. To assist them in developing this ingredient in their sound, I employ several approaches that I have found very successful.

Even very young players need to listen to music with sophisticated uses of vibrato. In our overproduced world dominated by pop music, the sound we hear is often full of different colors achieved not by one voice or instrument but rather by combining many sounds in rapid collections. It is important for young players to listen to classical brass players with wonderfully expressive use of vibrato as well as singers and string players. It takes a lot of listening to fully absorb how vibrato works in an expressive sound. With lots of listening, students can *immerse* themselves in this type of sound, and it will generate the need to hear it in their own playing. Do not underestimate the amount of listening this requires; it is a lot! This *tonal bathing*, as I call it, is an important component in the training of all players no matter their experience or place in the music profession.

In addition to the immersion listening for students that I advise, there are several self-awareness strategies you can use to help students hear and develop vibrato in their sound. A first step I often take is simply to create hand vibrato on my instrument for them to hear and then, using my hand, create it on their instruments while they sustain a note. Trombonists can use their slides to create this as well, and it is often a good first step in the realization process of what vibrato sounds like while playing. Of course, using hand vibrato is less efficient because you are actually varying lip compression with a secondary source (hand-controlled changes in mouthpiece pressure) rather than utilizing the primary source of your embouchure. Although embouchure control is dependent on the development of superior lip flexibility, hearing yourself make vibrato is an essential step toward that automatic natural connection between hearing sound with vibrato and playing with it.

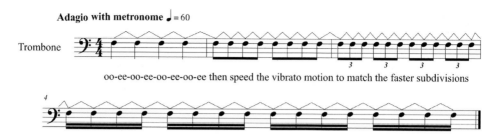

Figure 8.2 Vibrato realization/control exercise

To help create the lip control and movement required for expressive vibrato, I use several exercises in my practice and with my students. Lip slurs are at the center of this development, but there are some other focused techniques that are also helpful. Lip bends are wonderful to establish fine lip control. I like to start with half-step bends downward in the middle register and then work to the upper and lower registers. As with lip slurs, the softer dynamics and the upper register will offer the greatest challenges. Like lip slur practice, it is important to achieve the best tone quality on these bends as possible. Often in a new register, the half-step down note you *bend* to will not yield an open sound and will have less resonance. With practice and increased lip control, however, you will hear improvement in the sound quality of the bent note, and you can then strive for this model as you proceed to higher registers. After one semitone is established, you can then proceed by bending down two half steps while constantly striving for the best sound possible.

I also like to use a metronomic vibrato exercise to test lip control and develop the flexibility needed for expressive production. One of these exercises starts with quarter note vibrato motion and then progresses to eighth notes, eighth triplets, and finally sixteenth notes (see Fig. 8.2). Keeping the dynamics softer and gradually increasing the range will aid in the development of precise lip control. With enough repetition, this mental connection will become more natural to the player and, along with exposure to vibrato in other players, can lead to vibrato for expression and a more automatic relationship between the imagination and the physicality needed to create the sound.

Flexibility in Valve/Slide Use

When students begin mastering the sound and feel of efficient and gentle harmonic lip slurs, it is important to reinforce the same quality of sound when valves or slide movement is involved. In larger intervals especially, it takes daily attention to develop a consistency of sound when combining lip motion with valve or slide movement. The large upward slur, whether a lip slur or involving valve or slide changes, seems to be a problem for many players. First of all, I find that students either do not practice these slurs or do not practice them correctly. Young brass players often encounter upward slurs and, without enough time for quality teaching or practice, they will utilize secondary methods to make this note movement more secure. Among the fallback mechanisms the body will employ to accommodate the slur will be adding mouthpiece pressure, overblowing the air, smiling with the embouchure, and constricting the throat and oral cavity. Because these mechanisms might yield the successful sounding of the note and, if the lips are not yet capable of doing it correctly, students will repeat these secondary methods over and over, they can become normal in their playing. Of course, one can detect these methods by their impact on the sound quality, but unfortunately those changes in sound can also become normal and expected to both the student and even listeners if they are not identified and corrected in a timely manner.

In a similar fashion, larger descending intervals also can invite secondary methods into use to achieve a functional rendition of the passage. This is especially true in the lowest registers. Here too the lips have a role to play in shaping the aperture by the amount of resistance they present to the air. Oddly, I find that many brass players actually play with too much pressure in the low register. The lips become trapped between the mouthpiece and the teeth and are unable to protrude slightly to correctly provide the shaped resistance to the air. Again, secondary methods are employed that include overblowing, graphic loss of embouchure corner formation, and unnecessary over pivoting to produce the note. When these methods are used, the trained ear can hear the discrepancies in sound quality, pitch, and volume as well as the accentuation of the note change. Often the lower note of the descending interval is arrived at with an accompanying *thud* that is very noticeable. The player and listener, however, can, with much exposure to this sound, become satisfied that it is the proper way for such passages to be rendered. When the teacher later challenges this sense of satisfaction, it is vital to demonstrate the correct sound over and over to differentiate it from the incorrect one that relies on these less efficient, alternate methods.

Again, using models of efficient playing can be the best way to improve these larger slurs. Critical listening to smaller intervals and comparing them to larger intervals are important as is selecting etudes and exercises that include slurs of varying intervals to allow for clear comparison in terms of sound quality. Listening to other instruments that do not face the physical challenges of brass players can be a great reminder of how effortless such slurs can sound when playing large intervals. Listen to woodwinds when they employ the octave key and strive for this kind of reliability and sound quality in larger intervallic motion. Students also should be encouraged to play duets with woodwind and string instrumentalists and also play intervals on the piano to hear the flow of sound during skips and leaps as a model.

Development of sensitive lip flexibility is key to a vibrant and flexible sound. In my years of playing I have learned that there are certainly different schools of thought and teaching when it comes to brass tone production. Many times, I have found myself in an environment with both players and teachers who teach and play a more direct, less vibrant concept of sound. This is often the case in those whose experiences are dominated by commercial playing and also marching bands and drum corps.

During my first years of university teaching I would spend the academic year working at my university but would return to Eastman each summer to work on my doctoral degree. In the five years it took me to finish, I experienced an interesting phenomenon in my own playing. The vibrant and expressive sound production I reinforced in my own playing during each summer session became diluted over the ensuing nine months as I was surrounded with less vibrant tones from everywhere. Much of this less vibrant exposure was from my own students in the 20 or more private lessons each week, but it also came from other teachers, band directors, and professional players in my area of the country. The overwhelming concept was a brighter, very direct sound that often lacked vibrancy, even in the easy middle registers and in solo playing. This *hard* sound style was, of course, recognizable to me as I had worked so hard to eliminate it from my own playing. Despite this awareness, however, the constant exposure to hard sounds and the resulting adulation for those making them from many in the music profession would, over the course of nine months, begin to change my concept and make me question my own playing.

By May and the end of the university year, I consistently felt that my sound needed to be brighter, harder, and more like those I was hearing all around me. Off I would go to Eastman for the summer with these ideas but then would be reimmersed in the more vibrant sound predominant in that environment. Playing along with Butler and Geyer and others in Rochester, I would return back to the tonal awareness and the sophisticated playing style I so admired. These years taught me that no matter how developed you are, or accomplished your playing, your environment always has an impact on you, your playing, and your teaching. Just as our students need to be listening to great players both live and recorded, so do we who call ourselves teachers and professional performers. The dangers of complacency are great if you do not consistently seek to revalidate your concepts at the highest levels of the profession. The comfort that we take from how we sound at the moment must be constantly challenged by the discomfort of considering how our sound can be richer, vibrant, and even more expressive.

Exercises

- Sustain long tones with no vibrato or lip movement and listen to the color of the sound. Compare this color to a long tone with the smallest vibrato-style lip motion you can sustain. Gradually increase the speed and width of the vibrato to create different colors, and consider how these different sounds might be used to create different emotional responses.

- Practice soft ascending and descending intervals very slowly, listening to the quality of sound as you traverse the skip or leap. Work for consistency of volume and tone vibrancy as well as pitch. Compare lip slurs to similar slurs that involve changes in valves or slide positions for similar fluidity and consistency of sound.
- Play slow lip slurs, but once you arrive on each new note, gradually bend it down one half step with only your lip motion. As you move to more extreme high and low registers, try to keep the same control and reliability as in the middle register. Play them softly, and once you are successful with a one half-step bend, go for two half steps!

9

THE TOOLS OF ARTICULATION

"It's 'nu' tonguing man!"

Wynton Marsalis
Classical and Jazz Trumpeter

In 1987 while sitting with Wynton Marsalis on a bus ride from Montreal to Toronto during the Carnaval Tour with the Eastman Wind Ensemble, I asked him about his Grammy-winning recording of the Hummel *Concerto*. Since its release a few years earlier, my friends and I had all pondered whether he was slurring or tonguing during a portion of the second movement. In describing this passage in the work, Wynton said, "It's *nu* tonguing man!" I had never heard articulation described in this manner. For me, it was a great learning moment. As in many other components of brass performance, Wynton was bringing expressive techniques from jazz playing into classical performance. I have always envied the seemingly greater range of expression often stressed in early jazz training, and this seemed so simple of a concept that I wondered why I had not encountered it.

One of the greatest tools for expressing music on brass instruments is the tongue. Just like its use in creating a myriad of sounds in the speaking language, the tongue can help players achieve a wide range of colors and emotional responses with proper practice and exposure to listening models. As with all techniques, it is vital that students spend time listening to both brass performers and also other instruments and singers for inspiration.

The function of the tongue in managing pressurized air is multifaceted and can be developed with a variety of teaching methods. Essentially, our articulation is dependent on the tongue stopping the airflow momentarily and then releasing the now-pressurized air, achieving an accent in the sound flow. Donald Smithers describes this activity brilliantly in his article "Playing the Baroque Trumpet."[1]

The sound of the attack can be changed by the placement of the tongue, thus changing the amount of oral cavity space that pressurized air has to depressurize prior to reaching the embouchure. The more depressurization that occurs, the less percussiveness is heard in the attack (see Fig. 9.1).

Placement of the tip of the tongue is the best place to start the process of realization for varied attacks. The closer this placement is to the vibrating lips, the more pronounced the accent. Placing the tongue between the teeth is therefore the most percussive as the pressurized air is released right at the point of the vibrating lips. This *th* placement is never used, however, because it results in an attack that is too percussive and too disruptive to the airflow. The tip of the tongue behind the top teeth where it meets the upper palate yields the *t* sound, and moving progressively with the tip of the tongue along the palate toward the back of the mouth, we create *d*, *n*, and *l* syllables. With the back of the tongue, we can articulate further back with *k* and *g*. Dr. Leonard Candelaria, the longtime professor of trumpet at the University of North Texas introduced me to a great visualization aid in thinking about articulation and the sounds different techniques produce. As students now all see similar representations on audio programs like *Audacity*, it becomes a good tool to help them form concepts of the differentiation of attacks and types of articulation (see Fig. 9.2).

Dr. Candelaria references the three sounding parts of a note as initial attack, steady state, and decay. This illustration shows the role each of these three parts plays in achieving the sound of each articulation. To help demonstrate the initial attack

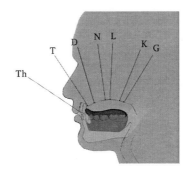

Figure 9.1 Tongue placements for articulation

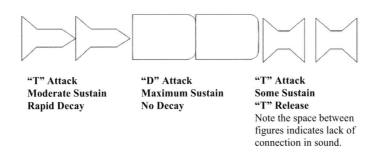

"T" Attack
Moderate Sustain
Rapid Decay

"D" Attack
Maximum Sustain
No Decay

"T" Attack
Some Sustain
"T" Release
Note the space between
figures indicates lack of
connection in sound.

Figure 9.2 Visual representations of note attacks—Candelaria

portion of articulated notes, have your students vocalize the various consonants; they can feel the tip of the tongue move in this course along the upper palate. Have them repeat *tu*, *du*, *nu*, and *lu* several times; it is easy to make the connection between the movement of the tongue and the change in sound. In more advanced students, you can also ask them to repeat *tu-ku-tu-ku* and *du-gu-du-gu* to feel and hear the same type of connection with double tonguing. With this realization, they can begin to experiment with mouthpiece buzzing and playing these articulations on their instruments.

The vowel component of the syllable is, of course, also part of this equation as it relates to the size of the oral cavity in which the movement of the tongue upward and downward facilitates different ranges and dynamics. You can create smaller oral cavity formations by forming the *ee* vowel sound, which raises the tongue, and this can assist in the high register and with softer dynamics. The *ah* vowel sounds drop the tongue down in the mouth, increasing oral cavity size, and helps in lows and louds. An *oo* placement is a more middle placement and can assist in middle register and mezzo dynamic levels.

I find that too often, brass players are not made aware of these different placements and how they can impact their sound. Once students can produce *t* or *d* readily, it is important to introduce the less percussive attacks as well. As brass instruments are perhaps the most suited to playing in an articulated style, it is clear that the greatest work needs to be in the area of lyrical, connected playing. This is especially true regarding the initial attack on brasses as they are the easiest instruments on which we can make strong, percussive attacks outside of the percussion section. Unfortunately, when the level of attack is much higher than the steady state and decay pattern, the audience only hears the attack as a percussive effect, and the concept of melody can be lost. This is often how brass instruments are featured not only in the band and orchestra but also in smaller ensembles like brass choirs, quintets, and even as soloists. Especially when playing rapidly with many tongued notes, we must strive so that we hear more continuity and not simply this percussive effect of the attack without a sustained tone color. It is in these moments a less percussive choice of tonguing can be helpful for both punctuating the music but also presenting an expressive melody. Wynton Marsalis on the *Carnaval* recording and in our tour set a new standard, in my view, for the melodic capabilities in even the most rapid articulation settings. In his playing, we still hear the attack cleanly, but because it is not at the highest level of percussiveness or *ping*, the melodic lines are more expressive, and the tone quality is richer and fuller.

Often in playing melodically, players allow too much decay of the sound, so the overall sustaining and carrying power of notes do not match the intensity level of the attack and the prominence needed in the brass melody. Even though the sound still rings a bit throughout, the large decay after a strong attack creates the sense of separation between notes. The result is a weaker presentation that lacks presence in large rooms and misses the opportunity to instill feelings of confidence that can be expressed with a more consistent flow of sound. By sustaining the sound with less decay, the melodic line gains more prominence without an overall increase in volume or attack level, and listeners generally prefer the more connected nature of the melody produced.

Barbara Butler refers to the loss of sustained sound because of too rapid of a decay as *gaps* in the sound, and truly, that is the impact in larger rooms of such playing. In solo moments, these gaps become more obvious, and I believe that they become a normal part of many players' presentations in part due to ensemble experiences and also because they have not done enough listening to themselves in comparison with great models. The impact of a *gap-filled* rendition of a melodic line and one that is more sustained is very audible, so be sure to listen intently to recordings of yourself to maximize your melodic presentation.

As a musician, I like to compare my articulation to the colors and techniques available to a painter. I think that a painter would not want just one color of blue but as many shades of blue as one can imagine. Look around you in the world, and see all the various hues and shades of blue. Can you imagine if there was only one blue color? To me, that is what it sounds like when I hear brass players who articulate exactly the same on everything they play. Although it might be impressive in its consistency, the impact on listeners will soon wane, and players will need to use bigger effects in other areas of their playing to hold our attention.

To ensure that you will develop the ability to hear and play different articulation types, you need a methodical approach to articulation that assures experience in all keys, ranges, techniques, volumes, and methods of attack. The Clarke *Technical Studies* are a great vehicle to develop articulation, but so are many other books and systems. As with all resources, success will come from how you use and adapt exercises in the resource as opposed to what simply appears in the printed material. The Clarke *Studies*, in print, are limited because they do offer enough varied articulation, and they do not cover the full range of the instrument. It is important to see beyond the printed exercises to use these patterns to *exercise* all of your articulation tools. In approaching articulation studies, you always must strive to change articulation styles, especially the consonant sound of attack. If you can imagine a technique or style of attack, you should try to achieve it using these patterns as a convenient vehicle. Of course the exercises as written work your fingerings and establish your abilities to hear in all the keys of conventional music, but they are also invaluable as a platform for developing articulation as an expressive tool.

One of the first assignments I give to serious students is to memorize all the Clarke patterns in all the keys. Although this seems a bit too much for some of them, the serious players achieve it quickly once they accept it as necessary. With the patterns memorized, students can focus entirely on their sound while they are practicing without the distraction of reading music. As a teacher, I often start lessons by randomly playing Clarke studies back and forth with students in different keys using different slur/tongue combinations and different attack styles. If the student cannot duplicate the study without the music, it is very apparent to them that they are not ready to gain the full benefit my modeling is offering. Only with consistent practice can they readily access these patterns and use them to make quick connections between the sound in their heads and the resulting sound on their instruments. If they approach their practice with the goal of becoming conversant in these patterns, they eventually can achieve a direct connection between their mental image and coordination of techniques on their instrument to realize it. Some students achieve this level in their playing and benefit greatly from these connections, while others do not and never understand how natural and exciting such playing can be.

Earn the Right to Tongue It by Slurring It First

As the tongue in articulation adds another component in sound production and melodic presentation, it also has the capability of causing disruption in the flow of sound. Articulation offers many players the opportunity to use a secondary method to gain security in note movement depending on the range, size of interval, and volume level that might be difficult to control with slurred lip movement alone. For example, if a student is unable to efficiently create a high note on a brass instrument due to insufficient lip compression or airspeed, tonguing the note in a very percussive manner, combined with added mouthpiece pressure, can be substituted. Unfortunately, this yields a less vibrant sound and severely limits expressive tools like dynamics and vibrato. It does, however, allow the note to be heard and can be used when necessary. In all registers, the tongue can be used to mask inefficiencies in lip use, so I find it good practice to use slurring as an initial strategy when working all articulated passages to ensure maximum lip control. I tell my students to *earn the right to tongue it* by demonstrating the ability to slur the entire phrase first.

By using this approach, we can isolate and work on issues with lip movement and airspeed without the additional articulation component. This focus on lip efficiency is sometimes quite challenging to students, especially in passages with extremes of range or large intervals. I find that once they can slur it without disruptions in volume, time, or tone color, adding the tongue motion is more likely to retain a more expressive and full tone. Even when they cannot slur the entire passage efficiently with perfect control, the process of working on it in this manner both helps them identify long-term goals in their playing and also enhances the eventual articulated rendition in terms of sound and expression.

Always remember that if a student can tongue a phrase but cannot slur it, that means that they are not making their best sound and will be less able to make some of the changes needed for musical interpretation. It is one of the easiest ways to evaluate how far a student is from the ideal efficient sound on any passage. When they can slur it with ease, more colors of articulation instantly become available because of the efficiency of the embouchure. This means there are many more possibilities for musical expression and fewer issues with endurance, pitch, tone color, and dynamics as well.

Articulation to Imitate Slurring

One of the most valuable tools for a brass player is also the ability to articulate in a manner that sounds like slurring. Especially for trombonists who must immediately develop legato tonguing due to the movement of the slide, this ability can be used in many instances to ensure security and facilitate expression.

Legato articulation of this nature involves a less percussive attack matched with a consistent steady state and little or no decay in the sound. As with the lip use mentioned in slurring, a precise use of the lips is also a necessary component of good legato technique. An obvious question that might arise is this: If you need to be able to slur it to demonstrate lip function, why would you use legato tonguing to replace that ability? The answer lies in the abilities of the players and the demands of the music. Some slurs are more demanding than others, and often players will use their legato tonguing method to bolster reliability and calm their worries. The use of legato tongue instead of slurring is used often in situations when players seek a bit of extra security.

Exposed slurs that cover large intervals are one of the situations when players might utilize their tongues for security. The larger the slur, the more extreme the range, and the softer the dynamic, the more likely legato tonguing is to be used. This is true in solo playing and also in ensembles. When more than one player is asked to traverse such slurs, it is more likely that legato tonguing can help accuracy as the subtle differences in sound between legato tonguing and actual slurring disappear as you add more players.

For example, in the opening of the *Fanfare for the Common Man* by Aaron Copland, three trumpets are required to slur from middle G to middle C to G on the top of the staff. As a student at Florida State University, I was delighted to be one of the three players who opened the concert in 1979 with Mr. Copland conducting! Though we were three skilled players, the interval from C to G was always problematic for all three of us to slur it right together with the arrival right on time and in tune (see Fig. 9.3). A solution to such a challenge is to have all the players use a combination of

Figure 9.3 Copland *Fanfare* opening

slurring and legato tongue to increase accuracy. As three players perform it together, there is no audible difference between slurring and legato tonguing in a big room for the audience. As a result, *du-oo-nee* might be a great way to try it and other like passages with your students.

Developing Multiple Tonguing

One area of brass playing that has retreated somewhat in recent years in early training is the development of capable multiple tonguing. Although certainly there are great resources and models available to students, it seems that band programs are stressing this skill less as we move away from the heyday of virtuoso brass solos like *The Carnival of Venice* for cornet or *Blue Bells of Scotland* for trombone. It is always sad to hear high school players who produce a wonderful sound but have no ability to double tongue or triple tongue. Of course, we only hear this absence when they attempt to play this effect in their chosen music!

Once students can single tongue with consistent airflow and a stable sound, they can begin the process of learning multiple tonguing. As with any muscular training, it is vital to start slowly to ensure proper function of the tongue and consistent support of the air. For students, it is very helpful to have teachers model the exact sound at slow speeds to realize how slow to start and to be certain that they are actually using the back of the tongue to achieve *k* and *g* attacks rather than just single tonguing everything.

It is also helpful to have students begin by vocalizing syllables for double tonguing and triple tonguing with special attention to a sustained vowel sound. This will assist proper airflow and avoid gaps once they begin to play on the instrument. After vocalization, have them do the same process without engaging the vocal chords but rather by simply blowing the air and using their tongues to create sounds only with the tongue's manipulation of a steady airstream. They should blow vigorously enough to feel the airflow on the palm of their hand from about one foot away from their mouth (recall Fig. 3.1). Blow on their hand for them, and then have them blow on their own hand for comparison. Blowing and tonguing in this manner are great practice, and I urge players to practice them while walking to class or when they are away from their instruments and wish to do something in their idle time that will help their development as players. This process helps them realize the impact of pressurized air on the movement of the tongue and prepares them for playing on the mouthpiece and instrument.

Two next steps can be to blow and tongue as described but also now attempt to sustain a buzz of the lips during process. This is very challenging, but it can help students understand how the pressurized air and lip resistance operate with multiple tonguing syllables. Buzzing the mouthpiece while multiple tonguing is the next logical step in this process and, as in other uses of the mouthpiece, very revealing to players. With experienced players working on advanced solos, I often simply ask them to buzz a brief passage on their mouthpiece to examine the efficiency of tongue movement and airflow. When they are unable to create a stable flow of sound, they usually realize that they tried to skip over the logical process of developing efficient tonguing, and until they address this basic weakness, such solos will be out of their reach.

As double tonguing is more predominant in brass literature, I suggest that you begin with this technique. After students adequately can blow the air and create the proper syllables, have them play very slowly with their lips, mouthpiece, and instrument focusing on sustained sounds, perhaps about one note per second to be sure. As they gradually speed up the process, be sure that if they cannot sustain the sound, they will need to slow back down. Tell them to think about flowing one note right into the next with no decay. This takes a lot of air, so they will need to do it slowly until they understand the sensation and sound of using the air correctly.

Because the *k* or *g* consonant sound is created with the back of the tongue arching to the palate, this part of the double tongue will always be a bit weaker because there is more space in the oral cavity for the air to depressurize prior to reaching the buzzing lips. There are some practice tips, though, that you can employ to make this syllable stronger and more equal to the *t* or *d* sound and create a more consistent flow of attacks. One idea is to accent the back of the tongue attack (*k* or *g*) in the process (see Fig. 9.4A). Do this with exaggerated accents to bring this tongue action further forward to create more percussiveness. You can also reverse the syllables, so instead of *tu-ku-tu-ku*, you can play *ku-tu-ku-tu* (Fig. 9.4B). Placing the *k* attack on the strong

Standard Syllables but Accent Back of Tongue

Connect with air. Start slowly and think legato style.

Figure 9.4A Accenting *ku* in double tonguing

Place K on the Strong Part of the Beat to Reinforce Strength and Accent

Connect with air. Start slowly and think legato style.

Figure 9.4B Putting *ku* on strong part of the beat

65

Use All K or G Consonants to Strengthen the Back of Tongue Attack

Connect with air. Start slowly and think legato style.

Figure 9.4C Using all *ku* in double tonguing

part of the beat will also result in more effort to make it a stronger accent. Finally, you should practice all back of the tongue attacks (*k-k-k-k*) and compare them to all front tongue attacks (*t-t-t-t*) (Fig. 9.4C).

Start multiple tonguing with only one repeated pitch and only move to pitch changes once they can control the tongue motion with sustained airflow. As you progress to moving diatonic notes, go for two or three repeated notes (depending on if double or triple tonguing) with note changes occurring on the strong part of the tonguing sequence. Finally move into note changes on all syllables and then into larger intervals.

I also like to steal an exercise concept from percussionists in working on all forms of articulation. Similar to how they work on single- and double-stroke drumrolls by beginning very slowly and gradually increasing speed while focusing on identical attacks, I like to start multiple tonguing very slowly, speed up to maximum, and then return to the slow tempo all in one breath. By establishing the connected sound with proper air use, you easily can identify if you lose this sound as you increase speed. For those students who cannot make an efficient sound when multiple tonguing at a fast speed, I find this to be a great diagnostic tool. Usually, the sound changes because they are closing their mouths as they increase the speed. The remedy for this is simply to use more air to maintain an open mouth and an open sound. It does take some time for them to abandon the closed-mouth process, however, because oftentimes they have been relying on it for years to play multiple-tongued passages faster than their true ability level would allow, and closing their mouths becomes a secondary method to the proper use of air and connection in articulation.

Flutter Tonguing

Flutter tonguing is a special effect that brass players occasionally encounter in their music, so it should be touched upon as a technique regularly in the practice routine. The rapid tongue movement across the pressurized airstream can be difficult to sustain initially as it takes a combination of consistent air support along with flexible response of the embouchure. Always start by rolling the *rr* without the instrument to see if you can vocalize in this manner. Once this is established, like other methods of articulation, you should start in the middle register and at mezzo forte dynamics. Migration to boundary ranges, both high and low, will prove more challenging as will flutter tonguing in the extreme dynamic ranges of *pp* and *ff*.

Because flutter tonguing, like all articulation, requires the embouchure to respond with rapid lip movement to sound consistently on the instrument, this technique can be used to realize and improve response as well. Most initial attack problems that are not related to inhalation issues are due to lack of immediate response in the lips at the precise start of the note. I have found that flutter-tongued attacks are helpful in working immediate response in all registers and dynamic ranges as it requires a more flexible embouchure along with tongue movement than slower, longer tones. Additionally, I enjoy working soft articulations of all kinds to reinforce my security in very soft playing. I first learned about such soft articulation practicing for over-all response from Charles Schlueter, the longtime principal trumpet of the Boston Symphony Orchestra who employs soft tonguing as a method of checking his overall embouchure responsiveness.

Pu Attacks

Another great articulation technique that will develop better lip response is to use air attacks to evaluate the commencement of lip vibration without the use of the tongue in the attack process. These *pu attacks* can help players find the perfect balance between airflow and lip resistance on any note in any range with any dynamic level. When you can attack the note in this manner with a clear, on-time start with no air in the sound, you can be assured that your lips are really responsive. With this ability, all articulation styles are possible because of the flexibility of the lips. When a player has done too much loud playing, the ability to do *pu* attacks in the softer dynamics is usually very challenging, and therefore it should be a focus when working to return the lips to the level of sensitive response this technique requires. Soft attacks such as this in the upper register are especially challenging to the lips as they need to create the sophisticated control that yields the smallest aperture in brass playing. It is important to have young players practice this and other types of soft playing to balance the overwhelming amount of loud playing they experience in band and other ensembles in school. With many years of neglect, the more delicate response and sounds of gentle articulation may never develop in players, and this severely limits their overall range of expressive capability as players.

Articulation is one the great resources for musical expression in brass playing. It is very important to introduce the different sounds that the tongue can assist in producing and developing the ability to make these sounds readily. Using scales and technical studies to coordinate embouchure, finger, and tongue movement is vital to begin the process. With repeated work and attention to proper sound color, players can create natural connections between their mental images and the sounds of articulation that allow brass playing to be as expressive as the use of language.

Exercises

- With as much connection of the sound as possible and starting at about one note per second, play a tonguing exercise that speeds up to your tongue's fastest ability and then slows down to the speed at which you started. Work on this accelerando and ritardando so that you can achieve it all in one breath. Play at softer dynamics to preserve air use and maximize response. Listen for any loss of sustain or openness in the sound, and once you can do it single tonguing, move to double and triple tonguing.

- Beginning in the middle register, practice starting tones with only the air, thinking about the syllable *pu*. Be sure that your inhalation and exhalation are in one consistent cycle, and strive for a clean, pure commencement of the sound without using the tongue. Softer dynamics are more challenging but also more beneficial to precise development of embouchure response. Practice these attacks in all registers, and you will find, as many professional players do, that this articulation style is valuable not just as a practice tool, but it also offers security in performance when a very soft, non-accented attack is required.

- Beginning with one repeated pitch, articulate using a *t* attack for two measures followed by two measures of *d* and *n* attacks. Compare these three attack styles, and listen for the different colors they create and also for reliability and consistency among each style.

Note

1 Donald Smithers, "Playing the Baroque Trumpet: Research into the history and physics of this largely forgotten instrument is revealing its secrets, enabling modern trumpeters to play it as the musicians of the 17th and 18th centuries did" (*Scientific American*, April 1986, Vol. 254, No. 4, p. 108–115).

10

EFFECTIVE PRACTICING

"There won't come a time when you don't have to practice anymore."

J. J. Johnson
Jazz Trombonist

Expression and Problem Solving During Practice

Practice sessions can offer brass students unlimited opportunities to develop playing wisely and realize on their instruments the sound that they already have developed in their imaginations. It is important that the approach to practice be the same focused yet reactionary process that we want to apply to all performance preparation. This takes constant reexamination of our playing against our mental models. Once we know what we want to sound like and also are aware of how we currently sound, the next step is a comparison of the two and the development of an action plan to bring the reality closer to the model.

Because we so idolize great players on our instruments and want to emulate their wonderful performances, we often lose sight of our own individuality in the improvement of our playing. Often, for example, students latch onto the routine or practice regime of a great brass player and think that if they simply copy the practice structure, they too will reach greatness. Although we can gain much from learning what great players do to improve, the attempt to systematize practice and preparation is this manner fails to recognize individuality in our skills and needs. We are all different in our playing and also different in our day-to-day playing schedule. Most routines are ultimate examples or snapshots of daily work done at one given time and offered in that context by great players. Their written form on paper does not capture the flexible nature of their practice and how they respond to the varying needs in their playing. A real routine is actually not routine at all but rather a mind-set that determines what and how to practice based on how you currently sound, what your goals are, and what playing demands are upcoming. It is also important to remember that it is impossible to play all techniques, keys, and ranges thoroughly each day, so the approach to practice planning must be based on long-range goals balanced with short-term needs.

Daily Practice Regimen

Each practice session always should begin with a few moments of focused thought in the same manner as meditation. Take the time to truly devote this block of time only to your playing, and *give yourself permission* to not think or worry about anything else. Although this state of mind sounds simple, it actually takes some effort to achieve. Our minds are constantly bombarded with worries and thoughts that can easily distract us from a task that requires maximum focus. If you can allow yourself to concentrate only on music for the practice session, without feeling guilty for not considering your sick boyfriend, math homework, or that fight with your mother, you can achieve great progress. To assist you in this process, choose a practice space where you cannot see others, and actually turn your cell phone and other devices off, or leave them outside the room. Whatever focused task you want to accomplish, use this approach, and you will see great benefits in your work. When you later decide to do math homework or some other nonmusic work, you will need to go through the same process to give yourself permission not to worry about your upcoming solo performance as well. My motto is always *work hard; play hard*. By that I mean that if your do focused work during the working portion of your day, you can then enjoy your social and relaxed time without the guilt caused by worrying about missed or inefficient practice and other work. If you plan practice sessions into your day and approach them with a focused mind-set, you also can fully enjoy life outside of music without the nagging guilt that accompanies nonexistent or unproductive practice sessions.

Be sure to apply logic and common sense each day in your practice sessions. Playing a brass instrument is a taxing muscular activity, and there are going to be differences in your ability to play depending on time spent playing and the type of playing you are doing. Central to understanding how this applies to you requires you first to understand efficient versus inefficient playing. Endurance grows steadily when you build on efficient use of your muscles but suffers under inefficient use of these muscles. Too often students abuse their lips with incorrect playing, especially in ensemble rehearsals, performances, and also in panic practice sessions, and these moments can actually diminish their overall improvement as players.

As you attempt to increase the amount of time spent playing per day, it is best to consider playing more sessions that are shorter in length rather than trying simply to keep increasing the length of one long practice session. Dividing practice time can increase attention span and also minimize the impact of incorrect playing that might come nearer the end of a long practice session. This method requires planning to accommodate several playing sessions and should be developed carefully in your overall schedule. During each session, focus on the efficiency of your work, and rest when you are unable to maintain your proper embouchure and the airspeed/lip compression formula. Forced playing with excessive mouthpiece pressure or overblowing of the air will not build solid fundamentals, like good tone reliability or endurance, so it should be avoided whenever possible.

Ideally, more experienced players try to schedule at least two sessions per day. The first is often the development and maintenance of technical abilities, that is, your *athlete*, and should be early enough in the day to ensure good mental focus. Subsequent sessions can then target literature and planning large-scale musical expression once basic playing mechanisms are well established. If you have an extraordinarily good day, with very efficient playing, and you spend a lot of time practicing, do not be dismayed if you have less endurance or production the following day. This is a normal muscular growth cycle and always should be part of your planning process. Remember also that ensemble rehearsals and other non-practice playing also fall under these guidelines. If you have an unusually heavy amount of this type of playing, it is sometimes necessary to reduce your practice time to accommodate it. No one is Superman, although there are certainly differences in endurance abilities among players. This is due to varying levels of muscular development, the ability to give consistent attention to efficient productivity, and also inherent physical gifts and talent. Beware of those often-repeated fairy tales about great players who never have to practice or who have great endurance without rest or consistent development. Most, if not all, are untrue, and believing in them can lead to a lack of resolve in both goal setting and sustained effort.

Method Books and Practice Materials

Always remember that it is not what materials you choose to practice but what you want out of them. There are no *magic* books or etudes that ensure your development as a player. The magic comes from the goal-oriented direction you use in choosing how to use practice materials to achieve defined targets. It is important to focus on what you sound like no matter what you are practicing. True improvement comes from this detailed focus in your product, not what etudes or exercises you are playing. Any etudes and exercises that cover all basic ranges and techniques can ably serve your technical needs. Often you even can reuse etudes to develop new areas of playing simply by learning how to transpose and adapt them in terms of articulation style, tempi, and register.

Basic patterns like scales and arpeggios should be familiar and memorized as soon as possible, so you can create variations on them to match the exact technical challenges that confront you. Many brass players use Clarke *Technical Studies* or the Arban *Complete Conservatory Method* as the point of origin for technical development. Like other books with technical exercises, it is important to make some adaptations to accommodate development. In areas of articulation, for example, Arban offers many varieties of patterns but in very few keys. It is important to transpose these patterns into all keys to cover the broader needs of a competent player. Clarke's studies, in their written presentation, often stop before reaching into the upper register, so it is important to transpose some patterns up one octave to better develop technical control in the high register.

When you do enough repetitions to memorize these basic technical patterns, you can then devote more of your focus to how they sound as your concentration is only aural rather than divided between aural and the visual focus needed for music reading. Remember that you are not simply trying to learn each new technique and key but rather how you sound playing in that key with different techniques. The more patterns and techniques you can learn in each key, the better equipped you will also be as a sight-reader because most of our music is constructed using these same patterns. True control in each key relies on an immediate connectivity in the work of our fingers, embouchure, tongue, and airflow with the mental images of sound in each tonality. Being conversant in each key is developed by way of this easy, immediate technical mastery and the expressive sound that will accompany it.

Always build your practice around self-questioning rather than books or exercises. Start your session by deciding what questions are important for you to address. There are central daily questions you must ask consistently, such as the following:

Is my sound flowing easily and with consistent quality?
Are my registers equal in presence and intonation?
Are my attacks precise and immediate?

But you also might have very defined questions for a specific practice session:

How fast can I single tongue with changing pitches on every note in the key of F#?
Am I playing with great pitch softly in the key of C minor?
Are there any closed notes that do not exhibit vibrant resonance in this passage?

Endurance

In earlier days, I felt that endurance was built simply by increasing the amount of time you played. I had many teachers who taught me to play until exhaustion and some who told me to play even when exhausted! Although it is certainly true that more playing contributes to increased endurance, it is very important that this is efficient playing. Once you know when you are playing correctly and when you are not, you have the key to building endurance in a substantive manner.

Efficient playing requires you to constantly examine your playing in small ways during the course of your practice session. Sometimes, when you are consumed with working out a small detail in a passage such as a fingering or articulation, you can lose your awareness of whether you are playing correctly or not. Be sure periodically to step back and check that you are still making a sound that is free and vibrant. You can sing, buzz, play softer, and employ other strategies to check up on your efficiency. If you find that you have lost the ability to play correctly, take a rest before re-embarking on the focused technical work. Develop some quick, memorized diagnostic passages that you can play readily to check on efficiency. I often play softer lip slurs or arpeggio-inspired figures throughout my playing range to double-check this ability throughout my day. I listen carefully to my sound, especially in terms of attacks, vibrancy, and pitch control to see if I might need a break. If the passage I have been practicing is very loud, I might switch to some softer practice to increase my efficiency. Later in your practice session you might feel that loud volumes are still easy to produce and control, but as you tire, you might notice yourself progressively playing everything louder to compensate for some loss of efficiency. Always be aware of your overall efficiency by engaging your favorite quick playing tests to assess response.

I believe that lyrical playing should be at the center of endurance building. Because slurring requires the greatest lip strength and control, it is beneficial to use lyrical etudes and passages to build your endurance. Use shorter and lower etudes to start, and gradually build to longer and higher ones. Always listen to your sound to see how successful you are in terms of playing correctly. Keep track of where in the music this efficient playing ends, and try to play past that point with it intact the next time. If you are working on an articulated etude, spend some quality time slurring it instead to examine how well your lips are doing in forming the notes and negotiating intervals with a consistent and even sound. Often, the tongue can disguise less efficient playing and therefore should be added after you have proven your abilities with slurring. Too often, players disregard this important relationship, and unfortunately you can hear it in their sound in articulated passages. Although they are playing in time with appropriate attention to articulation, the sound produced when tonguing is not pleasing due to a lack of vibrancy and ability to center pitch or vary percussiveness. Usually, they employ a more percussive articulation that is harder and heavier due to this lack of efficiency in their embouchure. They do this to make up for the inability of their lips to do the maximum in negotiating intervals. If they do not attempt to go back and slur the passage, they will likely not make sufficient progress toward increasing the role of the lips in making these movements and will miss out on more controlled and effortless playing. Their tone will also never achieve the easy and efficient flow that is possible when lip movement is maximized in negotiating intervals.

Proper management of the air and breathing is, of course, central to endurance for brass playing, as we will soon discuss. Although we already have mentioned problems associated with excessive mouthpiece pressure, there is one technique that can be helpful to remember regarding mouthpiece pressure and endurance. Despite our best efforts, there will be moments when, due to length of playing, conditioning, or demands of the music, we will increase pressure while playing. In these moments, it is important to remember that brief moments of excessive pressure are not as debilitating to endurance as longer periods of added pushing. If a player can remember to do something consciously to remove excess pressure following the moment in the music that precipitated its addition, they can increase their ability to keep playing. This is normally done with a quick *lift* of the mouthpiece away from the embouchure. It does not always mean removing the contact between the lips and the mouthpiece but rather a relaxation of the force with which the player is pushing. It can coincide with a breath, although often the intake of air is not needed. Such lifts can be very helpful in reestablishing a more efficient manner of playing and improve tone production and the flexibility needed for expression.

If players do not reduce excessive pressure once employed, they tend to continue to play with this extra pushing, even when musical demands are reduced. This happens often during high-register passages that are above the player's comfortable range. To make the notes sound, they push harder, creating the *artificial lip compression* needed to sound the note. When the high passage ends, however, they continue to play with added pressure because their setup has been altered. I call this *locked playing* because the amount of pressure seems to be stuck in place. I can remember times when I played long stretches in this condition, and it destroyed my endurance quickly. Once I learned to do some lifting at critical places in the music, my endurance was better, and so was my confidence.

Overall, I like to compare efficiency in playing to the manual transmission gears of a car. When in fifth gear at higher speeds, the engine seems less taxed and is highly efficient. If you were to drive at higher speeds in lower gears, the result would be higher rpms from the engine along with noticeable sounds of strain. As we tire as players, we tend to change gears to continue meeting physical challenges posed by the music. Most experienced players can keep playing through fourth, third, second, and into first gears. After that point, you reach a point where you can no longer form an embouchure, and the engine of our playing stops. Great endurance means playing in the highest gears possible for the longest period possible. Once you can recognize when you are playing in the less efficient, lower gears, you can respond with the right combination of practice and rest to increase efficiency and endurance.

Feeling Time

Our greatest musicians can feel and express time at the smallest possible subdivision of the beat. I remember when my jazz ensemble was playing with the great drummer Peter Erskine in a rehearsal. I remember him telling the players that all of them should do what professional drummers do: hear all the smallest subdivisions of the music no matter what your part looks like. This is the key to great time in all types of music. If you understand all the rhythmic levels of the music, you can feel where your part is within the greater rubric. Metronome work is essential to this development. Use it to subdivide at smaller and smaller units as you play and sing your part. In my experience, some of the worst time I hear in players is actually their rhythmic interpretation of longer note values. If you are hearing the underlying subdivision while playing these longer notes, this is never a problem. You should really hear the other moving parts while you are sustaining notes whether it is a drummer, pianist, violin section, or any other sound. This rhythmic listening ability is what distinguishes these greatest players from others.

When beginning your practice on a new piece of music, first be sure that you fully comprehend the rhythm of each measure down to the fastest subdivision. Too often young players guess rhythms in early attempts, thus postponing a thorough understanding of how to hear the melody. Instead, start with a slower, more methodical rendition during which you can clearly feel the beat, its subdivisions, and relationships between moving passages, sustained notes, and rests.

Expression in Practice

Often my students misunderstand me when I divide playing sessions on an instrument into the *artist* and the *athlete*. They wrongly assume that expressive playing is only the goal in the artistic practice of their solos and other performance pieces. When they are working on technique, they might feel that there is no need to consider expression in playing. I totally disagree with this separation of the practice philosophy. I believe that all playing is expressive with musicality, informing all technique and all approaches to even the most basic technical exercises.

I once asked Barbara Butler what she thought was the biggest obstacle to students playing expressively, and she replied, *"Because they aren't even trying to be expressive."* If we think only about technique for half of our playing time each day, we are missing too many opportunities to play more expressively and enjoy the art of music making. In the *athletic* portion of our practice, we focus on expanding our boundaries in technical terms, but all of this playing should also be expressive in nature. You certainly can play a scale expressively as you can any pattern. This concept is, of course, also vital in the earliest stages of learning music that will eventually be performed. As mentioned previously, you should lead with your mental ideas of what you want the music to sound like and what emotions it expresses. If you practice it only in a technical manner and then, at some late stage in the process, try to decide what it all means in a creative sense, you are missing a great opportunity to foster a more cohesive musical performance. This is actually a backward approach. Instead of technique growing from the musical needs of the piece, many practice with a technique-only attitude that limits their musical image to whatever sounds happen to be coming out of the instrument. Barbara refers to this as *leading with our problems.* The best way to avoid this backward method is always to lead with our musical ideas.

Singing is one of the best self-teaching tools a student can use for keeping musical ideas at the forefront of their practice. All teachers should sing for students and encourage them to use their voices as a preliminary tool in learning all music. The process of singing first, before even attempting to play in on the instrument, is a very helpful tool in developing a musical image that is not tarnished by technical limitations. Take out a new piece of music and, before trying to play it, sing through it, even if all the pitches are not correct, and look for the shape of the melodies and where target or stressed notes occur. Make decisions about how you want it to sound before attempting to play it on your instrument. Decide what the piece is about and what emotions it expresses. Once you have attempted your initial singing version of the piece, quickly verify that you are hearing all the correct pitches and rhythms as they will greatly impact your expressive decisions.

Most players do not start with this process but rather launch into playing a rendition of the music without much forethought. If the music is easy enough, this might be possible, but if it is more challenging, starting cold without any idea of what you want musically can lead to what I call *reactionary expression*. In this mode of playing, our musicality is often shaped or limited by initial technical ability rather than the product of a musical plan that allows the development of new techniques.

The process of deciding what a piece of music *means* is an exercise in creativity that should start at an early age. The connection to independence and responsibility for meaning in music can be fostered in all students in both private lessons and in ensemble environments. All music should be expressive, even technical exercises, so do not miss the chance to add character and emotion to all playing with students. Playing without regard to musical thought is an empty technical exercise, and do not be surprised if students are not enthused about doing that regularly.

Structure in Practicing

Younger players always will need more structure and prescribed practiced than more experienced musicians. Beginning brass players need more help to develop the physicality to play, and this usually means specifying how much time to spend practicing in technical areas of focus. When teaching younger players, setting goals in terms of time spent playing, metronome markings, and other benchmarks can allow them to understand the gradual progress they are making in their playing. Long-term planning can show them, for example, how a few clicks of progress on the metronome can bring them to a performance level in a matter of days. This organization will yield great benefits to them and also increase their desire to keep playing and improving.

Exercises

- When you enter the practice room, eliminate chances for interruption by turning your cell phone completely off and sitting or standing so that you cannot see through the window and others cannot see you.

- Before you start to play, focus your thoughts only on your goals for your playing for that session, and actually imagine all other thoughts and concerns being placed in boxes for safekeeping. Later you also can put your playing in a *mental box* as well when you wish to give your full attention to another project.
- While playing your basic patterns like scales and arpeggios, consider the mood you are in, and try to play in a manner that expresses this emotion. If you are sad, angry, or whatever, connect this emotion to everything you are playing. After a while, attempt to change this mood, and express a new emotional state in your playing of basic patterns.

11

USING FILTERS TO CLARIFY YOUR PLAYING

"The wise musicians are those who play what they can master."

Duke Ellington
Pianist, Composer, Band Leader

As we pursue the best possible technical mastery in performance, it is important to have redundancy built into the process of detecting and eliminating unwanted characteristics in our playing. We can compare this refinement process to the process of purifying a liquid by passing our playing through a series of *filters*. Just as our drinking water, for example, is made safe by a process of eliminating waste products with different filtering methods, so our playing can become pure by passing it through a series of processes that will utilize focused listening to verify the best possible results. As we may be surprised at the impurities that are removed from our water, sometimes filtering our playing brings problems to our attention that we did not know existed. Many filters will detect the same weaknesses, so using all of them builds in redundancy and also instills great confidence. The willingness to follow these methods and avoid the temptation of assuming there are no problems is a regular behavior of great players. In my experience, it is usually not the ability of the students to use this filtration method to hear and fix issues in their playing but their desire to incorporate such examination into their daily playing that determines their level of success.

The Mouthpiece

As mentioned earlier, buzzing the brass mouthpiece is an easy way to check on many capabilities in playing. Hearing the pitches correctly, using lip compression and airspeed without excessive mouthpiece pressure, centering the sound, and articulation are all highlighted with playing the mouthpiece alone. When a passage arrives that students do not want to check with this filter, it usually means that they already know there is an inefficiency that needs to be addressed, but they are not yet prepared to confront it. I often tell students that buzzing the mouthpiece is like looking at yourself naked in the mirror. You can no longer hide your issues with big baggy clothes or not looking. Now you can see what needs attention and how you can work on it to achieve your goals. Likewise, buzzing the mouthpiece takes away mouthpiece pressure and the note security of the instrument, forcing you to hear how close you are to the ideal. If you find yourself avoiding this process, it is important to confront why you would want to omit this valuable diagnostic tool.

Singing

All instruments are, in their origin, attempts to copy the expressive qualities of the human voice. Many of the great brass soloists continued their study once in the profession by studying singers to incorporate qualities of superior vocal style into their playing. It is important to use your singing voice as a teaching aid in your practice to gain insight into how you are hearing a passage and what work needs to be done with your musical image prior to engaging with the instrument. If you cannot sing the correct pitches, it is because you cannot hear them, and this, of course, will lead to unfocused playing and unequal tone on the instrument. Sometimes we can hear a passage, but our singing voice might not be able to realize it. I suggest you spend a bit of time each day training your voice to recreate what you hear in your mind, so singing can serve a more valued role in your practice and teaching. Not only will you improve pitch recognition, but also vocal practice will offer ideas for expression in terms of volume, flow of sound, articulation, and vibrato.

Often brass students avoid singing because it is new for them, and they feel that it does not allow them to show their best musical ability. It is vital to move them past this mind-set into the comprehension that singing will greatly enhance their learning regardless of their ability level. It provides a wonderful method for improving musicianship without the horn on your face, and this becomes a great companion to playing as it allows for continued musical improvement while resting the embouchure. Encourage students to use this filter daily to check natural connections between what they hear in their mind and how they can realize it aurally without the constraints of their instrument or technical ability. Once they can realize their desired sound with their singing voice, this can become their best aural model for subsequent instrumental renditions.

In singing instrumental music, it is valuable to use a *brass singing* style that involves singing consonant sounds for articulated notes and vowel sounds for notes that are not tongued. When brass singing through the music, students can demonstrate if they realize exactly where they will use the tongue and where they will slur as they will need to select the appropriate singing syllables for each note. In younger students, this is a wonderful way to reinforce their hearing of articulation and great practice to reinforce what they are learning on their instrument. For example, in the melody that follows, I would choose to articulate with the *d* consonant for the articulated notes and use the *oo* vowel sound to facilitate the midrange of the melody (see Fig. 11.1).

Figure 11.1 Brass singing

Singing in this defined manner also can be tailored to the strength of attack by changing the consonant sound to change the level of attack percussiveness on tongued notes. Stronger attack sounds bring the tongue closer to the front of the mouth and use consonants sounds such as *t* or *d*, while less percussive attacks involve the tongue striking further back, as in *n* or *l*. Choosing vowel sounds like *ee* for the higher, brighter, and softer colors and *ah* for lower, darker, and louder sounds also can be included to focus the exercise to mimic the best eventual sound on the instrument and the use of the tongue to achieve it. Brass singing also is a great way to establish *target notes* in each phrase and how nontarget notes will lean toward or away from them musically. Approaching music in this manner helps outline phrasing and also will establish the best expressive places for breaths when playing on the instrument. We will discuss this concept in more detail in ensuing chapters.

Many teachers tell their students that *if you can sing it, you can play it*. Certainly a singing rendition of a musical passage tells the listener much about what performers are hearing in their imaginations and what they are attempting to express on their instruments. It is vital that all brass players make use of the filter of singing as a vehicle for creating and evaluating musical ideas outside of the confines of playing the instrument. Many great brass performers use singing at the beginning of the preparation phase for new music as it allows them to imagine whatever they choose musically without the limitations of a first reading with their instrument. Just as conductors employ this method for score preparation before they have time with an ensemble, so we can also use it to establish what we want to say musically allowing us to bring focused goals into the practice room.

Conducting

I was fortunate at an early age to get the opportunity to become a conductor. In junior high school our teacher encouraged us to compete for the chance to conduct the band, and I was motivated immediately to investigate this part of music making. Through all my years of playing, I also have been a conductor of bands, jazz ensembles, brass ensembles, and trumpet ensembles. The connections that you make to bodily movement and musical expression as a conductor are very valuable investments that pay off immensely in your own playing and teaching in the studio. Using this filter, especially along with singing, can help you solidify technical and expressive qualities in phrases. It also helps students feel the music *leaning* that we will discuss later.

Most students can learn basic conducting patterns quickly if they already understand meter and basic rhythmic packaging. As with singing, conducting skill needs to be started at an early age and become a regular part of practice and learning. Once basic beat patterns are thoroughly connected to mental imagery, arm and hand movement can be refined to express mood and feelings more directly. These physical movements help internalize rhythm and expression in a way that enriches our concept of playing. On a basic level, you can ask students who are struggling with a rhythmically complex passage to put down their instruments and sing and conduct the same phrase. If they do not understand the rhythm easily, you will see this as a disruption in their conducting and singing. If they sing without conducting, you also will be able to hear their rhythmic weaknesses, but it is less obvious without the steady beat in their arms. Using conducting advances rhythmic understanding one level further than foot tapping as students will need to distinguish rhythm relative to the separate beats of the measure. With many such passages, in addition to poor rhythm, students also might be missing exact pitches, so the complete filtration process including singing along with conducting can help eliminate many types of mistakes.

First have the student sing only the rhythm and conduct the passage to solidify rhythmic understanding. You also can employ one of the many counting methods that music theory teachers often use to present rhythmic dictation. After you can conduct and vocalize rhythms, work on pitch security with singing and buzzing the mouthpiece. Finally, conduct and sing the complete melody rhythmically and melodically to express your music concept fully. Conducting in this manner can further visualize musical expression by emphasizing target notes and realizing changes in volume and speed.

Like most musicians, I have spent a lot of time sitting in ensembles with all kinds of conductors. Due to my early exposure to this craft, I have always been intrigued with how each conductor communicates the music to both players and the audience. As a result of this interest, I always prefer to watch them during rehearsal and learn from their efforts. When they are very skilled in expressive conducting, it is amazing how easily the ensemble responds with a cohesive musical performance. When they or their ensemble members are less skilled, they must rely more on spoken directions and singing to illicit the desired results. Even if they are very inexperienced or unprepared, watching them can always be instructive as you see what does not work! As in all learning, if you can learn from their mistakes, you can find shortcuts for your own musical endeavors. For this reason, bring a score to rehearsals, and watch the conductor instead of reading a book or talking to your colleagues, so you can maximize the learning potential in each session. Your musicianship and teaching will be greatly enriched, no matter who is on the podium.

Articulation Consistency

Often when I would see legendary teacher Vincent Cichowicz in a master class, he would help students clarify articulated passages by having them play the rhythm and articulation style on one repeated pitch rather than the written melody. Once the articulation was controlled and even, the student would then use this one pitch rendition as a model to influence the written passage. Despite the simplicity of this filter, there were always immediate results in successive repetitions by the student. This concept of checking for articulation style and consistency should be a mainstay in teaching and learning brass instruments. Although most players have seen similar demonstrations or even used them in their teaching, this technique also should be part of the normal filtration process for musical preparation. Using this filter on the mouthpiece can be even more revealing, especially in rapid passages like those that require multiple tonguing. Again, if your students resist using this well-proven teaching tool to help their playing, it is likely they are already aware of a problem and choose not to magnify it with such filters. It is vital that they confront these obstacles, first in their thinking and then in their actions.

As the tongue can be a disruptor of the flow of sound, it is also helpful to slur passages that are marked as tongued as a filter to ensure proper lip function and centering of notes as mentioned earlier. The ability to slur bigger skips and rapid note movement while maintaining a constant sound and dynamic level offers a relaxed, flowing model to compare to articulated attempts. Pay particular attention to passages that change register or involve several small motives interspersed with rests, listening for light and accurate articulation. If it is too heavy and disrupts the sound, return to slurred versions to keep comparing this model to the written version. When they are very similar in volume, pitch, weight of attack, and sound flow, then you are able to change the articulation as you please with the confidence of efficiency.

Tonguing through passages marked slurred is also a great filter to ensure proper time, especially those moments that involve rapid changes in fingerings and slide positions. Often in these passages, rhythmic stability at the subdivision level is challenged relative to less comfortable finger and slide movement. Articulating these strings of notes can reveal minor time issues that are less audible in the more blended sounds of slurring. The best clarity in slurring requires precise movements in both time and movement from up to down with valves or from one position to another on the trombone slide. When players take the time to articulate these slurred passages, especially with a metronome, they can make big strides in achieving true clarity in these technical moments.

Recording

Great playing starts with hearing what it sounds like in others and then developing your own mental image of your playing. The companion to this process, too often neglected by students, is to be able to know what they really sound like now so that they can develop a plan to move from there to the desired image. Teachers can help immensely with feedback, but self-examination via recording is an even more valuable tool. Technology for recording is as easy as selecting an app on your smartphone today. With computers, phones, and cheap portable recorders available to most, it is important to start early helping students to take ownership over their playing by evaluating recordings of themselves.

Most students wait too long to record themselves because they want to avoid hearing too many mistakes and confront so many issues in their playing. Just as delaying using other filters, waiting to use this valuable tool only prolongs your preparation process, and it may mean that you actually develop problems in your preparation that could have been avoided easily. I am always amazed at how differently students approach their playing just because they are aware it is being recorded. Whereas playing through passages with mistakes is easily forgotten and rationalized, listening to recordings containing mistakes is more impactful and lasting. Just knowing that you are recording tends to yield a higher level of focus and reduces mistakes. Once we go through this process, we can better focus on those spots that are not working and develop a plan to fix them.

Just as our own voice sounds radically different on a recording from how we hear it during speaking, so too our playing of an instrument sounds equally different. The physiological nature of hearing ourselves through our throats and ears, along with our rich imagination and comfort in hearing ourselves in this manner, requires that we seek constant input from recordings to balance accurately this prejudicial listening and disrupt our sense of comfort. How you sound on the recording is really how you do sound, and therefore you must become comfortable in charting improvement with that in mind. Recordings also can reinforce feedback from teachers and others who sometimes evaluate your playing differently from what you expected. My best students record their lessons as well so that, later in the week, they can remind themselves of how they sounded and the ideas we developed for improving their playing that were reactions to those sounds. Recording ensemble rehearsals and performances from where the audience sits is also important for a realistic evaluation of your playing. It gives you the opportunity to better understand comments from the conductor and also the feedback you get from audience members.

To deflect those emotional aspects naturally connected to listening to yourself on a recording, it is important to act more like a scientist during much of the process. Disconnecting from unfocused general feelings and choosing to listen for specific indicators can help you get past harmful personal feelings of disappointment. It is also helpful to compare your recording with the playing of others, being always mindful of the cutting, splicing, and sound refinement inherent in professional recordings. Charles Geyer once told me "recordings are the worst thing that ever happened to performing musicians." I found this very compelling at the time, but I now agree totally with this view. Because all recordings are technically cleansed of error or unwanted sounds, students learning to play unfortunately can develop an unrealistic expectations in their own playing that can be very destructive. Even *live* orchestral performances we hear on the radio are now cut and spliced between several live concerts to remove obvious mistakes or unwanted elements. Because the normality of our world is full of such *doctored* music, it is vital for teachers to discuss this with students.

Barbara Butler, while at Eastman, was fond of using a reel-to-reel tape deck to record students and then play it back at a lower speed. The result was one octave lower and twice as slow, so you sounded like a bad euphonium player. Add one level slower, and you were a bad tuba player! It was amazing how much you learned about both your playing and how to listen for indictors both at slow and regular speed from this process. With today's technology, you can now listen to yourself at any speed without changing the pitch level. This is a great learning and teaching tool should you choose to use it.

The Metronome

A concept of steady time develops slowly over years of playing and needs to be revisited daily to ensure reliability. In the highest levels of brass playing, like symphony orchestra auditions, exact time and the flow of subdivisions of the beat disqualify more players than any other technical matter. It is important to understand the flow of time in your music to the smallest subdivision to establish an exact understanding of how rhythms lie in the metrical scheme. Even with a consistent or easy rhythmic scheme, subdivision with the metronome in practice is needed to reinforce the concept of time. Oddly, many students get very lazy and do not use the metronome in their daily practice. The resulting time instability inevitably leads to unnecessary errors and can create the image that a musical work is overly difficult. By first establishing the tempo at which they can play passages without difficulty and then slowly speeding up using the metronome, the length of learning a new piece actually is reduced because mastery increases more quickly.

Maurice André, the famed trumpet soloist, often would speak of how he approached a new work for the first time. Even in the first reading, he would choose a tempo that was slow enough to offer him a flawless rendition, even if it was extremely slow. Each time he played through passages with no difficulty, his mind considered them easy to play. Upon establishing an initial flawless performance tempo in terms of a metronome marking, he would then, on subsequent passes, speed up in very small increments, preserving error-free playing. With each flawless rendition, his mind recorded the mental message that *the music is easy and I can play it.* When this process is followed, building all the way to performance tempo, the eventual onstage performance is very successful because technical accuracy has been achieved consistently, and the mind also is filled with positive mental messages that instill confidence and comfort.

Imagine the opposite approach to a new piece of music. Instead of first playing through it slowly without error, you instead try to play through it at performance tempo, creating many errors. Even if you are using a metronome, you have already registered one mental memory that *it's a hard piece of music that I cannot play* in your mind, and you also failed to find a baseline tempo at which you can play it error free. If during subsequent passes through the piece, you slow down from the performance tempo in small increments while continuing to make mistakes, you reinforce the concept that it is hard for you and you cannot play it. You are obviously wasting time compared to André's process. Even if later you finally gain some awareness and slow down enough to reach a flawless, controlled tempo and then engage that process, you have already filled your mind with many messages that the music is hard and you cannot play it. When you are onstage, it is much better to have less of these voices in your head and more of those that remember that *it's easy and I can play it.*

Sadly, despite the obvious benefit of starting slowly with a flawless performance, most players continue to approach music too fast with many errors, building up negative messages in their memories. This behavior is not only debilitating to onstage confidence, but it also wastes a lot of time compared to the slow, methodical approach. Not using the metronome at all also leads to wasted time and effort. If we can help students embrace the logic of this process and the discipline to practice with direction, they will see the results in their playing and will be thrilled to learn that it takes no more time to be successful than not.

Although musical expression often means that time is slightly altered during a musical passage, it is important when first learning the passage to establish rock-solid time. Once the rhythmic structure of the melody is completely understood and controlled, the process of using changes in tempo to express musical ideas can be developed. Often students, understanding that the use of rubato and other tempo alterations will be part of the final product, attempt to perform rhythmically challenging passages immediately with these expressive gestures. Unfortunately, they often make this leap without fully understanding rhythms and their realization in the metrical environment. This behavior can lead to learning incorrect rhythms as students *guess* instead of guaranteeing rhythmic accuracy with the metronome. Additionally, if the passage requires a technique that is not fully developed, players also may make adjustments in the tempo or rhythm to accommodate these weaknesses. The most logical sequence of learning starts with fundamental understanding of rhythm down to the smallest subdivision. The metronome is critical for this phase and also can be combined with self-recording for students to hear where they are rhythmically challenged or have difficulties playing in steady time. As with many other techniques, students *earn the right* to add rubato by first demonstrating rhythmic stability and understanding. This process of approaching expression by way of a thorough comprehension of time is vital to building musical understanding along with musicality.

When considering the use of tempo alteration in expressing the melodic line, study the great players, and you will find a naturalness to acceleration and ritardando that relates to note speed and musical style. I often ask students to compare the speed of changing notes to motion in the physical world to illustrate the *naturalness* of motion in music. A ball slowly rolling to a stop or gradually beginning motion from a stop is a great example. The shape of the ball and its momentum determine how quickly the slowing or speeding up occurs. The ball cannot suddenly jerk to a stop or accelerate suddenly either. Instead, the impact of gravity and the slope, combined with the dimensions of the ball, creates a measured sense of movement. The metronome, of course, cannot measure all of the slight changes that characterize an expressive performance, but it is important to understand the relationship between the concept of a steady pulse in music and the changing pulse used in expressive playing.

Bodily movement is also a valuable tool in understanding natural changes in tempo. Dancers, skaters, and conductors all can prove informative as we think about how rushing and slowing time can take on a relaxed and normal feel. Singing through passages also helps greatly in determining this natural rate of tempo change. Relating new musical passages to memories of other melodies and comparing our use of speech in dialogue also can be helpful in choosing how rubato can better express our feelings through music.

The Tuner

The tuner is another helpful filter to use in the preparation of music. Like the metronome, it is important to use tuners and other methods of pitch checking daily to continuously reinforce a good pitch center and to develop a sense for pitch relationships in all keys. Although it is tempting always to use the visual readout or needle, especially for visually oriented learners, it is important to keep in mind that music is an aural art, and the ability to listen and adjust pitch deserves our greater attention. When an emitted pitch is available, this is preferable to watching the needle or other readouts as you are using your ears to match rather than your eyes. Listening critically and matching the intonation of others are the goals, so practicing this process is the shortest route to playing with great pitch. Needles or other readouts are also so discerning that they can impair confidence in your playing, and when watching instead of listening, you are also more likely to adjust improperly and without maximizing honest playing.

An understanding of harmonic structure will help you use the tuner more accurately as you navigate the worlds of even temperament and just tuning. The security that roots and fifths of chords, for example, are always pure, while thirds are often lowered in just intonation, is important as you consider the use of this device. In playing through a melody, understanding where the melody line lands on roots and fifths of chords will help establish basic intonation, so you can begin to distill the tuning process. Start the process by playing root drones on the tuner to provide model notes for matching octaves and fifths. You can, of course, also simply check the needle for the accuracy of these important skeletal pitches as a place to start your examination. As you proceed, you also can continue simply to match each note to the tuner as a rough estimate of where you are placing the pitch as well. Although this equal temperament approach can offer a rough understanding of tuning tendencies, in environments where natural tuning is the norm, this method does not recreate necessary adjustments needed on the smaller level for success.

Spot tuning is also a great way to examine your tuning in the context of where you are in the piece. Too often students isolate and work on tuning despite the fact that context for a brass player means much in the tuning landscape. The best way to complete the tuning process is to play the full piece or at least lengthy sections with small fermatas on critical target notes to measure intonation accuracy. Often this exercise reveals important spots where tuning is not secure, and these moments many be related to endurance or technical demands. In these places, reinforce stability by singing and buzzing to slowly imprint the melodic flow of pitches. Examine the harmonic structure, and match those needs to mechanical tuning possibilities with slides and alternate fingerings. Remember that tuning issues will be heard often as unwanted changes in tone color, so these changes, along with other detection methods, are vital.

You also can combine the processes of self-recording and the use of tuning devices by playing back your performance and checking target pitches with the tuner. This is a great way to examine your playing away from the challenges presented while manipulating the instrument. Once you identify inaccurate tuning spots, check for what mechanical means you might use to achieve desired pitch level. Oftentimes, these musical moments occur later in the composition, and simply pulling out the main tuning slide as you tire might be enough to have a huge impact on your pitch and tone.

It is interesting to consider tuning relationships in a successful performance by comparing what we hear with what we see on the readout on the tuner. Tuner readouts are more sensitive than our ears, so watching them intently while listening to a great performer can easily demonstrate sophisticated tuning in high-level performance. Place the tuner next to the speaker as you play back one of your favorite recordings of a great soloist. Perhaps you can use the solo recording of the work you are preparing. Notice the needle of the tuner and where it reports pitches as you listen. You may be surprised to see many notes that, although they sound fantastic to you in context, the tuner is telling you are out of tune. This is illustrative of two characteristics of tuning. The performance of *natural tuning* means that not all notes will line up with the equal temperament demands of the tuner. Also, a rich, vibrant sound can be a bit out of tune and still be very successful. This knowledge will assist you as you use your tuner as a filter and reduce expected frustrations when *needle watching*. Such tuning experiments reinforce the aural nature of tuning and its importance in the performance of music.

The Piano

The piano is central to the understanding of pitch, and I use it every day in my practice and teaching. The sound of the piano is superior to synthesized notes, and learning all of its characteristics will aid you in your many performances with it. For most brass players, solo playing means playing with the piano, so understanding its tone capabilities and pitch limitations will enhance your performance capabilities greatly.

In the realm of articulation, it is helpful to consider the collaborative need for the brass instrument and piano to sound alike to achieve those moments in music that call for equal voices, as in contrapuntal moments. Play several articulated notes on the piano keyboard, and then compare them to your articulation style on the instrument. In most cases, you will find that the piano cannot manage the percussiveness of attack you might be making easily on the brass instrument. To achieve some equality of effect, the pianist will need to maximize his or her percussiveness at the keystroke, while you will need to reduce your percussiveness by changing your consonant attack sound (e.g., *d* instead of *t*) to achieve the desired equality. When I hear a soloist who truly explores the interaction of the piano and his or her instrument in this way, it is usually very rewarding musically to hear them play together.

Unfortunately many times the sophistication of such preparation goes unnoticed, and listeners prefer instead to focus only on the individual achievement of the soloist. In truth, all successful instrumental collaborations are built in phases. First players learn their individual parts, and then they must devote time and energy to learn how to match these parts in creation of a whole. Having pianos in practice rooms allows brass players to get a head start on future collaborations while also offering a filter in terms of pitch and articulation in their individual practice.

Playing Along With a Recording

Before helpful aids like *Smart Music*, it was commonplace to play along with professional recordings as a means to check accuracy in all facets of playing. This process is still helpful to players and should be used to help determine technical accuracy and gain awareness of interpretive possibilities. Unlike albums and turntables, digital recordings are stable and play back consistently at A = 440 or a pitch level very close. Playing along with a great player can be a fun and an instinctive filter for detecting issues prior to limited rehearsal time with accompanists and ensembles. While playing along, listen for anything that is different in terms of pitch, tone color, and rhythm. When you hear discrepancies, investigate what is different in your rendition, and seek fixes where desired. Musical interpretations are, of course, a more personal choice, although actually playing through the tempo and volume changes along with an expressive recording can help you understand the types of changes needed to be effective in relating musical ideas to audiences. In addition to solo recordings, playing brass parts with great orchestral and band recordings is the next best experience to actually sitting in a great ensemble. If you have trouble feeling time, matching your pitch, or making it through the big blows endurance wise, you will experience the same issues once you are in such a group.

Smart Music

Smart Music and similar accompaniment programs are well worth their small subscription price. Although the synthesized accompaniment does not always sound pleasing to the ear, it does render accompaniment in equal temperament just like the piano. In this way, it can help you prepare for those pitch problems this collaboration inherently poses. The ability to slow down and utilize the metronome and tuner on this program while playing is also an effective tool for examination of playing and preparing for performance. The recording feature also allows you to play along with accompaniment and then listen back for issues in time and pitch. This reduces separate processes into one easy step, and that makes it more likely that we will use it.

Some of the challenges in using such accompaniment programs might include the random inability to follow the soloist immediately or increases or decreases in speed that are more than the natural pace required in the music. It also does not, in any way, replace a real pianist who can follow and react musically to a soloist in ways impossible for the computer to duplicate. *Smart Music* is, however, a great addition to our preparation for that coveted time with a human collaborator, and as such, it is something we should all use as one of our filters.

Exercises

• Record yourself playing through your solo while replicating a performance. When listening back, circle the spots where you had technical or musical issues. Repeat this process several times using a different colored pencil to do the circling or highlighting. When you have done several recordings, note that your trouble spots are usually consistently the same. This can help you decide where to do focused practicing in your music.

• Sing through a melodic passage using *brass singing* style. If there are rhythmic difficulties, change to singing only rhythms without changing pitches. Once the rhythm is firmly established, add pitches, and then also conduct while singing to further establish security while experimenting with musical gestures that slightly change the time. Try to bring those same ideas into your renditions on the instrument.

• Sing through your melody while patting the smallest subdivisions on your shoulder or chest with your hand. Feel where the notes of the melody land on with these subdivisions. The mere act of doing these two actions together will help you better understand the combination of rhythmic and melodic flow in the music.

• Adopt a process of singing a passage, then buzzing it on the mouthpiece, and finally playing it on the instrument. Make it somewhat like a game with different levels that must be earned. If you cannot sing it, you don't get to buzz it, and so on. In a classroom setting, do the same in groups and individually to reinforce how these processes improve our instrumental playing.

12

PLANNING FOR PERFORMANCE

"Music is the shorthand of emotion."

Leo Tolstoy
Russian Author

Hierarchy of Skills

In preparing for a successful music performance, it is vital that players create a long-term plan that includes focused benchmarks corresponding to distinct time points along the way. The first and most lengthy process in this plan is practice room preparation followed by adding accompaniment and finally playing for others. It is vital for players to understand that during each of these three phases, there will be a new learning curve with new challenges that take time and focus to conquer. If there is a delay in starting any one of these three processes, it can negatively impact the likelihood of a successful performance, so it is important to start early and make a performance plan that accurately balances challenges in the music with the time needed to address them. Especially in the practice room stage, students and their teachers must set goals to ensure that they gain the technical skills and develop a musical plan in a timely manner because collaboration with a pianist and reaching confidence playing for audiences are phases of preparation that also will take valuable time and should not be rushed.

The first goal for the preparation of any music should be identifying the tempo at which all of the three basic parameters of rhythm, notes, and articulation are correct and easily repeated without error. With undergraduate students I consistently find that most of their high school experience in music preparation focused mostly on this first phase of musical planning. As a result of this experience, they believe that they are ready to perform as soon as they can play all the correct rhythms, pitches, and articulations in the music and plan their practice accordingly. During their own practice and in ensemble rehearsals, the vast majority of time in high school was spent fixing errors in these three areas with perhaps only a small amount of time spent on intonation and expression. My experience as an adjudicator reinforces the notion that many high school students are still challenged in these three areas of

91

playing up until the time of their one and only performance. Once in my studio, I stress that these basic three areas are now the prerequisite for serious musical study, so they must be addressed quickly in their overall performance planning. Of course, this should start with them first finding the tempo at which they can be sure that rhythms, pitches, and articulations are accurate before attempting faster speeds or working at performance tempo.

Students and teachers should construct a *hierarchy of skills* to help organize the practice room process for musical preparation. Depending on how you illustrate these skills, the beginning of the process should be the awareness and accuracy of rhythm, correct pitches, and basic articulation. Articulation in this phase refers only to the ability to distinguish between what notes are tongued or slurred and perform them accordingly. Once students have control of these three elements, even at a very slow tempo, further progress is possible as the tempo increases and as the other musical elements are engaged. If students, in the process of adding these elements, lose control of these three basic core elements, they must immediately slow down to restore them to absolute mastery. I like to create a chart that looks like the one in Fig. 12.1 to illustrate a divide between these three essential elements and more sophisticated features required in musical performance.

Teachers must work to reinforce the need for absolute mastery of basic elements by challenging students with tempo benchmarks. To be most successful, students should keep a record of these tempi and the consistent progress toward performance goals on their pieces. This level of organization will take time for students to embrace, but it is vital to incorporate it into their practice philosophy.

Once students have control of their music in terms of rhythm, pitch, and marked articulation with steady time as a firm foundation, they can consider interpretative colors of sound, differing levels or percussiveness in articulation, the use of vibrato, and small changes in time and dynamics that yield expressive melodies. When they

Hierarchy of Skills

Essential Elements   Rhythm (count, conduct, play)
Pitches (sing, buzz, play)
Articulation (slurred or tongued)

****

Musical Expression   Tone Color
Vibrato Use
Rubato
Modified Articulation for Expression
Playing With Accompaniment
Playing for Audiences

Figure 12.1 Hierarchy of skills

Bryan Goff : Recital Planning and Practice Record

Sunday	Monday	Tuesday	Wednesday	Thursday	Friday	Saturday
10 — 1.25 1.0 1. warmup/tone .30 2. tech .25 3. emb .25	11 — 2.5 2.50 [previous maximum was 2 hours] 1. warmup .5 2. tech 1.0 3. emb, 1.0	12 — 1.25 1.0 1. warmup/tone .30 2. tech .25 3. emb .25	13 — 2.75 2.75 1. warmup .5 2. tech 1.25 3. emb, 1.0	14 — 1.25 1.25 1. warmup/tone .75 2. tech .25 3. emb .25	15 — 2.75 3.00 1. warmup .5 2. tech 1.5 3. emb, including high notes 1.0	16 — 1.25 .75 [VERY stiff] 1. emb .75
17 — 3.0 3.00 1. warmup .5 2. tech 1.5 3. emb 1.0	18 — 1.25 1.25 1. warmup/tone .75 2. tech .25 3. emb .25	19 — 3.0 2.5 [very stiff} 1. warmup .5 2. tech .75 3. emb 1.25 [easy]	20 — 1.5 1.5 1. warmup/tone .75 2. tech .25 3. emb .5	21 — 3.25 3.25 1. warmup .5 2. tech 1.5 3. emb 1.25	22 — 1.5 1.5 1. warmup/tone .75 2. tech .25 3. emb .5	23 — 3.25 3.25 1. warmup .5 2. tech 1.5 3. emb 1.25
24 — 1.5 1.25 1. warmup/tone .75 2. tech .25 3. emb .25	25 — 3.25 3.25 1. warmup .5 2. tech 1.5 3. emb 1.25	26 — 1.5 1.5 1. warmup/tone .75 2. tech .25 3. emb .5	27 — 3.5 3.5 [poor response today, stiff] 1. warmup/tone 1.25 2. tech 1.0 3. emb. 1.5 [last ½ hour played only middle g !!]	28 — 1.75 1.5 1. warmup/tone .75 2. tech .25 3. emb .5	29 — 3.50 2.75 1. brief warmup 20" 2. DR [first actual dress rehearsal—sounded awful on last piece, couldn't hit high notes 3. emb. 20"[easy]	30 — 1.75 .50 .50 very easy emb. —felt bruised from yesterday's DR
31 — 3.50 3.5 1. warmup/tone 1.25 2. tech .75 3. emb. 1.5	1 — 1.75 1.5 [stiff] 1. warmup/tone .5 2. tech .5 3. easy emb .5	2 — 3.75 3.75 1. warmup/tone 1.0 2. tech [spot work on trouble places] 1.0 3. emb [including high register long tones] 1.75	3 — 2.0 1.5 [tired—poor high register] 1. warmup .5 2. tech .25 3. emb .75 [took it VERY easy]	4 — 3.75 3.75 [felt great at end] 1. brief warmup 20" 2. DR 3. tech 4. emb	5 — 2.0 2.0 1. warmup/tone 1.0 2. tech .5 3. emb .5 [easy at end]	6 — 4.0 4.0 [really wiped out at end] 1. brief warmup 20" 2. DR 3. tech 4. emb
7 — 2.0 1.75 [stiff today] 1. warmup .75 2. tech .5 3. emb .5	8 — 4.0 4.25 1. warmup .5 2. reh w. accomp 1.5 3. tech .75 4. emb 1.5	9 — 2.0 1.5 [very stiff today] 1. warmup/tone .75 2. tech .5 3. tone (warm down) .5	10 — 4.0 4' 1. brief warmup 20" 2. DR 3. tech 4. emb	11 — 1.5 1.75 1. warmup .5 2. DR w. accomp 1.25	12 8:00 Recital	

DR = run through recital with all rests, intermission, etc.
tech = practice on technical spots that still need woodshedding (i.e. learn the notes)
emb = embouchure building and tone studies: soft playing, flexibility exercises, some easy long tones

Figure 12.2 Bryan Goff recital planning and practice record

have a clear idea of their interpretation and can express it on their instrument, it is then time to share those ideas with the pianist who will collaborate in the performance.

Bryan Goff, my trumpet professor while at Florida State University, like most successful teachers and performers on brass instruments, developed a system of planning and record keeping that can assist players in long-term performance preparation (see Fig. 12.2). During each day, individual practice sessions are noted along with content like run-throughs of the complete program and also basic technical and embouchure work. When brass players take the time to keep track of their playing in this precise manner, it ensures much greater success in building the confidence needed for guaranteed success in the recital.

Adding Piano Accompaniment

When adding piano accompaniment to solos, brass performers will encounter new challenges that do not readily appear in the practice room. Because we hear in natural intonation when playing alone and because many of our recordings are solos with orchestral accompaniment, the fixed-pitch, equal-tempered piano offers new challenges to our ears and our technique. As the piano cannot adjust its tuning to accommodate chord and key changes, brass players need to understand that initial rehearsals with a pianist often will be more challenging to endurance, flexibility, and tonal expressivity than playing alone in the practice room. This is because brass players now have to match the equal temperament of the piano, and this involves both mechanical and physical pitch manipulation. If they have practiced too far from the pitch the piano provides, these new demands can result in missed notes and less efficient playing, resulting in less endurance and control. Too often, students even at the collegiate level are not aware of these intonation challenges if they are not aware of these tuning discrepancies, and they can be continually confused and caught off guard by them. It is important for young musicians to understand fully why they encounter new difficulties when playing with the piano, so they can address them in an organized and sophisticated manner. If they are aware of these issues, they will not be unduly surprised by them and will plan for extra time in their preparation.

Working with a pianist also includes sharing an interpretive vision that will determine precise coordination of the two voices. Good ensemble flows from knowing this vision well and communicating with both your playing and your listening. Prior to developing this synchronized approach to the music, there will be awkward moments that, like the tuning already described, can result in less efficient playing from both parties. Do not be surprised if your early rehearsals are characterized by more mistakes and less control than you experienced when practicing alone.

It is important to build a drop in productivity into the overall performance preparation schedule when moving toward working with accompanists, although there are some things you can do to preempt the impact of pairing with the piano. Knowledge of the accompaniment and the harmonic structure of the work certainly can help you know where there will be intonation challenges. Some composers of sonatas and other works conceived for brass and piano were very kind in writing for the combination of piano and a brass soloist. Accommodating thirds when possible and not writing unisons between the piano and solo parts are two strategies good composers employ to offer brass instruments the best opportunity to play in natural intonation, even with an equal-tempered accompaniment. Of course, piano reductions of concertos, because they were originally written for instruments with greater tuning flexibility, often overlook these opportunities, and these can cause the most problems for a soloist.

Playing along with a recording of the piano, either alone or with the soloist, is one early way to prepare prior to pairing with your accompanist. Another strategy is to make use of *Smart Music* or some other synthesized accompaniment because its equal temperament will give you ideas of the adjustments you will need to make when playing with the piano. In addition to preparing for slight pitch adjustments required by equal-temperament piano accompaniment, it is important to reinforce that success also will depend on your ability to have flexibility in your sound and efficiency in your playing. Minor pitch adjustments for players who do not possess these qualities yield more cracked notes, missed notes, and obvious pitch problems than for those who are more flexible in their approach to the instrument.

Scheduling rehearsal time with a pianist before the soloist can understand and play the part well on his or her own is much less productive and also unfortunately can invite the development of bad habits in brass playing. When students cannot hear their parts or play them up to tempo, such rehearsals actually can intimidate students and elicit the same inefficient playing they too often experience in ensemble rehearsals. If they have not gained an understanding for pitch tendencies, they will use more volume and mouthpiece pressure, play with a louder, harder sound, and articulate too heavily to *get through* the solo. When this happens, they are left with thoughts that the solo is *really hard* and that they must play in this forced manner to be successful. The pianist also is left with an interpretation of the piece that is louder, heavier, and likely slower. This experience leaves a lasting imprint on his or her memory. If the planning is done well and soloists can be better prepared, such early rehearsals can be much more productive and build better confidence in both collaborators.

Brass players also have to plan carefully when to schedule rehearsal time with a pianist. With the limited amount of time they can play efficiently in each day, it is important that they enter rehearsals with maximum strength and flexibility to meet the high demands of solo literature. Often, however, these rehearsals come after a heavy day of ensemble rehearsal playing that uses up their efficient playing for the day and the solo rehearsal is a bigger struggle chop-wise than it needs to be. The rigors of solo literature demand planning and preparation to maximize time with the pianist and also build confidence in the soloist, especially in his or her ability to have the endurance and flexibility to play well. For high brass players like trumpet and horn soloists, this is a much bigger issue than it is for low brass players like trombone, euphonium, and tuba soloists. Two hours of consistent playing for high brass players in a given day will make it less likely that they will be successful in a solo rehearsal, even if there is ample rest between playing times. When planning run-throughs of the performance, it is important to keep this in mind. Not doing so can impact the growth of young musicians in physical and musical confidence and can ultimately reduce their desire to participate in solo ventures.

Of course collaboration with a pianist is really a duet, a form of chamber music, not simply solo and accompaniment. Teaching should reinforce the equality of each participant in this duo and help young players understand that their preparation must extend beyond simply learning to play their solo lines well. Students should know the piano part as well as their own and be able to hear the melodies during their rests and even understand the interaction of the two parts when playing together. Although brass soloists are often much younger and less experienced than their collaborative pianists, they need to also realize that they must be leaders in the musical preparation of their work. Many rehearsals pair the soloist and pianist without a teacher present. In this environment, students too often rely on the pianist to do all or most of the decision making and correction of errors. As they gain more understanding and experience, however, it is vital for them to be able to detect and remedy issues in both the solo and piano parts and coach the musical interpretation.

Pianists who play for brass soloists are often overworked as they attempt to accompany dozens of players, with different soloists even playing the same literature. With so much music to prepare, they usually will not focus on the very detailed interaction that makes a superb performance without the direction of the soloist. For example, I have watched pianists schedule 16 or more rehearsals with soloists in one day. It looks like a factory operation with students coming in and out each 20 or 30 minutes. I tell my students to make their time special by entering the room with specific goals for technical accuracy and musical expression. All pianists respond better to those soloists who know what they want musically and can show it by how they play. When soloists come in who know the piano part, know how they want it to sound, and can communicate that to the pianist, the collaborator always will respond with a higher level of technical and musical playing. Pianists soon learn which students are those special musicians who come prepared and demand this higher level from them. They will seek opportunities to collaborate with them just as they might seek to avoid those who do not bring such focus to rehearsal and performance.

Playing for Audiences

In my weekly solo class, I always invite students to play all or parts of their solos for the other students to provide early opportunities for them simply to play for an audience outside their practice or lesson experience. The focus for these small performances is to offer students the chance to see if they can replicate something they have done well in the practice room or in the lesson in front of an audience of peers. Once players are confident they can perform a passage or entire work in the practice room, meeting their targets in terms of technical accuracy and focus on musical expression, it is time for them to see how the presence of an audience impacts their performance. Playing in front of others, especially trained musicians, is a skill that is learned, not simply an innate ability. Behaviors that appear in the live performance environment must be understood and accommodated in the same manner that we work on other technical issues in our preparation. It is a simple rule that those who perform for audiences more often are the most prepared because they have had the chance to adapt to the unique challenges that this environment poses.

Wynton Marsalis told me once that he was not comfortable playing a classical solo in public until he had done so at least 15 times. As you all know, 15 performances for audiences is a rarity for most players, especially students. The more performance opportunities we can provide, however, the more likely our preparation will result in more confident and precise playing. It is important that students fully understand that the impact of nerves on playing for others is reduced with more and more repetition in front of an audience. Teachers need to create many performance opportunities in front of others as a normal process for preparing students. Teachers also must help students understand that early performances might yield mistakes that can be eliminated by adapting mental focus and changing the performance preparation schedule. How teachers give feedback for errors is vital to building this awareness and preserving the confidence and ego that students need to become successful performers.

Playing for others, as in my solo class or in other organized groups, is critical to helping students share their fear of performing and also their strategies for overcoming it. Students need to be encouraged to play for each other whenever they can to reinforce the benefit of such exposure. At many great music schools, students constantly are knocking on each other's practice room doors and asking fellow students if they can play for them. The mere presence of another musician in the room creates the sensation of a real performance and reveals many new challenges associated with it. Performers at this level of training understand that performance preparation is continually in a process of development as new literature and new audiences are introduced. Small efforts like playing in front of another student in a practice room or playing a portion of your solo in front of the class are essential for great performances later.

Brass players should plan for the unique challenges posed by playing for others and also see it as a new phase in their performance plan that might initially negatively impact their precision and comfort. If they approach performance opportunities in this manner, errors will bring less emotional suffering and, instead, lead them to the logical and focused solutions they need.

As will be discussed in the section on overcoming performance anxiety, playing for others can be exciting and rewarding with proper preparation. Young brass players need to be aware that it is a skill that can be developed rather than a talent that you either possess or lack. This awareness only comes, however, with the successful performance that such preparation brings, and sadly some students rarely experience it. Those students who are unsuccessful are more likely to quit solo playing and maybe even withdraw from music altogether. As teachers, we need to do everything in our power to foster them toward prepared and successful performances on their instruments. Doing so changes their attitudes toward performing and instills a true joy in musical expression. It also prepares them for the challenges that musical performance and other public presentations will pose in their future.

This three-step process of *practice room, playing with piano, and playing for an audience* can offer students the chance to ensure a more successful performance. Encourage them to lay out a time line that logically targets successful technical mastery and musical interpretation in the first step. Then share these musical ideas with a pianist as you revisit some techniques to establish a unified interpretation. Finally, set up several opportunities to play for others, so you can see what being in front of audiences does to your playing with enough time to make adaptations prior to the most important performances. It is clear that this process will take more planning and require an earlier start than what is often done. Oddly, it actually will not take more time overall, just more focused, goal-oriented practice and preparation. The great players do not always practice more than others; they just maximize the time they do spend. If you do that as well, you will be amazed at the outcome.

Exercises

Develop a time line for performing a new solo using these parameters:

- Establish and record initial tempi with correct rhythms, pitches, and articulations.
- Plot goals for tempi with a schedule of days required to reach them from the initial established tempi. How about five clicks higher each practice session? If your first initial tempo is 60, and you wish to perform it at 120, that is 12 practice sessions! That could be as early as 12 days but certainly within three or four weeks. Your goal is a musical plan with technical mastery in that time period.
- Plan for at least three rehearsals with a pianist prior to any public performance. Record each of these valuable meetings to review and plan for subsequent adaptations. Know your performance tempi, and be ready to share them with the pianist as early as possible.
- Find at least five musicians whose expertise you respect to listen to you play your solo with piano accompaniment. Bring them to your rehearsal. You will need to plan carefully for this and also be persuasive. Play the hardest parts of your solo for friends, teachers, and family members until they become automatic.

13

MUSICAL BREATHING

"Blow freely!"

William Cramer, Trombone Professor
The Florida State University

Brass players, from an early age, are taught about the importance of the breathing process as it relates to playing their instruments. The physical mechanism of breathing usually is described and accompanied with exercises that aim to increase lung use and reinforce proper posture and body motion during the process of inhalation and exhalation. In some cases, these exercises are quite dramatic and involve a significant amount of structured movement and posing. I have found too often, however, that the importance of breathing as part of musical expression is not stressed enough. There seems to be a bit of a disconnect between the physicality of breathing and how it serves in the actual process of interpreting music. I also find the simple philosophy of consistent capacity breaths falls short in addressing all the needs of high brass players.

The Physicality of the Breath

The first point brass players should consider when playing an instrument is that they will need to move more air in and out faster than our bodies do under most conditions. The second concept is the need to blow air steadily out of our bodies at a variety of speeds. While some athletic exercises might require the process of moving more air faster, the concept of steady blowing is not required in any other normal physical activity. There are many good exercises using devices as simple as balloons and as complex as inspirometers and breathing bottles that students can use to work on these two processes. The most important early goals are to encourage relaxed, open inhalations and steady exhalations. An open throat and relaxation of the abdominal muscles should be stressed, and these points are made now in all breathing discussions for brass players.

Inhalation

Taking a relaxed and voluminous inhalation is vital to the process of playing a brass instrument efficiently. By creating a large oral cavity and relaxing the throat, this process of inhaling should yield very little audible sound, with only the movement of air creating noise. Closed mouths and tense necks usually can be distinguished in a more audible inhalation noise as the moving air passes through smaller, more constricted spaces. Because the physical process of blowing the air back out of the body tends to retain the dimensions and muscle tension used in inhalation, it is important to strive for a silent breathing process at all times. It takes daily effort to reinforce the proper concepts that lead to this process, and a few props can be helpful, even with advanced players.

One inexpensive breathing aid involves a small piece of one-inch diameter PVC pipe or similar plastic device that you can keep in your instrument case. Prior to playing, insert this pipe into your mouth, closing your lips around it and securing it with your upper and lower teeth (see Fig. 13.1).

The action of gently biting this pipe results in the throat opening, and by breathing in this manner for a few moments, you can feel the physiology of a relaxed inhalation. If you don't have a prop, you simply can put your first two fingers together and

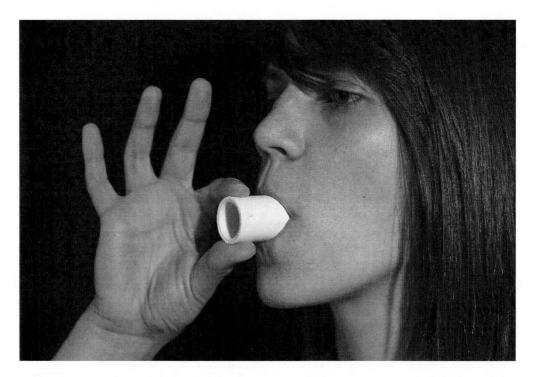

Figure 13.1 Using breathing tube for open throat

Figure 13.2 Using two fingers to stimulate open throat

place them in the same position as the tube to create this *bite reflex* (see Fig. 13.2). Recently, while teaching in Greece with Chicago Symphony principal trumpeter, Chris Martin, I was again reminded of this breathing aid as I noticed him walking with a pipe in his mouth for several minutes prior to his first playing of the day.

The lungs are amazing organs that basically will expand and fill with air to a degree limited only by how large a person can make the chest cavity to allow for this expansion. Young players usually focus on the expansion of the chest to make this area bigger, and this is of course part of the process we will need to play well. A bit more challenging is the process of allowing the lungs room to expand downward as well as outward, and this requires some illumination for players. Most players are aware that the diaphragm is the muscle that separates the thoracic and abdominal cavities, but less of them understand that it actually contracts downward and also is an *involuntary muscle*. It is important to understand that we cannot directly control the diaphragm but only effect its contraction downward by the manipulation of other muscles. Despite this reality, many music teachers still refer to *breathing with the diaphragm* and other concepts like *diaphragmatic vibrato*, and these ideas tend to give students the wrong idea about the function of this muscle. In breathing for playing a brass instrument, it is the *abdominal muscles* that are really the key to this downward expansion of the chest cavity. These muscles can be controlled actively, and their relaxation is key to developing a larger, more efficient inhalation because their movement triggers the movement of the diaphragm.

To reinforce the use of this process, place one hand flat across the abdomen, and inhale deeply while relaxing the abs (see Fig. 13.3). This will result in the front of the

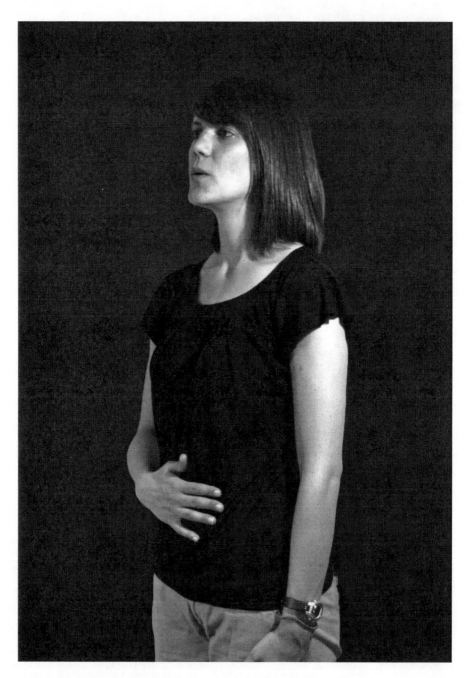

Figure 13.3 Using hand to sense relaxation of abdominal muscles

body centered on the navel region moving forward as the diaphragm contracts in response to this movement in the abdominal muscles. When this happens, organs in the abdomen also shift downward and forward to make room. It's okay; this movement of these organs is healthy and normal, but you might hear liquids in your stomach sloshing around when you do it! I always think this sound is actually a great indicator that you are inhaling well and engaging the diaphragm.

Thinking of filling the lungs from the bottom up is a great way to trigger this important component in the inhalation process and, along with consistent attention to the relaxation of the abdominals, should be stressed in the beginning of our playing day. Because we generally do not like the appearance of our bellies looking bigger than normal, we tend to keep these muscles contracted most of the time. It will require some coaxing to fully relax them when the time comes to play our instruments, so some focus on this process is helpful.

Avoiding Tension

One of the biggest enemies to the relaxed, silent inhalation is the creation of excessive tension in the neck and shoulder regions. Often, for example, students will raise their shoulders during inhalation, thinking that it might perhaps assist in lung expansion. This reaction, along with tensing neck muscles, is common when we try too hard in a new physical movement. One of the best therapies to counteract these habits is actually to first tense every muscle you can in the upper region of your body, so you can feel the sensations that this creates. Then, slowly remove all the muscle tension you possibly can, so you can feel the difference as you achieve a more relaxed state of physicality. Doing this as an exercise can help reinforce the correct, relaxed playing state and also help you identify when excessive tension creeps into your body.

Planning the Use of Air

Perhaps our greatest brass pedagogue for breathing is Arnold Jacobs, the famed principal tuba of the Chicago Symphony. Mr. Jacobs was very effective in his description of lung function and capacity breathing. His teachings in this area and also in the area of performance psychology are well documented in the book *Arnold Jacobs: Song and Wind* by his student Brian Frederikson, and it should be on all brass teachers' *must-have* lists.[1]

Along with the ideas of Mr. Jacobs and others, we have done good work in stressing the idea of capacity breathing and the benefit of filling up with air during inhalation. Unfortunately, there is too little discussion about the process of exhalation or blowing for brass players. Once the lungs are filled with air, it is also important to expel this air in a timely manner to maintain a relaxed breathing state. In tuba players, this is not much of an issue as their instrument uses air rapidly due to its large bore and mouthpiece. On the smaller-bore and small-mouthpiece instruments like trumpet and horn, however, the air is used less quickly, and often air can end up trapped inside the body, causing tension. More must be done to help these players maintain a relaxed use of air by teaching them to plan for air exhalation in the same manner that they plan for large inhalations.

Once inhalation is complete, and the lungs are filled with fresh air, the transfer of gases begins to take place as oxygen leaves air molecules, enters the bloodstream, and is replaced with carbon dioxide. As the air molecules now fill with carbon dioxide, the body senses the change, and receptors create a physical sensation to expel this spent air. Although we often think that it is the need for oxygen that creates this feeling, as when holding your breath for an extended period, it is actually the need to expel the carbon dioxide that initiates the physical response. In understanding this concept, we can return to that inhalation of a high brass player. If they take in a capacity breath, and if the phrase they play is shorter or softer, the next inhalation will be attempted with carbon dioxide–laden air still in the lungs. The result is a trapping of stale, deoxygenated air in the lungs that leads to tension in the breathing process and problems in playing. In many cases, breathing too often can be much more of an obstacle to playing than breathing too little. Also, always striving for a capacity breath is illogical in situations where the air will not be used in playing. It is important for brass players to plan their use of air, including when to breathe and how much air is needed to coincide with musical phrasing.

Imagine that your trumpet player has a solo that consists of an obvious two-measure phrase followed by a longer, extended phrase of 12 measures (see Fig. 13.4). If the student takes a full, capacity breath at the beginning, and he or she cannot play the entire 14 measures in one breath, what type of breath will happen after the first two measures? As the student took a capacity breath at the start, there is still much air in the lungs that is beginning already to complete the transfer of gases. Should he

Figure 13.4 Planning breath with phrase

or she take another capacity breath after only two measures? If the student attempts this process, the result certainly will be tension in the body during the longer phrase as the air currently in his or her lungs will be trapped.

Try this simple exercise to see what I mean. If you take a full, deep breath and blow out air for only a few seconds before attempting a second capacity breath, you can immediately feel the tension created by this action. Repeat this only a few times, and the tension will build as you continue to feel the need to expel the air that is still in your lungs and has become deoxygenated. This sensation is even more catastrophic when playing a brass instrument due to the resistance of the instrument and mouth-piece combination. Unfortunately, with our attention focused on other elements in our playing, this tension is often less noticeable as it builds.

Even if the trumpet player in our example tries to take a smaller breath after the first two measures of playing, he or she still is retaining stale air trapped in the lungs for the longer portion of the phrase. The player would need to expel all the air in his or her lungs to have any chance to *reset* to a more relaxed mode of playing. I truly find this type of stale-air playing everywhere, even in experienced players, because they are focused only on inhalation and capacity breathing and not on efficient air use.

Imagine if that same trumpet player instead took a smaller breath at the beginning of the solo, one that would offer just enough air to comfortably play the first two measures. When they player reached the end of the first short part of the phrase, he or she would have expelled that air and would be able to take a capacity breath of fresh, oxygen-rich air to assist in the longer phrase that follows. He or she would find that not only would the inhalation itself be very relaxing and natural but so would the playing during that second part of the melody. Try this yourself right now. Take a small breath, blow out for a few seconds as you did before, and then take a capac-ity breath. Feels different, right? Imagine how much this concept can improve your relaxation while playing an instrument. It is important to teach brass players about matching inhalation to exhalation and also to musical phrasing. Focusing only on big, relaxed inhalations and blowing exercises that do not recreate the true conditions of playing give players only part of the equation. It is important to replicate the actual process of playing to achieve the highest levels of efficiency.

Releases

One of the great clues to gauge if students are matching their breathing to the needs of the music is to pay careful attention to how they release notes prior to the next inhalation and the exact sounds they make during these transitional breathing moments. When you can hear them *depressurize* as they release notes, they might be blowing too vigorously for the resistance of the instrument, or their bodies may be attempting to release the stale air quickly. When it appears that they need to expel air prior to taking another breath, you can be sure that they are breathing more often than needed or using capacity breathing when it is not needed. At the end of several lines of music, they may also be *winded* and will exhibit several short bursts of air following playing as their bodies work to reestablish the correct equilibrium of fresh air in the lungs. Often I ask students to try to immediately speak in a calm, relaxed voice after releasing the final note of an etude or solo. When they have not managed their breathing correctly, they gasp for air and have difficulty speaking in long sentences without interruption as these short bursts of air cannot be avoided. I even ask them to sing the alphabet in a relaxed voice following their playing to ensure that they have planned for efficient use of their air. When they have planned their breathing correctly, this is easy for them, but when they are breathing too often and trapping stale air, this inefficiency can be detected easily.

High Notes and Breathing

The concept of air use for high notes on brass instruments is also something we must consider. Teaching often instills in players that high notes take *a lot of air*. Although this is certainly true in terms of velocity or speed of the air, it is not true when considering actual volume. Think about the air use differential between a tuba and a trumpet. It is clear that the larger aperture requiring larger lip vibrations of the tuba requires more air. The opposite is also true; smaller apertures require greater lip compression and faster airspeed but use less air volume, as in trumpet playing. This information becomes very important for players who are attempting to play in the high register. Brass players, for example, will often overblow and overbreathe because they are confusing the need for airspeed with the need for air volume. It is important to work with them to separate the need for inhalation and planned exhalations from the need for lip compression and airspeed. If the passage needs to be loud, of course, the volume of air used will increase, but in softer dynamics, it is actually amazing how long the air can last when the lips are well trained and the equilibrium among the airspeed, air volume, and the resistance of the instrument is reached.

We also must consider this phenomenon alongside the nature of many brass parts in our literature. Often, we play small motives interspersed with rests. The motives do not take much air, yet from an early age we connect the concept of resting with inhalation. One of the biggest problems I find in players is that they are breathing much too often for the music they are playing. They do so partly because of the capacity breathing philosophy already mentioned and also because they have not learned to let rests in music go by without always accompanying the pause with an inhalation. Consider a passage for horn that includes high, short motives with many rests as seen in Fig. 13.5.

Most players, without realizing it, will breathe in every rest when they play a phrase like this. When you consider they also may try to take large-capacity inhalations in each small pause, you can imagine the tension they will create in a short period of

Figure 13.5 Horn high notes with rests

time. When you combine that with the high tessitura that demands less air volume, you can understand why this music can be overly challenging to so many.

If the player takes a different approach and chooses to let the rests that are internal to the phrase go by without breathing, they can find such passages to be more relaxing and, indeed, easier. This kind of planning results in a better sound and better endurance and should be done in all levels of teaching. Often I will instruct a student to take a capacity breath and then not inhale during any rests but just keep playing until they have expelled completely the air in their lungs. They are usually amazed at how long they can actually play and how relaxing it feels. Of course, they will need to practice this approach often to counteract breathing during each rest that might have been reinforced for many years.

Lifting Without Breathing

Many high brass parts end in the upper register right at the moment when embouchures are likely to be the most tired. This condition further complicates our understanding of how to use breathing most effectively. It is important to experiment with breathing and blowing during these moments to help find the right formula for efficiency. It is important to understand the difference between the need to reduce the locked feeling that sometimes occurs during these playing conditions and the need for air. One helpful strategy is to learn to *lift* the pressure off the embouchure and, when necessary, *release* the pressurized air to reset in these challenging moments. It is best to first work these moments down an octave and at lower dynamic levels before moving too soon to the written version. Once the breathing strategy is planned, then it is time to try playing it in a higher octave. Unfortunately, early encounters of such moments are often in band rehearsal, and too many times the director only encourages players to *use more air* and *play louder*. Although this might assist in some situations, it also can compound problems in playing efficiency and create problems in embouchure development.

In terms of resting the embouchure, it is very important to introduce students to the concept of *lifting* the mouthpiece pressure off of the lips without always inhaling. Many times we confuse the need for some lip rest with the need for air. Wynton Marsalis showed me many times that this confusion leads to too much breathing and a buildup of tension. His long, technical displays in cornet solos were very relaxed, and I learned that it came from breathing less often but lifting more often. If you can integrate this into playing, you will find it very helpful in increasing endurance and maximizing relaxation. When playing in the upper register on a brass instrument, this combination of planning the breaths in size and duration along with lifting the pressure off the embouchure is truly revolutionary for security and strength.

It will take some practice to be able to make use of lifts without inhaling in your playing. When you do experiment with them in your playing, you will start to realize that this process can be helpful in disrupting the *locked playing* that often occurs when we do not manage our breathing correctly or use excessive pressure. If our air is stale or we are not using enough of it in the blowing and support process, our bodies immediately compensate by using more mouthpiece pressure and other adaptations. Once these compensating methods are employed, it is unlikely that you simply can increase the air to stop them and *unlock* your playing. If you sense this situation, you must lift the mouthpiece slightly from the lips to reset the level of mouthpiece pressure and also allow your breathing mechanism to return to better efficiency. Although we often get the level of blowing versus the needs of the music wrong, especially in practice sessions, the awareness to reset our playing and disrupt the locked condition is a vital tool in creating the most efficient performance.

Breathing in Time

Leonard Candelaria often asks master class participants to identify the location of the first breath in their solos. They usually point to a spot that is eight or so measures into the work. He immediately corrects them by reminding them that the first breath is the one you take before you start the first phrase. The importance of this first breath in preparing us musically and physically to play cannot be overstated. If we can be relaxed and thinking musically as we inhale for this start, subsequent playing is likely to be of the same quality.

The first breath of the piece often tells much about a player. Some players inhale over an undefined amount of time and then try to play the music in perfect time. Not only is this process awkward to hear and see, but it also reduces the naturalness of the start and certainly interferes with performance ability. Breaths always should relate directly to the pulse of the music, and when they do not, it indicates the previously mentioned disconnect between the physical action of breathing and its use in expressing music. It is not surprising that so many brass players develop problems with initial attacks. Although much attention is given to the tongue and lip vibration during these moments, it is actually the pace of the inhalation that is usually to blame.

When planning for musical inhalations, you should decide the rhythmic value of all breaths. Will the inhalation be an entire beat? Perhaps an eighth note in the tempo? Once you have determined what rhythmic value is needed for the inhalation, you need to practice this many times to develop relaxation in this process. Once you have committed to a rhythmic value for the inhalation, you are already on your way to better stability in performance for, now, the music starts even before you play your instrument.

It is valuable to consider the upbeat of a conductor's baton when conceptualizing inhalations. Great conductors give us the breath with their upbeat. In addition to providing us with the cue to inhale, they are also setting up the music in terms of tempo and level of intensity. Our inhalations without conductors should serve the same purposes. Each inhalation should foreshadow the music that is to come. When we are feeling the music, these breaths are more likely to be helpful. When we are overly focused on the technical aspects of playing, there is more risk that inhaling can become problematic. If players wait to think about musical expression until later in preparation, often the breathing used in early practice stages can cause unnecessary problems in their playing. It is yet another reason why we need to hear what we want to sound like before we try to get our instruments to recreate it. If we approach our works with musical expression built into our concept, our breathing is likely to be better from the onset, and the path to great playing is shorter.

I mentioned earlier the issue of initial attack problems related to inhalation. It is important to pay close attention when examining inhalation to be sure that the intake process is occurring over the entire rhythmic time allotted. You might find that problems in making such attacks coincide with inhalations using less than the full time planned from the beginning process of inhaling to the first note played. This type of inhalation is a bit rushed, and there ends up being a small amount of time between the actual process of bringing in air and the changeover to blowing it back out through the instrument. These dead moments are truly disruptive to the process and can lead to *locked playing*. Initial attack problems are actually the same locked playing described earlier, but they occur at the beginning of a passage.

The best way to eliminate these issues is to be sure that the inhalation uses the full rhythmic value that you have planned for the breath. That means you need to be certain that you are always inhaling or blowing out, never pausing in between. For most players, this means a more relaxed approach to time during the inhalation, especially if it is in a slow tempo and also if it is the beginning of the work. When there are problems, it is because the inhalation is rushed, and the lungs fill too early, leaving the pause that causes tension. Always think of the continuous cycle of inhaling and blowing out as a constant in your breathing. As we tend to be the most nervous at the beginning of our performances, it is here where you will need the most preparation to ensure that the cycle concept is successful and the inhalation matches your musical plan.

Quick Breathing

One of the great challenges to wind players is getting efficient inhalations with short, full breaths during rapid tempos. Under these conditions, planning your breathing is even more vital as is practicing for different levels of capacity in rapid, physical movement. No tempo should be too fast for you to practice breathing and the changeover from inhalation to exhalation. During your practice time, be sure that you also are addressing these quick and efficient breaths that are so necessary in much of our literature.

In very fast pieces without rests, it might be necessary to locate a suitable, longer note whose time you will *cheat* to allow for a rapid inhalation. With each new circumstance, you first need to identify the breathing plan and then be aware that it might take many practice sessions to realize it efficiently. Especially with rapid inhalations, you need to get the amount of air in the lungs right to develop a relaxed breathing process. If planned correctly, breaths always should be points of relaxation rather than moments of stress, even in rapid, physical activity. In some instances, players need to understand that a capacity breath is impossible, so they will need to plan for smaller inhalations or *sips*, as in small drinks of fluid. When there are no rests and continuous playing, several of these *sips* will be needed to replace larger inhalations. Make sure to practice this style of inhalation as well, so it is part of your breathing repertoire. Not only are these *sips* helpful in planned moments, but they also come in handy when you have miscalculated your air needs and need just a small quick *air booster* while playing to finish a phrase.

Exercises

- Practice scales and other technical patterns at varying tempos using a metronome. Plan the first breath as a rhythmic unit, and practice breathing in time, using the entirety of the time allotted for inhalation to ensure a cyclic and uninterrupted changeover to exhalation. With longer exercises, plan also for breaths internal to the exercise for their rhythmic value, and practice them, adhering to these decisions. It will take many repetitions, especially with faster tempos, to make each breath a point of relaxation.
- Play through an etude or solo that has many rests internal to the melodic phrase, and practice lifting the instrument slightly away from the embouchure without losing all contact between the mouthpiece and the lips and without breathing. Do this especially in higher passages that have rests interspersed with short, melodic units.

- Take an average-size balloon, and practice inhaling in time and then blowing into the balloon for a defined number of beats in time. Try different tempos and different amounts of beats, but always try to fill the balloon and expel all the air in the allotted time. Pay attention to the constant movement of air between inhalation and exhalation by observing the balloon movement, and also notice that, when there are dead moments, the balloon will not immediately begin to fill.
- Play through sections of your music, and listen carefully for the sounds of releases, especially those prior to inhalation. Work to eliminate abrupt endings or unwanted changes in pitch or tone color. Challenge yourself especially in the upper register and in softer dynamics in this process.

Note

1 Brian Frederiksen and John Taylor, *Arnold Jacobs: Song and Wind* (Gurnee, IL: Windsong Press, 1996), 276 pp.

14

PLANNING YOUR INTERPRETATION

"The art of interpretation is not to play what is written."
Pablo Casals
Cellist, Composer

One of the keys to building successful performances is the creation of a long-range plan that creates a musical story for the audience incorporating compositional characteristics of the piece and how the player chooses to highlight them. This requires careful study of the music's structure and harmonic nature along with the sounds the instruments can make in interpreting it in performance. For many players this process begins by studying recordings or live performances of the work by others, while other times it requires a truly original interpretation of the music and what you want it to say to your listeners. This type of *informed creativity* is a mental process that is valued not only in music and the arts but also in all professions.

Start your musical planning process by considering the music from the listener's point of view and how you think the music should stimulate his or her emotions and imagination. If you listen to recordings of the piece, this can help you identify emotional responses, although always remember that these are created by another musician's interpretative decision making, so do not let them subdue you own ideas. There is a big difference between simply copying the work of others and imagining your own images for the music. If you study recordings, try to listen to several versions of the work to understand the variety of options available in bringing a story line to audiences. You also can wait to listen to the work of others until you have taken the time to examine the music and imagine an interpretation on your own. This often preserves the artistic opportunities the piece offers and reduces influences from *experts* who, although they have likely informed ideas about how the music should be played, should not dampen your musical individuality.

You can start by constructing a simple time line of the piece that shows the progression of feelings that you believe the music can stimulate. Take special note of where you think the emotional response in the listeners will change because the sound of the music changes. Look especially for long-range repetition, the return of prominent melodies and motives, and other structural elements that you will want to emphasize in this string of emotions.

On a smaller level, within an emotional area, identify subtle changes in accompaniment figures and style of articulation, especially in repeated melodies. This form of focused examination will help greatly as you formulate a plan for your expressive strategy. Where are the *big moments* of the work, and how will you emphasize them? Will you slow down as you crescendo to the climax of the recapitulation, even if these directions are not offered in the score? Will you choose to create a softer echo in a repeated motive? How about the relationship of your solo line to the piano accompaniment? Is it truly melody and accompaniment, or do the parts function as equals in polyphony? These are all features the composer included to help express the feelings he or she hoped the music would stir in listeners.

With the reinterpretation of each performer, these original intentions are always subject to personal taste, even when there are definitive performances already in existence. Music is so unique in the arts because of this continual rebirth of interpretation and we should always remember this as we play brass music so that it does not become simply an attempt to recreate an earlier performance. Because this is already done too often, live performances of art music are in danger of disappearing from the vibrant entertainment choices in our cities. Be sure to retain the uniqueness of *you* as you plan the interpretation of *your* music. Approaching preparation in this way also reduces performance anxiety because, once you are onstage, you are saying something new and original rather than taking on the impossible task of trying to recreate an earlier, edited, recorded, and thus artificially perfect performance.

Such musical planning should start earlier in the preparation process rather than waiting until later. With younger students, teachers can take time to point out different themes and where they return and where changes in the themes occur. Discuss and demonstrate strategies for marking important transitions in the music, so students can recognize them and begin to form their own ideas of how to emphasize them. Remember that technique is finding a way to get your instrument to create the exact sounds that you are already hearing in your imagination. Likewise, planning an interpretation also must begin with strong, imagined ideas about how you want the piece to sound and what emotions are connected to it.

The musical sounds you create in your mind, based on solid knowledge of compositional construction, will become focal points that will govern the creation of your unique interpretation. If you are constantly guided by a concrete, well-informed sound image of what you want to create, practice will be focused and productive. Too often students practice without such informed, internal musical guidance, and they do not know exactly what they want to achieve in terms of sound. If we can help them construct a mental image of what they want to sound like, with modeling and focused listening, they will be more motivated and goal oriented as they create and practice their musical plans. In this the role the teacher can help them understand these concepts of goal setting in a musical sense rather than only in an abstract development of technique. The teacher also can help them to volunteer their own ideas of what emotions the music should express and how their technique can advance those ideas.

Informed creativity involves more than simply playing *what you feel* as this alone is not enough to develop a sophisticated and successful interpretation. I have heard many performances and watched the players writhing around, seeming to be feeling very strong emotions, but because the movement did not match the construction of the music, it seemed out of place and actually distracted from the listening experience. It is important to know as much as you can about the form, rhythm, and harmonic structure of your music as this awareness increases your ability to convey a coherent plan to audiences. Start by looking for some basic features to understand large-scale construction and then move toward smaller, more detailed changes to enrich them with musical intent. The things we learn by studying music theory and music history can be extremely helpful as we develop our music ideas and construct our performance plans.

Variety and Repetition

At a basic level, I believe that all successful music needs to carefully balance the need for variety along with the use of repetition. Depending on the experience level and training of the audience, performers must consider this basic balance when selecting music and preparing what they hope will be a successful plan for its expression. Let me begin with a related story. I have taken many long trips with my brother, who is one year older than me and has no musical training. Our choice of music while driving easily demonstrates how musical experience shapes our reactions as listeners. When I am behind the wheel, I enjoy classical orchestral and opera recordings as well as small group jazz with extended solos. My brother prefers pop music or country artists. Oddly enough, we both tend to fall asleep when not driving and characterize each other's choices as *boring* as a contributing factor to our sleepiness. This situation is totally logical considering my professional music training and my brother, who has no musical experience. When he attempts to listen to my music, his inability to comprehend the great variety of sounds presented results in a loss of interest and then boredom. When I listen to his more simplistic music, it sounds too predictable and overly repetitive, causing lack of interest, boredom, and then restful sleep.

Novice listeners need more repetition and less variety in music as they require repeated sounds to help them organize what they are hearing. Experienced listeners usually prefer more variety and less repetition to provide continued stimulation and interest. Performers should not forget this basic *law of listening* as they need to cultivate and inspire audiences of all kinds with their performances.

During my doctoral studies at the Eastman School of Music, I found myself in yet another music theory course investigating 20th-century compositions. I already had taken a similar course at Florida State University and at the University of North Texas and found myself in familiar territory. In each of these courses, the teacher followed a canon tracing atonal music along with a heavy dose of 12-tone music and other adventures in serialism. Just as my many courses in Romantic music totally ignored Tchaikovsky, so these 20th-century courses all skipped over Hindemith, one of my favorite composers. With the several-day examination of the dodecaphonic *Variations for Orchestra, Op. 33a* of Arnold Schoenberg completed, my professor distributed yet another 12-tone work of Schoenberg for us to analyze. I must have had quite a sour look because he asked me why I looked so distraught. Fortified with the fact that I already had a great university teaching position, and this being the end of a long, academic, music career as a student, I decided to share my true feelings with him and the class. I asked the 25 experienced musicians in the graduate course how many of them actually listened to Schoenberg outside of the requirements of the course.

I also asked how many had played or paid to hear 12-tone music in their entire lives. Their lack of response—no one raised a hand—led me to my next questions for the class: "How many of you play or would pay to hear Hindemith? How many of you listen to Hindemith on your own?" The response was unanimous, a stark contrast to the Schoenberg question. I then handed the teacher a recording of *Mathis der Mahler* by Hindemith and challenged him to tell me why, after three degrees in music, I had not had the chance to analyze such composers. I asked him to consider skipping the next Schoenberg and analyze the Hindemith instead. I am happy to report that we did just that, and oddly, *Mathis der Mahler* also ended up as one of the score recognition examples in my doctoral written exams!

Although Schoenberg's music is a marvel of organization, it unfortunately often misses on the balance of variety and repetition, even for most experienced listeners. Unless you have devoted a lot of listening repetitions, or you spend most of your time listening to 12-tone music, you will likely not seek it out as art for enjoyment. This is due in large part to the mere fact that audiences do not have much or any experience listening to this complex system, and so they quickly become bored due to lack of understanding. Although there is certainly some repetition, the very language of the music requires melodies to be repeated many more times in one rendition to provide the currency needed for audience understanding. Eventually, of course, the desire to compose in this manner faded, largely due to lack of interest from performers and audiences. It remains central in music theory study because of its innovation and because its analysis works out like a logical puzzle, something that theorists tend to delight in, even if audiences cannot easily detect them.

In evaluating works to play for audiences, I always consider the audience and strongly feel that there should be something on the program that even novice listeners, like my brother, can understand enough to hold their interest. You always can balance the program with some more adventurous listening, but offering too much variety without the repetition to organize sounds will usually lead to much less success in widening our audiences and attracting listeners to our performances.

Know the Form and Structure of Music

Music theory does do a wonderful job of teaching performers about the structure of music, and such analyses provide essential tools in making decisions regarding expression. Although we can play music and have emotional feelings while doing so, the greater our understanding of what we are playing, structurally and historically, the greater our opportunity to present something very special to listeners. The form of our music, and its organization of repeated and varied sections, is vital to fully understand when making expressive decisions. Most music follows a well-known path of presenting melodies, moving away from them and then returning to them in some manner. This concept of departure and return is a central theme in the arts and leads to good music making. The reason that the sonata form, even in long, developing compositions, works so well is that it follows this plan of leaving and returning to familiar themes and textures. If these themes are well established in the beginning, you can offer many excursions filled with variety for listeners prior to the repetition of thematic return. It is vital for students to understand thematic construction in their music and how they need to *package* these melodies for listeners. The emphasis that comes with the triumphant return of themes is like the return of characters in the movies who appear after a long absence, a moment for special treatment.

Great composers, of course, know this better than anyone, and they usually provide compositional help for expressing important moments with carefully crafted melodic and harmonic structures to help set them apart for listeners. It is well worth the effort to spend time with your students to help them understand these features and what performance techniques they might use to highlight them. Those compositions that achieve, through their structure, a balance of variety and repetition that appeal to the greatest amount of listeners become part of the repertoire, and those that do not disappear as players will not want to perform them and audiences will not want to hear them.

Many times in master classes I have heard *never play the same music the same way twice*. This is good advice always to remember, even for achieving small-scale balance between repetition and variety. I think you will find that, especially in shorter repeated melodies, successful performers will find ways to vary the presentation for each melody. In Baroque music, for example, melodies often repeat due to song structure of the period and also the influence of dance on music. Experienced players use dynamics, articulation, and also ornamentation to vary the tune, giving listeners variety to go along with each repeated melody. This is especially necessary if you are listening in a concert setting as opposed to dancing, the original purpose for much of this music. In larger repeated sections, like the exposition of a symphony, the exact repeat is more warranted to assist listeners in understanding the more varied thematic structure of these larger compositions.

In popular music, the concept of varying repeated melodies also connects to the longevity of songs and their singers. The Beatles, perhaps the most revered and longest-lasting popular group of the 1960s, achieved this status primarily because their music offers listeners a carefully crafted balance between variety and repetition that may not be readily understood by many. The song "Lucy in the Sky With Diamonds," one of their big hits from the album *Sgt. Pepper's Lonely Hearts Club Band* in 1967 is a great example. In this song you can hear changes in meter, instrumentation, number of singers, harmonization, phrase length, and recording techniques all in the context of a three-minute rock song. Although the Beatles were certainly a social and cultural phenomenon, it is also the craftsmanship of their songs and recordings that has resulted in their continued appeal with listeners. Although all listeners do not easily detect many of these variations, it is certain that the Beatles, as performers, carefully planned for subtle variety in their music. Without the benefit of changes in instrumentation, recording techniques, and other variants, the demand on instrumental soloists to create variety in their melodies is, of course, much greater.

Note Grouping

All melodic notes should function in one of three roles. They should lead up to a *target note*, or high point, serve as a target note, or lead away from a target note. If you can remember this basic rule, you will save a lot of time in developing a coherent interpretation of your music. Music, like language, is divided into groups based on harmony, rhythm, articulation, accompaniment, and the necessity of breathing. Also like the recitation of language, there are many ways to perform the same melody by choosing different target notes as a speaker can choose different words in each sentence to stress.

Many musical phrases follow the path of leading to a center target note and then leading away from that high point with a small diminuendo. This is often the first step toward understanding the need for constant movement in music. These early melodies often also move up in range with the highest note in the target position, and this simplifies the process of leaning toward and away from it in a musical expression of the phrase.

Of course, as we encounter more complex and longer phrase construction, there are also more options for expression, and so it is important to dig a bit deeper into the musical construction to find inspiration to choose target notes and plan paths to and away from them. The tonality of the work can be helpful in this process. The return to tonic is always an option for emphasis, but so are sudden departures from the key that show up as accidentals in the music. Leaning toward these color changes can be rewarding in most applications, so be sure to consider them in choosing your targets.

On a larger scale, look for repeated passages and also sequences that take a smaller motive and repeat it moving up or down in range. Just recognizing repeated motives and sequences is a good first step. Once you have identified them, determine their destination and if they increase intensity toward a bigger target or decrease intensity away from one. The range is helpful, as are dynamic markings, but like the punctuation in sentences, these markings do not make all your decisions for you when it comes to musical expression.

Harmonic changes also can help you determine how to create your phrasing plan. Think about how modulations up at the end of pop songs increase intensity and are helped by an increase in volume, vibrato, and urgency in the singer. Spend some quality time examining changes in harmony and key to guide your decisions about how much stress each of these changes should receive and how these compositional devices impact emotional responses in listeners.

Motivic construction is an important smaller-scale component to consider in your expression of the music. Some composers gradually alter motives in music in a way that eventually yields a new theme that emerges in a very organic manner. Beethoven, Brahms, and Bartok are all famous for this concept of *developing variation*, but many works for brass instruments also develop melodies in a similar fashion. Sometimes the germinal motives are short (think the beginning of the *Fifth Symphony* of Beethoven) with added length and complexity as the composition continues. Some are longer and more complete but create variety with changes in the internal notes and rhythms of the melody. Using your ears and studying the score can reveal many such relationships in your music, and then you must decide how to present this method of construction to the audience. Look in the piano part as well to see if some of the organic creation of melodies is shared between the soloist and the pianist. Once you start to see these thematic derivations, you can think about where the arrival of an important melody occurs and how you would like to add emphasis to that moment. Especially on a smaller level, understanding themes in this way helps you make decisions on balance, volume, and articulation in either a solo or ensemble setting.

Establishing Characters

Many of our brass compositions lay out melodies in the manner of a conversation. Call and response with repeated ideas and question-and-answer formats are two styles of conversation from our use of language that can inform our melodic interpretation. See if you can imagine different melodic portions as words being sung by different characters in an imaginary musical or opera. Continue this process by thinking about how these characters might look and how their voices might sound.

Male, bass voices, female sopranos, large, menacing bodies, slender, delicate ones—these details can help you decide exactly how you would like the music to sound. Many melodies have two distinct sections, often in different keys or at least with different harmonies. This makes them ripe to interpret as a conversation between two people. The more detailed your image of these characters, the more opportunities you will have to inject expression into your playing. Image how they will move and use their bodies as they sing each melody. Imagine their facial expressions and how they manipulate their voices. Watch opera and musicals to gain some insight into this process, and then look up videos of the Canadian Brass and Mnozil Brass on YouTube to see how successful they are in creating such characters as they perform instrumental melodies.

By the time you reach the performance phase of your preparation, you need to have a plan that you can follow while onstage. This plan will be the culmination of much investigation into the music and matching your desired sound to your technical abilities at the time. The plan should include a succession of thoughts and feelings to occupy your thoughts during the performance. This planned string of mental triggers needs to coordinate directly with the music in real time and should accommodate the entirety of the piece. Using such a storytelling process keeps our minds focused on positive mental images and contributes to informed and confident playing. In addition to creating this thought sequence, it is important to practice playing through the work with it fully engaged and in confident control of our minds. There is, of course, always a gap between the *theory* of how to play musically and the real *practice* or ability to create that theoretical rendition with security. It will take many repetitions to learn how to stay focused on your mental plan, especially when encountering performance anxiety. It is when we do not maintain control over our thoughts and feelings by concentrating on a musical plan that fear, doubt, and apathy can enter our minds and disturb our playing, causing mistakes. Work hard to create and practice your mental/emotional plan to tell the best story possible while negotiating through the music. You will find that this makes onstage experiences more predictable and fulfilling for both you and your audiences.

Negotiating Technical Challenges

When brass performers encounter greater technical challenges in music preparation, it is often also more difficult to focus on musical ideas. This is especially true when we are asked to perform fast passages involving advanced finger and slide work and also rapid articulations. The process for these moments often requires that we take a step back from the musical plan and solidify our technical abilities to accurately negotiate the three basic elements of rhythms, correct notes, and correct articulations. As mentioned earlier, without this basic control of the written music, working on the subtleties of musical expression is impossible. There are some basic technical strategies, though, that can help brass players stabilize such passages and begin the path to the controlled elegance sought for in musical expression.

When encountering a fast-moving passage, especially with same value notes, it is usually better musically and technically to slightly elongate the first written pitch in performance. This concept of making the first note longer leads to a more relaxed and elegant melodic rendition while also calming anxiety about technique. String players do this all the time, and it is wonderful to watch the physical movement of their bow arm as it begins a long string of notes. This movement seems so natural and elegant visually as the momentum increases in a quick, smooth acceleration much like you can see in a golf swing or the outstretched arms in dancing.

Brass players who encounter a rapid string of notes almost always rush the time, especially at the beginning of the passage. The anxiety of technical demands can be alleviated by this practice of elongating the first note of the phrase and also notes that begin a change in melodic direction. By overdoing these elongations for some time, players can become more comfortable with the flow of notes, after which they can reduce the amount of stretching to musical taste. It is important to find the balance between playing technical passages in strict time and making these small elongations and then subsequently pushing the time. Although the ability to play in strict time is always an initial goal, once players have familiarity and security instilled, they can concentrate on how their interpretation of the melody might include small changes in time. Making these changes often decreases technical difficulty while also offering better chances for expressive playing—a great combination!

Exact time in technical passages, as in all melodic presentation, is actually quite lifeless and stale compared to incorporating small changes in time to outline phrases and increase and decrease intensity. Listening to Bach unaccompanied string and woodwind works as performed by world-class players reveals a slight stretching and pushing in the time that makes the solo voice much more interesting. Understanding the style of music, its composition structure, and your technical limitations will all impact when and how you alter the exactness of subdivisional time.

As mentioned earlier, the athletic focus of daily practice should rigorously work basic technical patterns in all keys, speeds, volumes, and ranges. If a player can focus the exactness of time on these patterns, encountering them in literature will be an easy transfer of this ability. As most music for brass instruments repeats simple patterns over and over, the time it takes to work up a piece for performance shrinks as the player gains command of the these oft-encountered patterns. I prefer to focus my technical efforts and frustration in this athletic session to spare such feelings when working on my solo or ensemble passages. Of course this technical mastery is not the end of a process but really the start of implementing rapid technique to enrich our musical ideas. When possible, I prefer that practice time devoted to performance materials be filled with musical expression and the exact sound of the melody without undue thoughts of technique. Even in the technical drill section of my practice, once I have control of technique with clarity and exact subdivision, I then shift my thoughts toward making the string of notes more expressive. I continue the pace with a metronome but allow for slight alterations in the smallest subdivision pace, outlining note groupings and harmonic motion. Performing Clarke studies, or scales, like the fast passages of *Carnival of Venice* and other solos are, in the end, all the same to me. They are all simply melodies.

A well-crafted interpretation considers the technical capability of the performer along with the structure of the music and its connections to larger historical and cultural influences. As communication, musical performance ultimately tells a story to the audience, so with much preparation, brass players can prepare a performance plan that incorporates elements inherent in the music and its time with ideas unique to the performer. It is this uniqueness that makes all music performance exciting, so be sure to keep it at the forefront during the many hours of preparation. By retaining this concept of ownership over our playing, we can reduce anxiety about performing and retain the emotional stimulation that drew us to this art in the first place.

Exercises

- Analyze your solo work by first identifying major changes in key, tempo, texture, and technical demands. Once you have found these transitional moments, draw a simple diagram of the form, and look for repeated melodies that you might connect to imaginary characters or emotional moods. Consider where peak moments are based on range and dynamics, and label the precise moments where these occur. Once you have these guideposts in your piece, construct a chain of emotions that match these musical changes.
- Experiment with melodies by assigning different characters to them, and play them while imagining how each character looks and moves. Practice singing the melodies, and allow your body to move as if onstage theatrically to inspire more ideas to bring into your instrumental rendition.
- Watch video of string performers to see and hear how they use elongation to make fast technical passages more elegant. Study their body movements as well as they play. Work on familiar rapid technical patterns and then passages from your music, experimenting with elongation at the beginnings of sections and as notes change direction to gain a more flexible and expressive feel for these melodies.

15

TOOLS FOR EXPRESSING
EMOTIONAL PEAKS

"Music expresses that which cannot be put into words and
that which cannot remain silent."

Victor Hugo
French Writer, Poet

"Music directly imitates the passions or states of the
soul. . . . When one listens to music that imitates a certain
passion, he becomes imbued with the same passion . . ."

Aristotle

With enough practice and technical mastery, players can begin to make immediate connections between emotional states and the physical manner in which they
play the instrument. Feelings of anger, for example, might bring louder volumes and
heavier accents, while gentle thoughts might illicit more lyrical articulation and softer
dynamics without the need to consider technique directly. To make the emotional
changes needed for an expressive performance, players must develop automatic
physical responses to be able tell a story through the music and maximize audience
impact. Making the instrument a true extension of our feelings in the same manner
as we use our voices requires both the development of facile technique from countless
repetitions but also lots of experience connecting our emotions to different types of
playing on the instrument. The more often we can attempt to express a feeling in our
playing, even on basic technical patterns, the more equipped we will be to call upon
the natural connection of emotion and technique in performance.

As in our use of human speech, even if you practice pronunciation and pacing to
promote clarity and effortless delivery, if emotional intent is missing, this usually can
be detected because there is a lack of validity in vocal dynamic, tone, and the accentuation of syllables. When individuals try to mislead you with their comments, for
example, the emotions they are actually feeling usually contrast with those normally
associated with their intended deception. In this way, it is easy to detect lying as we
sense the lack of naturalness and congruence in the delivery. Likewise, when we are
hearing speakers who are passionate about their words, the delivery seems genuine,

and we easily interpret their emotional intent as it achieves a certain congruence and viability in delivery.

Playing honestly with musical expression requires the performer to share honest feelings with their audiences. To be able to adopt this mind-set onstage, all preliminary technical preparation phases need to be completed. You should be as *over-prepared* technically as you possibly can be so that connections between thoughts and instrumental technique are automatic and instantaneous. If you have developed your thorough musical plan for each work, you just need to have the courage to stick to it and allow your mind and body to repeat the sequence of feelings and related physical playing motions it easily remembers.

Musical sound to me is like a living organism in that it is constantly moving including when we are simply holding longer notes. Even when our playing is at the lowest levels of intensity, the sound is still changing in the same way that our breathing and pulse moves our body. When expressing a melody, the slight changes in dynamics, tempo, vibrato, and articulation happen constantly and follow a natural, flowing path in great players. If the performer does not keep the melodic line *moving* at all times, the feeling instantly becomes static, and if there are no other musical lines that take over the obligation to move the sound forward, the audience will lose interest, and emotional projection will be diminished. There are some players who, when speaking, singing, or playing an instrument, intuitively keep their sound alive with expressive movement, while others seem less able to do so easily. These players are somehow able to express emotions freely while speaking or playing. We might refer to them as extroverts, although I have on occasion encountered students who seem overly shy and reserved until they have the chance to play an instrument, and then their whole persona changes.

When teaching the concept of expressing ideas while playing instrumental melodies, it is important to start with some basic technical maneuvers to help players connect the physical act of playing a brass instrument with the expression of emotion. I like to begin with several tools that they might think of as technical ways to increase and decrease intensity. By practicing these techniques individually and in small melodic moments, they can begin to relate them to the emotional gestures they can imitate.

Dynamics

The easiest place to start is with the use of dynamics to better express shorter melodies. The concept of crescendo toward a high point and decrescendo away from that high point taught to most beginners easily can help a student understand the idea of constant motion in music. Begin by sharing the basic axiom that music always should be either getting louder or getting softer and that it never, or rarely ever, stays static or at the same level of intensity. This concept necessitates that they constantly make decisions about every note and whether it is leading the listener toward something or away from it. Although not all phrases follow the crescendo to middle or decrescendo to the end plan, many simple melodies studied in early years do. Do not wait to bring these ideas to their attention. The difference between a young player who does such dynamic motion and one who does not is quite striking. Of course, there are physical abilities that must be developed and controlled to keep the sound moving effectively in this manner, but development of these abilities will be enhanced greatly by the recognition that they need to be part of all playing. In most beginning methods, students are instructed to play long tones that crescendo and decrescendo. Such exercises not only solidify the embouchure and build strength; they also instill the concept of a constantly moving sound even at this early age. Adapting this concept from held notes to melodies should be an easy step once they have the strength to play the notes.

Along with this process, players should be encouraged early on to select *target notes* that act as focal points for this process of moving toward and away from them. Even if they do not choose the most logical high points in each melody, their concept of movement to and from targets is vital to establishing this concept in their playing. There is always more than one way to express a melody, and so the concept of individual expression through choice also should appear early in the training of musicians.

I use the term *leaning* to refer to this movement toward and away from target notes or high points. The physical act of leaning toward someone or away from them is something that is easy to demonstrate with your body motion while singing or playing the melody. When appropriate, I will demonstrate leaning by singing the melody and even pushing my hand against a student's shoulder as I approach the target note and then reduce the pushing as I retreat from it. Musical conductors also mirror this leaning with their bodies as they lean toward their ensembles to increase intensity and lean back to diminish it while conducting. It is a very natural sensation in the body because it is experienced in so many everyday movements so it is logical to connect the concept of musical expression to these *natural* physical actions.

When I describe *leaning*, I am not only referring to the concept of crescendo and decrescendo but also to several other expressive tools as well. The most effective leaning we hear in great players is a sophisticated blending of several techniques used together, making the movement toward and away from target notes more powerful and also the connection to our bodies and emotions stronger.

Rubato and Time

Although we must spend a lot of time training players to play perfectly in time with metronomic accuracy to develop reliable control and technical mastery, it is also important for them to understand the flexible nature of time in most musical presentation. As mentioned earlier, playing melodies perfectly in time is a great start for players to understand the rhythmic construction of the melody and to be sure they can control note-to-note movement along with demands of range, articulation, and other obstacles. Once players can control these techniques and keep steady time, however, we must then also encourage them to experiment with moving the time faster and slower slightly and to amplify leaning toward and away from target notes. The combination of crescendo and decrescendo with these slight changes in pacing intensifies the leaning and the expression of target notes in the melodic presentation.

As with most emotional performance, the humanness of musical expression is most vivid when it departs from total control and predictability. The duality of being able to achieve a perfectly steady tempo with the realization that, in most musical environments, it needs not to be exactly steady is vital to shaping the musical thinking of young players. Again, listening to emotionally compelling performances and then dissecting them to glean how they manage time in leaning toward and away from high points is very helpful in gaining this awareness. In most cases, you will find that those performances that evoke the strongest emotional responses generally mimic human emotions as they rush to high points and slowly come down from these emotional peaks. This mirrors the natural acceleration toward emotional peaks and the graduated return to a less-charged emotional state.

Articulation

Articulation also can play a role in musical leaning, although it is usually subtler and requires rapid natural connections between the desired sound and exact tongue placement. The length of notes and their shape in terms of style of attack, intensity of continuity, and release are all valuable tools in enhancing our emotional messaging. The weight of an attack is, of course, the result of a careful combination of airflow, tongue placement, and lip tension. The coordination of these processes to create articulation sounds imagined by the mind is only possible with many hours of technical drill, as in the acquiring of correct pronunciation in language. Heavier articulation, for example, can add weight and intensity to notes, especially if they are also lengthened in delivery. Movement toward this type of articulation can combine with an acceleration of time and an increase in volume as we lean toward a target note. Articulation on a brass instrument offers countless variables available to the player in the same way that spoken language does. Just as our enunciation can progress as our spoken voice displays emotion, we also can employ subtle changes in articulation to increase or decrease intensity in our playing.

The interplay of slurring and tonguing for a brass player, like the pronunciation of words for a singer, is a complicated combination of these physical movements. Even within the context of a slurred passage, the tongue can be a great tool for emphasis if the player can keep the flow of sound constant and the level of interruption in volume is appropriate. Often students have asked me if I tongued a particular note in a lyrical passage that was all marked as slurred. My initial response sometimes is that I do not usually remember what part my tongue played. Upon repetition with a different mind-set, I sometimes find that I did use a very slight articulation such as the *n* tongue position to help define a target note in the phrase. Although it may sound strange to some players, when I am allowing myself to focus on emotional intent, I let my body respond as it wishes. The connection between emotion and how the body uses the tongue is natural and automatic now, although it took me many years to build and strengthen such a direct path.

Vibrato

Perhaps the most sophisticated tool a brass performer has is the use of vibrato in tonal expression. The color that vibrato creates in our sound through variations in its speed and width can communicate increases and decreases in emotional intensity to listeners. In terms of *leaning*, vibrato normally increases width and perhaps speed as we lean toward a target note or peak moment. Likewise, leaning away usually includes a reduction in speed and possibly, width. Listening to great brass players, again, can be very instructive into this use of vibrato as part of leaning. If players have developed the proper lip flexibility and have listened to expressive playing regularly, the natural use of vibrato in this manner is possible. If they lack the physical ability to easily vibrate their sound, however, the connection of this manipulation to emotion is impossible. Even with the lip flexibility ability, they will need guidance in developing the immediate connection between a feeling and the physical action of the lips. This is best done with listening and experimenting. The opportunity to study with a teacher who can demonstrate this expressive tool in close quarters is vital to this guidance.

Imitating Human Emotional Peaks

Think about how an emotion like anger builds up inside us and what happens when it reaches a peak that results in a dramatic response. Initially, the sensation might appear as a mild irritant that you can ignore and deflect. If the initiator of your anger persists and increases the intrusion, these feelings can begin to accumulate, occupying your thoughts and overcoming your ability to deflect them. Eventually, with continued increase from this irritant, you can lose control and raise your voice, change your use of language, and even physically respond to the emotional state created. Because we usually do not intend to lose control, its loss signals a high emotional state that usually seems to appear too suddenly. When we lose control of our actions in such moments, the last erosion of remaining resistance seems to disappear at an accelerated pace. We think we can withstand the challenge, but suddenly things seem to happen too quickly for us to control, and our emotions *get the better of us*. The pace of this buildup to an emotional peak usually follows a path that includes this accelerating path of increased intensity. This is true in the most profound human emotions. It is why we cry in movies, even though we try so hard to avoid it. It is why we cannot stop sexual urges past a certain point. It is how people end up in violent confrontations. It is what makes strong human emotions so human.

When musicians stir these very human feelings with their musical presentations, the results can be powerful indeed. Longer buildups to emotional peaks make the final arrival at the peak more impactful and lasting. When a peak emotion is reached, such as intense anger, passion, or sense of loss, the return to normal emotional states takes time, just as our bodies take time to return to a normal state following an emotionally charged moment. The calming process is related directly to the power of the emotional peak and requires the proper amount of time to de-intensify. Musical players must consider these concepts when developing their musical maps and experiment with how quickly they should lean toward and away from intense moments. Movement toward peak moments is enhanced by increases in dynamics, slight acceleration in time, heavier accents, and faster, wider vibrato. Movement away from peak moments often includes a diminishing of volume, a relaxation in tempo, a softening of articulation, and a slowing vibrato with reduction in its width. In some cases, the end of the process is a *disappearing act* of the brass sound as the vibrato decays in speed and width until it is a true straight tone and the volume decreases until it is inaudible.

This complex leaning takes great technical control and easy connection between emotional intention and automatic changes in physical playing. Some phrases are short, and planning how to lean is evident. In more complex compositions, the process of working toward musical high points often takes more thoughtful planning based on compositional structure and decision making about how exactly to express larger movement to emotional peaks and away from them.

Great musicians understand that music does not always build intensity in a consistent manner but also in *waves* of ups and downs that grow and diminish in intensity. As in human emotion, we do not move toward peak moments at a steady rate but rather in waves that become more intense as our control mechanisms respond to stimulants, attempt to control them, and eventually succumb to their power. Just as first appearances of emotional response can be resisted by our conscious control, so early building of emotion in music can rise slightly and return to a more relaxed state. As we approach the loss of emotional control, these waves restart at a gradually more intense level and move higher in intensity and faster in repetition until our resistance is depleted and control is lost. Planning of our musical expression often should consider this emotional course in a composition that presents longer melodies over a longer time period. Reaching peak levels of emotional expression too early makes the eventual high point anticlimactic and less impactful. For brass players especially, we need to seek points in the music to reduce intensity to avoid *topping out* too soon, especially in our use of loud dynamics. By studying the music carefully and considering larger-scale emotional impact, we can use the concept of *informed creativity* to maximize how we use our technical abilities to express these waves of feelings. It is also through our understanding of peak emotions and the ways they can be expressed that we develop greater technical abilities as we seek to match the maximum expressive properties of our instrument.

Emotional Exercise

When I taught beginning band in Texas, I often would encourage shy students to imagine themselves to be another person, while their instrument was in their hands. I gave them *permission* to be more aggressive and often challenged them to express themselves, both while playing and with their speaking voices in that manner. I found that loud, aggressive students tended to express themselves on their instruments more freely than others, while many of the quiet and shy students needed more encouragement. Some students were obviously conditioned to be quiet so often in their upbringing that they had somewhere lost the ability they had when very young to really *let themselves go* emotionally. When these students relaxed and really played in the full band, expressing freely, it was truly a life-altering moment for them.

Many writers have discussed the changes that happen in children during latter years in elementary school into middle school as they reach adolescence. Prior to the beginning of this maturation process, they often play and sing freely without fear of quality or audience. As they become more aware of themselves and the society around them, however, the tendency for many is to become overly concerned about what others think about their singing and other public behaviors. How children are encouraged and supported during this important stage of their lives influences their later ability to express their emotions freely in performing and ultimately can lead to participation decisions. Central to fostering expressive development during these years are opportunities for children to experiment without the fear of undue evaluation and freedom to make mistakes along the way.

During my teaching, beginning band was a sixth-grade class, and I found this age group to be much less inhibited than the seventh and eighth graders in our middle school. The impact of puberty and the focus on self-esteem that it brings changes many students and their confidence in expressing their emotions in front of their peers. Although they can be extremely loud and aggressive outside of the moment they need to play their instrument or sing, I found that it took more encouragement to get them truly to express their feelings through music. Thankfully, this seems to subside slightly in high school, but it is important that teachers adapt to these changes so as not to lose those valuable years in fostering their ability to be expressive players.

To help in this development, students should be encouraged to play in front of each other often from the very beginning of their musical study. This takes careful classroom control and planning, but it is vital to their developing the confidence to honestly share their playing, whatever the level, with others. How these moments of individual performance are presented and evaluated is crucial to building the confidence and comfort to perform. Remarks from the teacher and especially their classmates need to be supportive and given in a caring environment. Students who are really struggling need to be helped outside the class time to better prepare them technically and emotionally to be successful when they play for others. Assignments also need to allow students to be successful often in their early years. It is not just about helping them play the notes, rhythms, and articulations correctly but also developing a connection to musical expression on their instruments in front of others.

I think that studying connections between personality type and musical expression in performance would be an enriching endeavor. As a trumpet player, I am constantly labeled as aggressive, confident, and wanting to lead. Guess what? That is who I am! I also am aware of how many trumpet players become band directors or principals and also assume many other leadership positions. Perhaps it is partly due to the demands of playing this loud, easily noticed instrument. It is hard to know if the trumpet influenced my personality or if I chose to play the trumpet because of it. Certainly there are some undeniable truths buried in all those jokes and characterizations.

Overacting

If you ever have ventured backstage following a theatrical production, you might have been struck by the appearance of the stage characters at closer proximity. Onstage, they looked very natural while speaking their lines or singing their arias. Backstage they look almost comical. Their makeup is way overpowering with bigger, more colorful features and boundaries. Because the makeup and costuming is intended to create an impact from 50 feet away or more, the exaggeration is necessary to achieve the intimacy you would normally experience in close contact.

If you have the opportunity to be close to musical performers while they are delivering their lines or singing their melodies, you also would be struck by the exaggeration in their volumes, colors, and accentuation. Again, it must be remembered that they are tailoring these sounds for the audience farther away to recreate the sensation of being close to them. Unlike movie actors, theater and opera performers do not use microphones or camera close-ups, so they are more dependent on such exaggeration for success.

Great brass players also must *overact* depending on the distance between their placement and their audience. The bigger the room, the greater the awareness must be for such preparation. Sitting in a professional orchestra for the first time is a true learning experience in this regard. My reaction was disbelief at how loud and big they played but also how softly they played in contrast. Likewise, as a soloist onstage, you must constantly revisit your interpretation to make sure you are not underplaying for your audience.

Because students spend most of their practice time in very small practice rooms, the awareness of this facet of performance often can be overlooked. I often diagnose students with *practice room syndrome* as they come to a lesson and play everything in a very small dynamic range that usually is between mezzo piano and mezzo forte. Even the smallest changes in dynamics are abundantly evident in the practice room because there is always a wall, a floor, and a ceiling within five feet. Even in my studio, this distance is much shorter and the space much smaller than in any performance venue. Usually when I demonstrate expressive passages for them, especially in the louder dynamics, they are stunned and bewildered. In the smaller room, it sounds like too much change for their ears. Like those actors backstage, however, they must consider the eventual performance and the experience of their audience.

The best remedy for practice room syndrome is to play in bigger spaces whenever possible. It is important for soloists and also for ensembles. It is critical to understand that overacting is a normal part of performance and not some unusual behavior. When you feel that your performance is very solid technically but is not getting the proper response from listeners, this is the first place to look for more improvement. It is rare that I have watched a performance and had the feeling that it was *too musical* or way *too overacted*. Most often, we are left wanting more in this department.

If you play with a microphone, this changes the overacting formula somewhat. As the microphone is actually like another instrument, you must learn how it impacts the sound for the audience. The playback system, size of the speakers, volume levels, and acoustical considerations of the microphone all become active components of the sound. Many jazz artists even bring their own microphones with them on tour to ensure the sound quality and reaction to volume they desire. In general, microphones allow the player to play more intimately as if in a smaller space. If the sound system is well matched to the acoustical space, the result can be very pleasing for performer and audience. Unfortunately this is often not the case, so be sure to practice in a large space with the microphone to learn how to use this instrument, along with your own, to make the most expressive product.

Connecting the use of dynamics, time, articulation, and vibrato to musical expression should begin early in the development of brass players to ensure a more natural connection in expressing melodies. In fostering the desire to be an expressive player, teachers have an easier time motivating technical development because students will understand the need for technique to express emotions. With musical goals instead of purely technical goals, students will be more invested in their playing and more interested in its advancement.

Exercises

- Once a basic technical study or etude is learned, challenge students to attach an image or emotional state while playing it. Encourage them to try to make listeners *feel sad* or see imaginary *crickets jumping* when they play, and review how they change their articulation style and other elements of playing in doing so.

- Practice *overacting* elements in your music by playing really loud *fortes* and also playing really soft *pianos*. Take a simple melody, and push the time much faster to the peak while moving from *pp* to *ff*. Then slow way down and diminuendo to your softest playing afterward. When you believe you are overdoing these elements, ask another student to listen to your phrase, and see if he or she agrees. Also add vibrato that gets faster and wider toward the peak and diminishes in width and speed as you move away from it. Really overdo it!

16

IMPROVISATION TO EXERCISE
CREATIVITY AND EMOTION

"Improvisation is too good to leave to chance."

Paul Simon
Singer, Songwriter

The world of the classical musician continues to migrate to an environment where all recordings are flawless and the concept of making errors as part of performance, or even development of playing, is hidden from the public. All *live* performances on television also are following the path set by overproduced popular music as even some classical musicians have begun to fake their playing along with a safe, prerecorded track. The extreme pressure to present the perfect performance is everywhere in music and is increasing because of our edited recordings and reluctance to discuss the mistakes as a normal part of playing. In response to this pressure, many professional players and even students turn to drugs to calm their nerves and fears that they will make mistakes that might hurt their ability to earn money or position in the highly competitive world of music making. As in many of life's endeavors, it seems that music has retreated to a tightly controlled and risk-free activity with a high premium on lack of mistakes.

It is no wonder that encouraging students to engage in activities that will yield many errors in the learning process is difficult. This aversion to mistakes that permeates our field unfortunately dampens creativity and reduces free expression in the music learning process. Improvisation on an instrument, by its very nature, demands rapid creative thinking and decisive action that sometimes yields great results and sometimes does not. It requires ample time for the performer to become comfortable with a process that naturally involves trial and error. While I was directing a collegiate jazz ensemble, many of the players were stubbornly against trying an improvised solo. It was clear they had not had any experience, or at least enough experience, to get past the initial fear of mistakes to be able to embrace the benefits of creating music on the spot. In professional, classical orchestras, it is somewhat entertaining to witness the fear that permeates the group when a pops concert requires a member of the brass section to solo with only chord changes provided. This invasion in an environment that has become a *land of controlled and perfect preparation* with ample time to scrutinize every note is now an unwelcome intrusion to most, so the chance to truly improvise is avoided instead of embraced for its offer of freedom and individuality.

I believe that all musicians should engage in improvisation as a normal avenue of discovery for their creative process. I am not referring to jazz improvisation specifically but to a more broad exercise of creating melodies either by using defined guidelines or even with no guidelines whatsoever. This process allows for a direct line of connection between the sounds we hear in our imaginations and the realization of those sounds with an instrument. Especially for classical musicians who scrutinize every aspect of technique during most of their preparation, this exercise of creativity and emotional expression is vital to the preservation of these elements in our playing. As with many self-discovery exercises, I think the process of improvisation should begin in the safety of the applied lesson with only the teacher and the student in attendance. The teacher should model the process and interact with the student in regular attempts to improvise melodies, accompaniments, and variations.

In beginning stages of improvisation, it is valuable to give a very limited range of options to the student so as not to overwhelm him or her with too many choices. In jazz improvisation, we often only use a few notes, like the minor pentatonic scale or even just the first three notes of the blues scale. When improvising in the classical style, perhaps only a major scale or its first three tones can be an initial start to improvising. By keeping choices within easy hearing and control, students will be more courageous in developing this new skill. I often engage students in improvised duets with selected keys or target notes. They are more likely to gain confidence when the improvisation is a shared experience and they can react to what the teacher is playing.

Call and response between the teacher and student in this improvisation process can be a superior method just as it is in traditional jazz improvisation. The quick response to ideas presented by the teacher really helps students develop their technical abilities to reproduce something they are hearing and also using their imaginations as they alter the music with their own changes. The private lesson offers a safe starting point for this type of creative exercise, so be sure to include time in each meeting to depart from the *correction of errors* method that can overwhelm your time together.

In my university studio class, I often explore improvisation with a variety of assignments suitable for group settings. One of these is a simple 12-bar blues over which I require all students to improvise. With their easy knowledge of music theory, it is really only a matter of courage for them to play newly composed melodies in front of others. With basic prompting using *guide tones* and other constructs, I give them structures that will offer them a safe haven with limited choice as they gain more confidence. As classically trained musicians, the predominance of rules and expectations are so defined that it often takes many repetitions for students to adopt a mind-set that will allow them to improvise freely. This mind-set is vital, in my view, for musicians to move into a more free and expressive manner of playing both in improvisation but also in their approach to written music as well.

In another exercise, players take a preexisting melody that is performed and then improvise upon it utilizing musical features of the original. They can use elements in the original melody to stimulate variations and extensions of its components. This is also a convenient vehicle for some interesting emotional response work. After the original rendition of the melody and a brief discussion of its emotional impact, the player might be asked to change the melody to achieve a different emotional response in listeners. In addition to possible rhythmic and articulation changes, they are also free to experiment with any of musical features, including changes in dynamics, tempo, or even harmonic language. Any element can be altered to achieve their desired expressive outcome.

From an early age, we as listeners are culturally imbued with conditioned emotional responses to musical sounds of all kinds. The sounds of instruments themselves tend to portray characters in our imaginations because we have heard those connections reinforced thousands of times in movie and stage music. The trumpet as the hero, the trombone villain, the pastoral nature of the horn, and the comical possibilities of the tuba are well established in our emotional reflexologies. Basic musical structures and even the intervals themselves also contribute to these cultural connections. The perfect fifth, the *heroic* interval, when also played on the trumpet is hard to misinterpret. The interval of the sixth, however, usually means *love*! For some quick evidence, do a quick examination of the movie music of John Williams, our most celebrated soundtrack composer, and you will see how these musical triggers work very well indeed.

In the lesson or with groups of students, you also can try exercises that are much less organized and a more free expression of emotions. One favorite is to provide a student with an emotional response term such as the single word *lonely* on a card they draw from a hat. Only the selected student knows the word, while the rest of the class is unaware of the assigned emotional response term. Following a brief amount of time to prepare, I ask the class to close their eyes, or I turn off the lights, to avoid students interacting with each other. The performer improvises anything he or she wishes with no restrictions whatsoever. Their only assignment is to try and express the emotion of the chosen word to listeners.

In the past 30 years of doing this exercise, I have witnessed two interesting outcomes. First, student performers, while improvising without rules or cumbersome evaluation, often play with better sounds and display better technical skill than in their prepared etudes and solos. Sometimes their playing really surprises the other students and the teacher as well. The other outcome is the amazing amount of times that student listeners, when asked to tell the class what emotional term came to their minds during the improvised performance of their colleague, offered the same or very similar term as that on the drawn card.

One of the great benefits of improvisation is how it hard wires our mental images of sound to what we do with the instrument. Imagining something to play and then making the instrument realize it is exactly what we need to be doing in all of our playing. Creating new music on the spot while improvising reinforces this concept as we strive to increase technical ability to make our desired sounds a reality. Like sight-reading and playing from memory, improvisation should be a regular part of our musical experience because each of these processes amplifies the need to connect our physical manipulation of the instrument directly to the sounds and accompanying emotions we wish to create. I often refer to reading music as an obstacle because the additional distraction of looking at these symbols takes a large portion of attention away from how the music we are making actually sounds.

Likewise, improvisation offers great benefit in connecting our emotions to instrumental performance. By starting with emotional terminology or telling a story with our invented music, we shift the focus away from reproducing something that exists on paper accurately to expressing our thoughts and feelings directly. When we play well-known printed music, the level of expectation is dominated by the desire to reproduce an earlier performance, and this easily can overpower emotional expression. It is important to remember the value of creativity in playing, and this often should pivot attention away from technical evaluations toward freer expression using improvisation.

As students progress into more demanding classical music training, smaller and smaller details are scrutinized for exactness to prepare them for the competitive environment that awaits. With so many restrictions on much of their playing, it is vital for them to find outlets to exercise creativity in a free and less judgmental format. By finding time to allow for unfettered improvisation and use of playing abilities, we can reconnect with that powerful sensation of expression that drew us to music in the first place. The feeling of freedom, along with the carefree manner of approaching music experienced in these moments, can also positively influence our approach to written music and our attitudes toward it.

Focus on Emotions During Performance

For me, there is still something *magical* in the concept of expressing emotion with an instrumental performance. I often ask my students how they possibly can stimulate an emotional response in a listening audience if they are not actually feeling any emotion while they play. In reality, I think that humans still have many powers of perception that are not fully understood. One of these involves listening to music as a form of communication from one person to another. Just as we sense emotion in the sound of the human voice under a great range of circumstances, we also can sense emotion in the sound of an instrument. Although actors can practice the technique of emotional expression with their voices, there is a stronger connection when they truly are feeling the emotional meaning of the words rather than attempting to engage a series of vocal techniques absent these feelings. With the delivery of words that truly express honest emotion, there is a connection between the actor and the audience that is so special that it is hard to understand or describe. This is precisely why great actors spend so much time and effort to discover their *characters* and allow themselves to think and feel as that persona.

When musicians truly feel an emotion or become a character as they play an instrument, a similar special connection can be made between the player and the audience. Although most of our music is abstract and without programmatic connection, the emotion felt by the player, translated directly to the audience using instrumental sounds in the same ways actors use words, can be very powerful. This magical connection will stimulate listeners to imagine their own manifestations of the emotion from memories or invented scenes. Truly feeling an emotion while performing also leads to body motion and facial expressions that reinforce the way the music is conveyed to audiences.

I believe that more teaching must be dedicated to this emotion-centered process of music making because it is so central to our ability to play expressively. There must be a balance of high levels of technical execution, the engagement of the imagination, and the personal expression of feelings. This requires a special type of courage; it is important that students have the opportunity to perform their works as often as possible, so they can practice engaging their emotions while playing. Encourage them to share their emotional goals for the piece with listeners, and reinforce their commitment to this frame of mind during the performance. I often refer to it as *the trance of performing*. It takes a few moments to prepare mentally for this intense use of the mind, so ask students to take that time backstage and especially onstage prior to playing to adopt it. If they tune onstage, for example, they should take time after tuning to gain the proper mind-set. It is important to set the mood for the performer and also for the audience to have time to clear their thoughts as well. Like many musicians, I prefer to settle tuning backstage so that I can begin the performance mind-set fully as I walk onstage.

One easy way to help stimulate an emotional response or a story line through your music is to add some markings on the page that help trigger your feelings. In 1997 when Princess Diana was tragically killed in a car accident, I was preparing a recital that included a beautiful and elegant slow movement from a sonata. My emotional ideas for these melodies were still forming, and I found that thinking about Diana put me in the perfect emotional state while playing them. The music was reminiscent, a bit sad and reflective, but also pure and delicate. I found that thinking about this one person triggered all the subtle emotions I wanted the music to express. Above my first entrance in the music is still written "Diana," and it will likely be there for some time to come.

A few years ago, one of my university students who had struggled with establishing and holding an emotional mind-set onstage brought a trumpet solo, Enesco's *Legend*, to our group class for a performance. The assignment that day was to describe the emotional feelings the students wished to convey to the audience prior to playing the work. The student shared with the class a personal story of a good friend who had died recently in a tragic car accident. His normal tone of voice changed immediately as he began to relate the story, and his emotionally charged words brought the room to immediate and utter silence. As he began the slow, soft introduction of the C minor melody on his trumpet, it was incredibly intense. This performance on this day was something new for this student as he was able to focus on his emotions despite the many technical challenges this work demands. His performance was truly inspiring, and he and his colleagues all recognized it. As we look back on this performance, we all see it as a turning point in his ability to play more expressively onstage. With subsequent performances of this work in our university honors recital and for guest artists, he was even more successful in playing expressively by establishing and maintaining this emotional mind-set, even though these subsequent performances were in more high-pressure situations.

Philip Smith, the principal trumpet of the New York Philharmonic, is one of the very best brass players at achieving this high level of emotional communication with his playing. I have seen him perform live often, including a one-week recital tour in Missouri that I organized for him and Joseph Turrin in 1997. Phil speaks often in his master classes about focusing on emotions and extra musical images, and his playing both as a soloist and in the New York Philharmonic demonstrates the incredible results one can achieve with this approach. During such performances, the listener's attention is taken away from any technical evaluation and invited into the imaginary world of emotion. In this environment of *the trance*, technical mistakes are not as disruptive because both performer and audience are immersed in another mind-set. In listening to recordings of the recitals presented by Phil Smith and Joseph Turrin during this tour, I was very surprised when, during a very technical listening, I heard some obvious errors. In all honesty, I did recall hearing errors in the performance and had no recollection of them. This is not unusual when musical expression is at the forefront of our intent. Earlier in 1997, Mr. Smith gave a solo recital at the International Trumpet Guild (ITG) Conference in Gothenburg, Sweden, on the last day of the event. Prior to his concert, we had heard many solo performances by many fine trumpet players. After each of the earlier recitals, my colleagues immediately conversed about some of the errors and unsuccessful moments in the playing. After Mr. Smith played, however, the conversation was all about the emotions we felt during the concert. There was no mention of technical matters.

The success of such performances has much less to do with technical abilities of the player and much more to do with musical focus. At the aforementioned ITG

Conference, the other recitals demonstrated great amounts of technical skill and all those attributes that we respect in a purely technical evaluation. Unfortunately they were lacking in the expression of emotion compared to the presentation of Mr. Smith. The ability to enter the trance of emotional feeling is truly the difference and requires amazing trust in your preparation and validity of your presentation.

Exercises

- Select an easy key, and after playing through the scale and arpeggio, engage your student in playing an improvised duet. You begin and ask them to enter after you play for four measures. Give them the idea of a V-I starting pair of notes, and then encourage them to create their own melodies. Because you are playing along, you can choose to inspire them with your melodic creation or reinforce and imitate theirs to help them in the process. Repeat this idea often and in different keys.

- After students can play a simple eight-measure theme, encourage them to create their own variations by changing melodic notes, rhythms, and articulations. Once they have some experience creating variations, ask them to vary in a way that directly expresses an emotional response term like *angry* or *joyful*.

- Provide your student with a one-word emotional term like *sadness* or *sneaky*, and ask them to express the term by playing anything they wish on their instrument. You can do the same with some imaginary movie scenes like *first kiss between lovers* or *escaping the evil wizard* for two examples. Start a discussion about what things they played that were most successful and why. You can also talk about the techniques they used in their emotionally directed improvisations.

17

UNDERSTANDING PERFORMANCE ANXIETY

"I think it's healthy for a person to be nervous. It means you care—that you work hard and want to give a great performance. You just have to channel that nervous energy in the show."

Beyoncé Knowles

Through my years of playing and teaching, I have encountered many nervous moments, both my own and those I've observed in the actions of others. As with other high emotional states, the way we react to anxiety is as individualized as fear itself. I have seen people pass out, throw up, pace uncontrollably, get angry with those around them, flee the scene, cry, get drunk, assume various yoga positions, chant Buddhist proverbs, shake uncontrollably, run to the bathroom . . . well, you get the picture. By the way, many of these observed behaviors were of professional musicians!

It is important to realize that those feelings of nervousness that accompany a performance situation are normal human reactions. It is simply because the act of playing is important to you that you have these sensations. The more important the performance to you, the more intense nerves can feel and, if you do not work to channel this energy for positive results, the more debilitating they can be to your performance. The excitement or fear of performing impacts players in different ways and changes over the course of the preparation period and the actual onstage event. The more you know about yourself, the better equipped you will be to prepare for an exciting and rewarding performance experience that you will want to repeat again and again.

The physiological cause of our anxiety can be traced to the release of adrenaline into the bloodstream. This results in many bodily reactions related to fight or flight responses. It is possible to work on the front end of this adrenaline impact by reducing the fear that might be associated with performing that stimulates its release. The first strategy is to be overly prepared in technical and musical terms prior to the onstage event. As mentioned in Chapter 12, create a long-range plan that includes stages for individual practice, working with your pianist and other collaborators, and then testing your preparation in front of others. Well-planned practice sessions combined with playing for friends and teachers can go a long way in reducing the sensation of fear for the performance and thus impact the bodily release of adrenaline.

Concentrating on expression of the music and the audience's enjoyment of it also can go a long way in allowing you to shift your performance focus away from solely an evaluation of you as a player, a thought process that often disrupts a positive performance. Keeping the music and its expression foremost in your thoughts will help reduce the anxiety felt, especially in an evaluative environment. Having a musical plan for each piece will allow you to direct and maintain this focus and block the entrance of judgmental commentary into your subconscious mind-set. Because we all have the critical voice inside us, we must engage in thoughts that will not allow this part of our thinking the opportunity to comment while we are onstage.

Despite all our thoughtful preparation, it is still likely that the adrenaline will show up in our blood, especially if it is the first performance or an important moment in our career. In the world of music, this is often the case as many performances are offered only one time and usually for high stakes. In music degree recitals, solo ensemble events, concertos with bands and orchestras, and auditions, we often have only that one chance to play at our peak, and this situation, of course, is totally unrealistic. Could you imagine if the only race the runner competed in was during the Olympic finals? How about a political candidate only giving one speech during a campaign, and it is at the televised convention? Of course, this is not what they actually do. Runners run many races in preparation for the Olympics, and politicians try out speeches dozens of times before they ever reach the convention. In the same way, musicians must manufacture many repetitions of their performances in front of audiences, so they can examine how nerves will impact them and what they can do to counter these tendencies. It is unlikely that you will take your senior recital on a 20-performance tour, but you should arrange for as many run-throughs in front of learned listeners as you can. Wynton Marsalis told me once that he was not comfortable performing a solo work until he had done so 15 times in public. Only then did he feel like he was ready for a great performance onstage. Imagine if we all could have so many chances to improve our presentation onstage in front of an audience.

Live performance is a *skill* that takes great preparation but is also something that continues to evolve. We can improve as performers if we can remember that it is a *skill* and not merely a *talent*. In our early attempts to perform music formally, we can play through it in the practice room, changing our focus by imagining being onstage. Even with many successful repetitions of practice room run-throughs, however, there always will be surprises in our playing and mind-set changes once we are in front of others. This is a totally logical response and should be expected in all players. If you are truly ready to play your music without difficulty in the practice room, bringing it to the audience is the next step in its evolution. As you evaluate these initial public performances, you can respond to challenges that arise by first returning to a more scientific mind-set to log what happened and where you were not successful. You can address these moments in two ways. First, establish in technical terms what you did incorrectly, played too fast, tongued too heavily, and so on. Practice these sections in isolation, but this time place an emphasis on playing the *opposite* of these incorrect techniques. If you rushed the tempo, drag it ridiculously. If you tongued too heavily, tongue it is as lightly as possible. Adopt this *overacting the opposite* mind-set for these parts of the work, and insert them into your overall performance plan for the piece. The second way to confront mistakes is to work harder to focus on your *musical plan* while performing. Be sure that you can mentally stay with your sequence of thoughts and feelings, even under pressure. It sounds easier than it is, but with mental practicing and repeat performances, you can increase this focused mind-set and reduce unnecessary errors that come when it is lost.

Sometimes when discussing performance anxiety, I ask my university students to imagine that they will be required to walk naked through the halls of the school as part of their graduation requirement. This always brings an interesting response from students, but I mention it with purposeful intent. Would they walk hunched over, trying to hide their private parts from the gaze of others? Or could they decide that their bodies are whatever they are and strut proudly without concern down the halls, sharing the fullness of their bodies with all who cared to look? Once I have allowed them to visualize this concept and the feelings of embarrassment and fear that usually accompany it, I then relate it to playing a brass solo onstage. The audience always will be able to *see and hear everything*. You can try to hide your playing from them by using the music stand, your placement onstage, or your body position, but these will not actually interfere with their ability to *see and hear everything*. You really have the same two choices as the naked student in the hallway; you can either try to hide who you are or share it openly and without worrying about their judgment.

Our playing, at whatever level it is, is not about comparison to others but only about where we are in our development. It is vital that players learn to present who they are without allowing such comparison to debilitate them. Our physical bodies are the result of genetics and lifestyle. How they appear, fit and lean, obese and puffy, and everything in between, is *who we are*. Our ability on a brass instrument is also a unique combination of our inherited talent, hard work, and level of experience. We are all different as players, and we are *who we are*! The ability to understand onstage performance as an individual glimpse at us alone is vital to our path toward acceptance and confidence in what we are doing.

When asking students to reveal their playing honestly each day in their practice, I also relate it to looking in the mirror without clothes (I'm not a nudist . . . really). An honest evaluation of our playing means that we do not avoid listening to bad sounds or skip those techniques that cause them. Just as carefully chosen clothes can disguise the true nature of our body, so too can our choice of what to play and how to play it *dress up* our true playing to our ears. Of course, when considering what to present to an audience, we can and should present music and playing that best suits our ability levels. When we are working to improve our skills in the practice room, however, we must have the courage to consistently measure our abilities in an honest and focused manner.

Teachers Need to Put Student Needs Before Their Self-Image

As a teacher, the realization that people react differently to nervousness is vital in helping prepare students to be performers. Your own personal experience as a performer can help you, but you need to be prepared to look outside your personal experiences for alternate strategies for others. Let's be honest for a moment; performance anxiety causes many musicians to stop performing, turn to medications, or exhibit strange behavior around concert time. At all ages and levels of experience, the thrill of playing offers many opportunities for us to join in such music making or back away from it.

In the media-drenched world music students now live in, they are surrounded by music but have little experience with true live performance. All prerecorded music is scrubbed clean of mistakes, run through pitch correction software, and delivered as a perfect rendition. Even performances that we think are live, especially on television, are actually prerecorded, cleaned of error, and *lip-synched* onstage. Do not think for a moment that it is only pop stars who do this. Modern classical and jazz musicians also feel the need to *protect their image* by not risking the truth of a live, unaltered performance. As a result of constant exposure to these *caricatures* of live playing, students develop a sense that players can reach a level when all mistakes are totally eliminated. This misperception is incredibly harmful to their self-esteem because they continue to make mistakes as they play and learn their music. In essence, many professional musicians actually are hurting the next generation of players in an attempt to maximize and often cash in on the promotion of these unrealistic, contrived images.

Not only does such behavior paint an inaccurate picture of being a musician, but when performers have the courage to actually play live, the mistakes they make sometimes become the focus of ridicule and derision (think YouTube). The pressure all seems to be focused on avoidance of true live performance, despite the tremendous excitement it brings to human existence.

Let's take the example of the *live* orchestral performances we can hear on National Public Radio by the leading ensembles from America and Europe. Did you know that they are actually edited? Most big orchestras have a committee of musicians who listen to multiple weekly concerts and then determine edits among performances when there are errors that might detract from the *larger-than-life* image of the orchestra. When the doctored product is presented on the radio, however, they do not mention this part of the process. Listeners are left to assume that they are truly hearing a live, unedited performance. Just as Photoshop is ruining our images of face and body, such behavior in music has a devastating effect on young, hopeful players.

I also have worked with music teachers who do not play publicly, do not play in lessons, and seem to have forgotten altogether the challenges that playing poses. When their students make mistakes, especially in performance, these teachers often respond with surprise and displeasure. In coaching students, they choose not to share past mistakes and also prefer not to risk making new ones in front of them. Like doctored recordings and fake live performances, these teachers and professionals are trying to advance and protect their *image* and *marketability* at the expense of the very people they should be trying to help.

As a student, I also have had the great pleasure of working with teachers who perform frequently and model daily in all lessons. These teachers fully understand that helping students comprehend the challenges of playing means sharing in personal successes and failures. I still remember a lesson with Barbara Butler at Eastman during which I totally failed in a technical passage of an etude. Her response was this: "Oh that used to happen to me all the time in places like that. Here is what I did to keep it from happening." She then promptly picked up her trumpet and offered a model of what to do. She played both the passage from the etude and then also created an improvised pattern based on the challenging passage that she repeated in different keys and ranges. She did not play all of these patterns perfectly, but the quality of her sound and control of the technique was amply evident. This experience, compared to earlier lessons in my life when my mistakes were only met with the response, "Why can't you play that?" with no demonstration or sharing of common weaknesses, was amazingly supportive. I will never forget the difference in the way I felt as a hopeful musician in these two very different styles of lessons.

Applied study still retains the *master and pupil* model that is centuries old. Apprentice musicians spend much time and money seeking out great masters with whom they hope to learn the craft of becoming a musical performer. It is important that such masters share honestly the entirety of the craft, including failure and the perseverance needed to overcome it.

A high school band director in my state recently shared with me a visit by a university faculty ensemble that played a short concert and offered a clinic to his band. He was troubled because one of the players, a senior professor of music, responded to a question from a student about practicing by saying that she *never practices*. The band director was, of course, upset by this response, as he feared it sent the wrong message to his students. Actually, I know that this faculty member in reality practices all the time, and the ensemble, a regular part of her teaching load, also rehearses several times a week. Why would she respond in such a manner? The unfortunate truth involves the same self-image and value game mentioned earlier. It is hard to believe that someone whose profession is helping others to understand the path to musical performance would put his or her image above the welfare of such young students.

143

Unfortunately, I see this same behavior throughout our profession in conferences, rehearsals, and performances. The competitive nature of music brings out these untrue messages that teachers and students must recognize and overcome.

What is interesting to me is that the highest-level performers with whom I have worked are overwhelmingly honest about the humanness of performance. They choose to share honestly the challenges of performance and the times that things did not go as planned. These players, and teachers like them, are the best asset a young player can have. It is important that all teachers share their challenges in an honest and straightforward manner with their students. In doing so, they also can share how they overcame them and became successful performers onstage.

True Live Performances Are Essential

When my students do their first big degree recital, I always shake their hands afterward and say, "Welcome to the club." I do this because only at that moment do students fully understand the experience of playing many solo works onstage in a row. This challenge is the biggest that exists in brass performance and also the most exposed a player will feel. In fact many of our lauded players who reside in orchestras or brass ensembles rarely expose themselves to this type of performance due to the great challenges it poses. It is also important because once musicians go through the process of preparing and presenting a solo recital, their understanding of others going through the process is deeper, more realistic, and more compassionate. I also believe that players who have been too long without this experience begin to lose this understanding and compassion for those who are doing it.

Live performance brings great excitement to performers and audiences alike. There is an element of risk and reward that, like sporting events, engages the humanity in all of us. If we knew, before the concert starts, that there could be no mistakes, the experience would be much less interesting and thus less human. This is why so many big television music productions bore us. We already know the performances will be without error as they are faked. It's only the dancing or movement onstage that is in question. I would rather watch figure skating any day. At least it is totally live and real!

Exercises

- Ask a friend to come into your practice room to listen to your solo performance. Tell them they have no other purpose than to make you nervous. Record the performance, and compare it to a rendition when you were all alone in the same room. Note where you had problems, and realize that these reveal tendencies when you are playing for audiences.
- Mark your music with emotional stimulators and other terms that will assist you in focusing on your musical plan. Practice playing through your solo while

following this planned sequence of thoughts until you feel comfortable with the process. Bring the solo to others who will serve as your audience. Play a run-through while focusing on the prescribed sequence of thoughts. After you finish, note where you had trouble keeping focus on your musical plan, and work harder during the next performance to concentrate during these moments.

18

MODELS FOR CREATIVE PLAYING

"If a composer could say what he had to say in words he
would not bother trying to say it in music."

Gustav Mahler
Composer, Conductor

The Importance of the Human Voice

Comparisons between tone on a brass instrument and the sound of the human voice
are vital when striving to be an expressive player. If we take a moment to consider the
endless sounds made by our voices and the manner in which these sounds can express
feelings, we can see the great possibilities for our tone production on our instruments to do the same. Our sound on an instrument, like our voice, exhibits qualities
uniquely our own. It is possible for even the smallest nuances and changes in our
sound to connect with our emotional state in the same manner that our voice does
with mood changes. They key to playing an instrument expressively is the development of immediate and natural technical connections between our feelings and the
manipulation of the instrument and, more importantly, the ability to allow a central
thought or feeling to trigger these appropriate physical responses in our playing.

Imagine for a moment an actor given several lines to read for a theatrical production. For the most part, the words themselves are easy to read and speak aloud. The
specialness, though, comes when the actor actually becomes a *character* with a focused
emotional state of mind prior to the reading. Reading the lines from this perspective
unifies the tone of the reading and also invites nuanced inflection in the application
of the words. Over the course of years and years of development, our voices become
direct extensions of our feelings. The technique of speaking and mastering the sound
subtleties of language develop through thousands of moments of trial and error.
Although we had the ability to create emotional sounds even before the development
of language through crying, laughing, and other vocalizations, the sophistication of
communication that language adds takes many years to master. At the heart of this
communication is the immediacy of vocal technique response to emotional triggers.
Actors learn to control all the numerous inflections of the voice through a central

emotional state or sense of character. The pace of speaking, the volume, exact diction, and use of accentuation all flow from the brain as it directs the body to create those physical responses needed to produce just the right sound. The effectiveness of this communication is honed in our development as we assess the impact of emotion in our voice on listeners and adjust our vocal sound for the best results.

Instrumental musicians, of course, have a greater learning curve in making direct and immediate connections between emotional state and expression in playing when compared to speakers or singers. The techniques used to create sounds on an instrument take many years to master, and it is the subtleness in playing that develops last, at the highest level of our mastery. To equal the work of actors, we must develop similar, immediate connections between many instrumental techniques and mental triggers. In doing so, the instrument and its myriad of sounds can become more directly responsive to our emotional thoughts. Like the manner in which our voices can communicate excitement merely by thinking an exciting thought, so also can our instruments communicate this emotion through the immediate connection of volume, inflection, articulation style, vibrato, and other physical movements to our emotional states.

In the 1980s we saw the introduction of synthesizers capable of mimicking the sounds of brass instruments. The Yamaha DX7 was groundbreaking in its ability to sound like a horn, for example, and we began to hear it often in pop music and also as a replacement for our instruments in musicals and other venues. There were many in the music profession at this time who warned that such devices would mean the end of the rich variety of instruments and players of them. The future would now be keyboard players who could play all the parts and create the sounds of all the instruments. Although synthesizers have replaced instruments in some venues, it soon became clear that it was very difficult for a synthesizer to replicate the incredible number of variables in sound production that are needed to create an expressive melody. The slight changes in vibrato, airspeed, volume, lip tension, and articulation are impossible to replicate with the touch of a finger on a single key. Synthesizers could not capture the humanness of an instrumentalist, and just as we did not hear many synthesized singers, we really cannot hear a synthesized solo instrument that approaches the human expression we can create as brass players.

Often I speak to my students about the expressive value of *imperfection* in the sound. In a purely scientific sense, it is our ability to uniquely mix imperfect sounds into our melodic presentation that makes for an expressive performance. Machines have a long way to go before they can match the amazing control of sound choices heard from an accomplished musician. If you play pitches on a tuner or other basic machine, for example, you get a very stable sound wave that comes close to perfect output in terms of wavelength and frequency. Although we work hard as instrumentalists to achieve steady sound output, to duplicate the *perfectness* of the tuner in delivery of a melody would surely be met with great distaste. It is the presence of imperfection or variation in the sound, especially vibrato, that provides the human quality and makes the melody truly expressive. The myriad of *imperfections* that can be created in the sound both attracts listeners and individualizes players at the same time.

Because our own voices have developed over many years and are directly tied to our brains and their expression of emotions, they should be vital and constant tools for use in improving our playing of brass instruments. From beginning-level players to accomplished professionals, singing should be central to practicing and teaching brass sound concepts. Although many students are shy about singing, especially in front of their teacher, the teacher must constantly model singing for them and also find ways to give them the security and courage to sing as well. Even if your vocal quality is not great, the very act of expressing with your voice and expressing then with an instrument has a positive impact, with the instrumental version always lagging behind the vocal one in reaction time and naturalness.

In the creation of a warm and sonorous brass tone, we know that the throat should be open, the oral cavity larger, and the muscles in the upper body relaxed. Singers, of course, strive for the same physiological setup because both the sound of vocal tone and the sound of brass tone are enriched by it. I find it helpful to work for a full and rich vocal tone with students to influence their instrumental sound concept and physical setup. In the process of developing this tone, it also can be worthwhile to experiment with less sonorous sounds by closing the throat and tensing musculature and other impediments as a means of demonstrating the difference in sound quality. Depending on the gender and age of the student, you should seek out the singing register where he or she can create the best vocal tone and develop his or her voice in that range first. Just as you strive to first create a relaxed sound in one range on your instrument that you can use as a model when expanding range, you can do the same to develop your singing.

Depending on the student and his or her chosen instrument and the closer he or she eventually can come to the range of the instrument in singing, the more direct is the comparison to vocal and instrumental tone. Constantly encourage students to increase their vocal range and ability to more closely match that of their instruments. Of course, many times this will mean different octaves, but when possible, go for the same octave.

As a trumpet player and a male, much of the sounding range of the trumpet is above my normal singing range. As a result, I have worked diligently on my falsetto voice and found that it is a great teaching tool as I can now create an open and resonant falsetto to demonstrate higher passages required in trumpet playing. My female students usually are surprised when I first encourage them to start singing and find that I can emit a bigger, more open tone than their natural soprano voice. I must admit that it took some time for me to be brave enough to use my falsetto in teaching, but the moment I did, I became a better teacher for my students and for myself.

Creating Lyrics for Instrumental Melodies

Singers have a great advantage over instrumentalists in finding inspiration for expression in performance. The presence of text facilitates the storytelling process and enables them to focus their thoughts on emotions rather than just techniques. In the case of larger vocal productions like operas or musicals, they are further blessed with story lines that place their melodies in the context of what often is a powerful set of dramatic events. When they sing Puccini's "Nessun Dorma" from *Turandot* or "I Dreamed a Dream" from Schönberg's *Les Misérables*, the ability to sing expressively is enhanced greatly by the words themselves, the characters onstage, and the broader stories in which these words appear.

By crossing over into the realm of the singer, brass performers can benefit from similar emotional inspiration by creating an imaginary story line for your piece with defined characters and plots. If you take time to change the concept of the music in this way, you can help yourself make interpretive decisions and also deflect your concern about technical difficulties. On a smaller level, creating words for your instrumental melodies can allow you to *sing through your instrument* in a process that follows a more concrete musical expression plan. Developing story lines and lyrics for instrumental melodies is a great exercise in creativity, and it adds a new element of motivation, which is always welcome as you strive to illicit emotional responses by manipulating a piece of pipe!

A valuable tool for preparing instrumental melodies is to directly borrow the concepts of text expression from vocalists. To start the process, of course, we need to create the words that they already have provided for them. Going through a process of writing lyrics to instrumental melodies that express intended emotional states and whose very sound reinforces the melodic line can be extremely valuable for guiding technical work and preparing for onstage success. In teaching the value of creating words for instrumental melodies with my students, I have developed a process that starts with first having them perform vocal melodies on their instruments.

In our weekly solo class, they bring a vocal piece to perform and provide the class with the melody and original text. After they perform it for us, we have a discussion about how knowledge of the words influenced their interpretations of the melody, similar to the process that many singers use. We discuss word choice in terms of sound and their meaning to a larger story line. How do the words help determine high points and low points? Do they show a progression of emotions? We discuss the emotional responses words can illicit and how those emotions can be enhanced using instrumental techniques. We even think about the sounds of the words themselves. Hard consonants versus softer consonants and the subtle differences in vowels are explored with a focus on the pronunciation in different languages.

My teaching is heavily influenced by many years exploring vocal music in school. Most notable was a doctoral course at Eastman in German Lied. Can you imagine that course as part of a doctorate in trumpet performance? In examining the sophisticated connections between text and music in art songs, I realized that instrumental musicians could benefit greatly if they could apply similar concepts to wordless melodies. Although we often remark that our playing should *tell a story*, it is less likely that we take the next step in clarifying that story and applying it directly to how we play the instrument.

Once students have some experience in interpreting the relationships between text and music in vocal and brass performance using vocal literature, I then challenge them to create lyrics for instrumental works with special consideration to word sound and meaning. As you might imagine, the results from some students are disappointing and trivial, especially in the beginning. It is vital, however, that you establish a good environment in your lessons and classes so that students will feel comfortable stretching their efforts in this direction without fear of ridicule or negative feedback. What is wonderful is when the first student presents lyrics that really match the melody and greatly improve their playing of it on the instrument. The other students instantly recognize when this happens, and the result is a renewed effort to use this new avenue of musical expression to help their performances.

To start creating words for your instrumental melodies, you should first identify the emotional responses you wish to create with them. Limit these emotional response terms to true emotional responses such as anger, loneliness, or mischievousness. Once you have a sequence of emotional response thoughts that follow the music, then begin thinking about words that might express them. Examine the melody for high and low points and compositional features, such as downbeats and cadences, that can guide your choice in matching words to notes. Experiment with words that sound well together; tell a story using words whose very sounds elicits your desired emotional response. This process forces you to consider about how to divide and connect phrases just as in language punctuation, and this needs to relate to where the high and low points of the music occur. It is musical mapping at a very sophisticated level, so it takes time to develop. Making this strong connection between music and emotional response through words can start with beginners as they surely can connect basic feelings and words to their melodies. By starting this creative process early, they will be more comfortable with the concept of singing and expressing their feelings to others throughout their development. It is important for them to understand that there is great freedom in choosing your expression plan and the words that accompany it. The feeling of ownership this process imbues will empower them as performers, and they will feel this onstage when sharing it with audiences.

When you step onstage to play that solo, if you can *sing the lyrics* you created in your mind while you play, you will find a great inspiration to create expression and a mental focus that will occupy your thoughts so completely that the nervous voices in your mind are totally silenced. Again, this takes much preparation and practice. You have to create this mind-set in the practice room repeatedly so that it becomes your only approach to performance of the piece. Once you are successful with that part of the process, you need to invite colleagues into your practice room to test your ability to practice that mental focus in front of them. This begins the important process that will culminate in a successful telling of your story to audiences.

String Models

I have been fortunate to be onstage when great string players like violinist Joshua Bell share their beautiful playing. The great expression in his playing inspires me to bring as many of those sounds to brass instruments as I can. It is not surprising that string artists command such attention from listeners and other musicians alike. The literature and the capabilities of string instruments offer much for brass players to be inspired by and also much to copy.

String instrument performances provide excellent models for brass players for many reasons. The wealth of string melodies and presence of string instruments in the soundtrack of our daily lives are an important and consistent influence on our understanding of instrumental melody. Unencumbered by restrictions from breathing and endurance, string instruments present a free, rich sound in all registers. Perhaps the most valuable characteristic, however, is that tone production is all quite visible through the physical manipulation of the body and its relationship to the instrument. The ability to connect sound to physical motion is helpful to brass player in many ways.

The basic process of bowing on a string instrument by itself is rich for imitation. The decision of when to use up bow versus down bow requires string players to be more sophisticated from the very start in their conception of stressed and unstressed notes in a melody. Imagine if, for every phrase in a brass etude or solo, we were required to make similar decisions and mark the music. Although this level of consideration may seem extreme to some, our use of stress in our presentation of melodies should really be equally informed and start early in the process of learning an instrument.

The weight of the bow on the string and the stroke of the bow across strings is also a wonderful model for our concept of articulation. Take for example the motion from pitch to pitch in an articulated passage. If the ring of the string is comparable to the flow of a brass player's airstream, when a violinist moves from note to note, the string of the first note continues to ring until the second note sounds. The length of the sounding note is directly connected to the stroke of the bow.

With note-to-note movement on string instruments, you can visualize the connection and consistency of sound. Bow action shows how strings achieve their flowing melody with consistency of speed and stroke. In brass playing, one of the biggest challenges is air and tone connection of articulated notes. Because students constantly are challenged to maintain a steady airstream and have to learn how to keep it consistent when encountering new technical challenges, they sometimes develop a disjointed manner of blowing that creates gaps in the sound. As most of early brass playing is in ensembles of large numbers, this manner of playing can persist and become imprinted because in this environment, it is harder for teachers to detect the lack of tonal continuity. Because the difference in air connection is not something that can be seen, it is more likely overlooked in brass players as opposed to string students. To alleviate this obstacle, it is vital that teachers spend quality time listening to individual players and motivating them with great modeling on an instrument.

Articulation on string instruments is much more sophisticated than in wind instruments, and early on they learn terminologies for different methods of articulating along with physical movements that achieve them. The choice of how the bow strikes the string and the use of up and down motions of the bow in achieving different sounds are visible, so the connection to sound and movement is readily seen as well as being heard. The differences between the weight of the string on the bow and the distance used in striking the string with the bow all contribute to this rich variety of articulation sounds. Brass players usually learn about fewer types of articulation, in my view, in their early years, often using only one consonant syllable for tonguing even through high school. As with singing, the first step is exposure to string players, preferably in close proximity, so the students can easily see connections between body movement and the resulting sound. You also can start by watching some of the many videos online that show close-ups of this playing and then make attempts to mimic the variety of articulations that you hear and see in their performances.

Vibrato is another facet of playing that is very visible during string performances and directly transferrable to brass instruments. The speed and width of vibrato are seen in the motion of the left hand on the fingerboard. Although there are rare moments when there is no such motion, overwhelmingly you can easily see that the left hand stays busy creating vibrato throughout a performance. If you look closely, you even see this hand motion preceding the bow stroke on the string and also continuing after the bow motion has stopped. In terms of releases, this is comparable to the *spin* or *shimmer* in a brass sound as a note is released. If brass players consider the concept of the follow-through of this vibrancy, the room ring created in release will be enhanced just as it is in string playing.

The speed of vibrato related to intensity of emotional response in string performance is also valuable to examine. As intensity grows we can see the motion of the hand increase in speed and width. The use of vibrato to express emotion is evident, and it is worthwhile to examine string melodies to see where performers increase and decrease intensity. With the help of this visualization to accompany the sound, you can then listen more critically to wind performers to determine how they similarly use vibrato to aid in expression. Of course, then you should apply this listening and awareness to your own playing and use of vibrato.

In discussing ensemble tone for brass players, the concept of vibrato is sometimes that none should be used unless you are in the role of soloist. Many feel that if all members of the section use vibrato to enrich their sound, there will be distortion to sound and pitch clarity. If that is the case, then why, when we see orchestras play so beautifully, do we witness all the left hands of the members of the violin section moving together? The answer to this question really lies in the speed and width of their vibrato. As mentioned earlier, a narrow, middle-speed vibrato or *shimmer* serves to enrich the sound, assist in its projection, and allow for matching of pitch with tone colors. A sound that is totally devoid of vibrancy is cold and hard to the ear, much like that pitch emitted by a tuner that we mentioned earlier. Not only is it not pleasing to the ear, but it is difficult to exactly match pitch and also restrict its ability to fill the room. Brass sections in ensembles can learn much about vibrancy by considering the string section and how it works together to create group vibrancy.

The concepts of *leaning* and expressing *target notes* in phrases also are enriched with string instrument observation. Notice how the head, shoulders, arms, and trunk of the body move in string playing. Not only the process of downbeat and upbeat with the motion of the right arm but also other accompanying physical movements illustrate the intensity of music. The physicality of playing, like the movement of the conductor, is instructive to observers and helps convey emotional expression during performance. Because brass instruments can be played technically well without extra bodily motion, we often strive for *making it look easy* to a fault. The focus on continuity in sound and equality of technique at some point must shift to allow derivations that enrich melodic expression. Without the physical connection to phrasing inherent in conducting and string performance, brass players need to work harder at visualization and imagined movement to inform expression. Of course, experience with conducting, dancing, or playing an instrument that thrives on bodily motion is very helpful in instilling the physical connection in our imagination. Remembering this concept of visualizing musical movement, even without actually moving while playing, can positively influence expression for brass instrumentalists.

Observing string technique and the sound it achieves should start at an early age for brass players. Students can see and hear the differences between string performances of articulated passages and then compare them to their manner of playing similar passages. By using their airflow to achieve the same sound on brass instruments, they will increase lyricism and the options for expressive gestures. They also will decrease the likelihood of mistakes, such as cracked notes and pitch and tone inconsistency.

Teachers of brass instruments should make an effort to bring string players into the applied lesson and classroom, so students can engage in call and response practice with them. Encourage individual playing with attempts to imitate the connection of notes while articulating, and ask the string players to share their approaches to up and down bow decisions. This is especially important if there is not a string program in your school as it may be the only chance for students to benefit from this influence.

In university music programs, find the time to play duets with string instrumentalists, and also ask them to play some of your brass melodies to give you a new perspective for interpretation and musical direction.

Visual Imagery

Motion pictures and television also can inspire the expressive process as they provide background stories and direct emotional connections between images and musical themes. As a boy I learned many movie themes by ear and played them often, just for my own enjoyment. Among my favorites were the main themes from *Raiders of the Lost Ark*, *Star Wars*, and the beautiful trumpet solo from the television show *Dynasty*. The attraction was to express the characters and their stories by learning and playing these melodies. As I began teaching and doing master classes, I found that these themes were very successful for demonstrating technical and musical ideas to students. I also learned that while performing them, I was never nervous, and their renditions always were spirited and exciting. While playing them, I realized that I really was thinking only about the images and characters and their accompanying emotions that were so well instilled from viewing them. Furthermore, as I had learned these melodies by ear and had never seen them notated on paper, the process of learning them had eliminated this part of the normal preparation process, making a more direct connection to my emotion from the very beginning. In the ensuing years, as performing many solo recitals often brought more nervous moments and stress, I realized that perhaps I could find ways to bring the melodies of a classical concerto or sonata into the same process as my beloved movie themes.

The visual richness of opera and cinema can be great inspiration for musical expression of our instrumental melodies. With or without the addition of lyrics for these tunes, considering the clear visual images that they create can help to make decisions on how we will use technique, so we can evoke similar feelings in our performances. By focusing on the picture we hope to paint in listeners' minds, we can move our own focus away from technical matters and toward the emotions that will be mirrored in our playing, facial expressions, and body movements. In most cases, the conjuring of a visual image can be connected to words, as already discussed. In other instances, a *scene* alone might suffice to inspire creativity. Operas and musicals, of course, combine singing with great visual production, and so they can be amazing influences on young instrumentalists. Oddly, I find that many instrumental teachers do not develop a fondness for this type of musical production even as their marching bands strive to increase the visual aspects of their performances with similar body movements, elaborate props, and costumes.

Many musicians have discussed the benefits of musical imagery in performance. Others also have talked and written about focusing the mind on expression or storytelling and even *tricking* the mind into not focusing on technical matters. At one point during our Eastman Wind Ensemble tour with soloist Wynton Marsalis, I asked him about his thoughts onstage while performing cornet solos that were very challenging technically. Among the advice he gave was a simple bit of misdirection. He told me to find the small exit sign that is always above one of the doors in the rear of the hall. By seeking it and finding it while playing, you can take your focus away from the technical aspects of playing and allow your mind and body to do what they are capable of doing without interference. I already had come to a similar conclusion in my very first recital at Florida State University. The first work on the program was the Haydn *Concerto for Trumpet*, and I was beyond nervous! During the long piano exposition, I was trying to focus on all the technical processes that I had worked on with my teacher and in my practice. Although I was playing from memory, I still could see the notation clearly in my head, and I was scrutinizing it as my entrance approached. The fact that it was my first performance of it from memory made the nervousness even worse, and I wasn't even sure what all the notes were as I began to play. As you might imagine, the first few phrases were a mess as I grappled with all the minute technical thoughts swirling in my mind. What saved me was . . . the exit sign in the rear of the concert hall. One of them fluttered, and it caught my attention as I played. My mind was now preoccupied with this sign. Why is it fluttering? Why haven't they fixed that sign yet? At some point, I realized that I was playing the Haydn as well as I ever had, remembering it without difficulty and expressing the melodies as I had so carefully prepared. The exit sign had taken my conscious attention away from *micromanaging* my technical playing, and this allowed my mind–body connection to operate as trained.

This lesson in mental misdirection was very valuable to me and has been central to my playing and teaching ever since. I also have learned that the most valuable and rewarding way to direct our thoughts away from technical playing is to focus on thoughts and images of musical expression. This seems so obvious and necessary, but the processes involved in achieving such focus takes training and practice. I have found that just trying to be *musical* or to think musically in an abstract manner is not strong enough to withstand the challenges of a high-stress performance. To fully prepare for this type of challenge, the musical plan must be more fully defined and connected to the music. You also must practice the process of musical focus, first in your practice room and later in front of ever more discriminating audiences. Creating and following a plan for the sequence of thoughts and feelings for the entire work must be practiced in context until it all seems natural and the connections between your feelings and how they direct you to play the instrument are reliable and automatic.

Exercises

Create Words to Your Instrumental Melody

- Examine a small instrumental melody like an ABA form for high and low points and changes in harmony and articulation.
- Sing through the melody using *brass singing* techniques, and decide what basic emotional state it expresses to you.
- Create lyrics for the melody that mirror the sequence of emotions you feel the music creates.
- Sing the melody using the lyrics.
- On your instrument, consider how the emotional state can impact your manner of articulation, vibrato, dynamics, and use of rubato. Think about how the meanings and sounds of the words can influence these choices.
- Play the melody on your instrument while hearing the words being sung in your imagination. Allow yourself to concentrate only on the words, and let your body play the instrument using only this focused thought process.

Mark Up and Down Bows

- Take an etude or solo, and decide which notes should be stressed and which notes should not in each melody.
- Talk to a string player, and ask him or her to mark a copy of your music with the bowings he or she would use to express each melody and discuss how that can influence your brass performance plan.

Observe and Imitate Bowings

- Have a string performer demonstrate bowings and styles of articulation for you, and then try to mimic the same exact style of attack and note length on your instrument.
- If you cannot find a player who can do this, view one online on YouTube or one of the many string sites.
- Pay special attention to the connection of the notes and the gaps between notes in sound as the bowings and articulations change.

Create a Small Opera From Your Music

- Take an etude or solo, and assign the different melodies to characters as in an imagined opera or musical.

- Imagine how each character would appear and what his or her voice would sound like.
- Use this imagery to inspire variety in the way you present these melodies with your instrument.
- Train your focus to see and hear the imaginary characters singing each melody, and let your body simply play the instrument in response to these thoughts.
- You can enrich this further by creating words for these characters to sing as mentioned in the previous exercise.

19

ADVICE FOR APPLIED TEACHERS

"I'm going to help you play the trumpet for one hour a
week and for the other eighteen hours, the teacher is you!"
Bryan Goff
The Florida State University

Leonard Candelaria, emeritus trumpet professor from the University of North Texas,
is a very through thinker and brings an all-encompassing philosophy to his teaching.
Many times he outlined his concept of the applied lesson to me by saying: "A teacher's
job is to help students identify what needs to change in their playing, describe how to
improve it, and give them an aural example of the desired sound when it is successful."
In following this approach with students, he was always playing in lessons, making sure
that they understood the differences between his demonstrations and their renditions.
At all levels, teachers need to follow this simple plan for helping their students. First they
must be able to help them identify what they wish to change in their playing. Then they
must be able to recognize what the desired result should sound like. With this awareness, they need to find exercises that will lead to these outcomes. At each step of this
process, the teacher is vital to helping students fully understand the process by offering
both aural modeling and, when needed, verbal description.

As mentioned in Chapter 1 I want to recall the two characteristics that are vital
to teaching as espoused by Charles Geyer. First, teachers must be totally honest in
dealing with students, including assessment of their playing and the challenges of
the career field. Second, teachers must truly care for their students and their futures.
These two traits must remain central in teaching, and if you have them, you can be
a great mentor to younger players.

There are many approaches to teaching, but I have found that the most effective
ones always include an honest sharing of all the challenges we face as musicians
and brass players. It also requires a genuine concern for students and their lives,
even if it might mean some sacrifices to your own image and the image of the
profession. Although there are some top players who balance the great demands of
virtuoso playing with teaching a small number of students, in many cases, teaching is

impacted directly by both the number of students taught and the frequency of professional performance activities of the teacher. At the collegiate level, for example, there are many studios with well-known performers who serve mainly as *artists in residence*, and they maintain a busy playing career while also trying to teach a full-time load of students. Although certainly much can be learned from any contact with accomplished players, great playing does not always equate to great teaching. All students need a teacher who is willing to provide mentoring beyond the parameters of the weekly lesson in an honest and patient approach. Because the focus of teachers is the advancement of their students, I prefer to evaluate music teachers much less on their personal performance skill and much more on the accomplishments of their students.

As mentioned earlier, young players develop an unrealistic image of perfection because of heavily edited recordings and performances. Because of this orientation, they need experienced guidance to understand that mistakes are actually part of the learning process and also part of the life of a performer. In this learning process, teachers need to share their own weaknesses and failures with students honestly along with how they overcame them. Some teachers, unfortunately, do not feel comfortable with this level of open honesty. They hide past failures and those less-than-stellar performances and also limit their playing in lessons to create an image for their students of the teacher as a *great and infallible player*. This obsession with self-image certainly is influenced by the culture we see all around us in politics, media, and even in the arts. The best way to reduce the impact of these ridiculous messages is consistently to offer music students the reality of live playing and the mistakes that naturally come with learning.

In some ways, this more open approach is a bit counterintuitive to what we might feel we need to do to build our own careers as performers. For me, it is part of the philosophy of wearing many hats in the profession. Of course, as a performer I want to instill in audiences the sense that music making is effortless and fun. They usually do not know that I have played the music dozens of times before or spent countless hours in preparation. They also missed out on the many times I attempted parts of the performance in practice and failed miserably. The magic of the performance transcends the challenges we face leading up to a quality performance, and it is proper that we only present a part of the story to our audiences.

As a teacher and mentor of young performers, however, the focus must be completely different than the *act* we portray onstage. They must be aware of the entire process that all great performances require from start to finish, and we must be completely honest about the challenges involved in this process, especially our own personal experiences. Some teachers seem to want to treat their students only *as audiences*, emphasizing the *show* and not sharing how they had to overcome challenges to their playing along the way.

In my years of college teaching, I have brought many guests to perform and work with our students. Guest artists who appear frequently on recordings and regularly play with the best symphony orchestras are great for helping students understand that even these great players sometimes make mistakes in live performance. They also learn how the impact of these mistakes is lessened by the musicality and deliberateness of their presentation. When students fully appreciate that great players do make mistakes but also find practice methods that reduce them or their impact, they immediately see their future as players in a different light. Likewise, if their studio teacher shares the challenges to superior playing along with ways to overcome them, students will be energized and empowered to do the same. Unfortunately I often see and hear guests or fellow professionals say things like "Oh, I never practice" or "Gee, I haven't touched my horn in days" to students when it is totally untrue. Most of these players are practicing like mad and warming up more than others. This choice they make to deceive rather than share honestly reveals a self-centered desire to build up their image at the expense of the needs of the next generation of players. Although such choices might be of value in building a career as a performer or celebrity, they are devastating to students and their learning. I avoid hosting these players and prefer simply to admire their onstage performances as they seem unable to step out of that world when it is needed to help others.

I always have had a great respect for superior players who are laser focused on their performance careers and choose not to teach regularly. They often do this out of respect for the needs of students but also because they recognize the rigors of a performance career. Any time spent playing their instrument that is not devoted to their own improvement is a distraction that takes a toll in terms of chop time and preservation of only the highest-quality sound images in their minds. In short, great players need to be more self-centered about their playing to maintain the high levels required by the profession. It is important for them to choose when and how often they need to protect their playing and their listening and how much time and effort they can really devote to teaching those who are less experienced.

Most students, however, need and deserve their teacher to model correct playing for them—and often. This is especially true for students who have not yet developed a concept of their *model sound* in their imaginations. There is no substitute for live, up-close observation of a skilled player, and students need this stimulation frequently in their learning process. Veteran teachers, especially brass players, understand that providing this modeling comes at some cost to their own playing. One of my colleagues refers to lesson playing as *negative practice*, and I feel this is a great descriptor. In the process of playing with less experienced, less capable players, you are consistently hearing less efficient sounds with pitch and sound production issues. As brass players, the physicality of playing means there is a real effect on our endurance and production of tone when we play with these students. Even though we know where to place the pitch, for example, it takes great awareness to place it correctly when the student is not. This *sympathetic playing* that characterizes all great players works against us in these moments because we inevitably want to match them if they cannot match us. As I usually play second to my students in duets and also play a lot in unison, this phenomenon is magnified. It is inevitable that this will impact your playing negatively, but remember that your advanced playing also is impacting the student in a very positive way. The teacher is giving and the student is receiving in this model. This, of course, is the logical and proper arrangement, and teachers need to prepare for this as part of the profession.

Because teaching many students subjects the instructor to many hours of *negative practice*, it is vital to counter with processes that help preserve musicianship and the high level of playing that your students need and audiences deserve. Try to separate your personal practice from teaching with time and mental focus. Plan for those periods when you will need to shift more focus to your own playing and away from lesson playing. My students always sense when I have an important performance coming up as my playing in their lessons is reduced. Because I understand the great benefit of playing in lessons, the choice to not model for them is very difficult. Sometimes I have to put a note on my trumpet case that reads *NO* or even leave my instruments at home. The delicate balancing act of playing for them and playing for yourself is hardest when, like me, you are teaching more than 20 hours of lessons per week. Even if you find the chops and time to also practice for two hours per day, you are still only matching 20 hours of negative practice in lessons with 14 hours of focused repair practice. If you want to play a solo recital, you will need to plan carefully for a time when you can shift your focus from lots of modeling to teaching without that component. If your students are very advanced, or there are less of them, this balancing act is much easier than if they are less experienced and numerous.

Many in the teaching profession unfortunately react to this delicate balancing act by either not playing in lessons at all or, on the other end of the equation, discontinuing their performing altogether. I have worked with teachers in both situations and have found them somewhat lacking in their ability to help their students.

Teachers who give up public performance soon forget about the pace and challenges of preparation, and this limits their compassion for students. As with all activities that happened in the past, they begin to romanticize about the process, usually forgetting about their own struggles and failures. Teachers who choose never to play in lessons lose the most effective tool for modeling that their students desperately need. I believe that all teachers need to understand fully the needs of their students and decide if they are really willing to make the necessary continued commitment to them in terms of demonstration playing and modeling performer behavior.

Some teachers who do not play in lessons also do not sing or provide any other aural model for stimulation. They are reduced to lengthy descriptions of what they want from students, resulting in a crude, less-focused form of teaching. From these experiences as a student came a resolve to always give my students better. Although former players may have much to offer in spoken advice, not giving students good models to copy reduces the overall impact of study. It is important for those who are no longer playing to find alternative ways for students to gain this listening experience. Guest artists and older graduate students can, in some cases, help provide the needed modeling that should be an important part of applied study.

All students learn in different ways, and teachers need to be able to motivate using a variety of approaches. Playing, singing, buzzing, conducting, and describing should all be on the menu. Combining such an all-encompassing approach with opportunities to hear skilled performers in close proximity and in live performances can lead to a superior learning environment for students as they develop images of quality sound production and musical expression.

Use Students as a Resource

Students learn as much or more from their colleagues as they do from their teachers in productive learning environments. In all great music schools, the culture of the institution fosters much student collaboration and encourages cross-learning opportunities. Weekly studio solo classes can include weekly performances for each other and feedback from student to student. Practice time can be greatly enriched if you can seek advice or consolation from a fellow student in a nearby room as you work to overcome challenges faced in your music. This type of collaborative learning is enhanced in a residential campus because of the close proximity of living and learning centers. In some universities, the large and impersonal campus with many commuter students can unfortunately reduce opportunities for students to engage in this type of collaborative learning that is vital to their future growth as performers. In these schools, teachers must do more to put students together in less-formal settings to foster group learning and offer more cross-learning opportunities.

Students also can be more engaged while in secondary school music programs. In my high school experience, student officers in the band regularly conducted the band, planned and judged chair challenges, and helped foster new members in their playing. We were in the band room before school, during lunch, and after school listening to music and working together on our music projects. The system capitalized on the experience and talent of older students to help each other, new members, and the band director to create a great learning environment. It is not surprising that many of these high school students went on to successful careers in music performance and teaching. Their advanced levels upon entering college were a direct result of the environment created by their teachers and fellow students.

In all levels of learning, collaborative experiences can be included to enhance the experience of individual students. Teachers should take the time to contact their colleagues and develop time for their students to be together to share best practices and play for each other. It is clear that, where this is part of the teaching plan, students are learning faster and gaining the confidence that they will need to move forward. It takes more time and effort from the teacher, but it should be a regular part of the learning environment.

Perseverance

Learning to play brass instruments well inherently involves consistent effort and improvement that is often measured only in small gains in ability. Like athletes, brass players will endure moments when their physical capabilities fail the desired musical goals due to fatigue, lack of preparation, or their development of poor playing habits. Because music is connected so strongly to our emotional selves, it is more devastating when we fail to play well or feel that improvement is not coming fast enough. Teachers can be a pivotal factor in students learning lifelong lessons through these musical challenges as they show students how steady, incremental growth is achieved with consistent effort.

When students encounter emotional low points in their playing, it is important to help them focus on positive actions they can identify with while struggling with new challenges. Often I ask them to be more *scientific* about their playing and use logic to counter the emotions that are creating these feelings of inadequacy. If they are not playing efficiently with good results, they need to reduce the passages attempted to basic components in a manner that allows them to reassert control and confidence. This can include playing passages in context but much more slowly or even playing a fermata on each individual note to ensure the proper sound production. When things are going badly, this *divide and conquer* process can help turn students away from reaffirming their inability to play the music. Finding a stable point in each passage through these and other methods must be an immediate goal when frustration threatens to halt improvement.

Learning from mistakes and failure is part of any profession, and musicians need to understand that poor playing is the result of miscalculation in preparation, and it can be remedied in the future. The overwhelming response to poor performances is too often a general self-effacing evaluation based on unfocused emotion (I suck). It is vital that teachers assist students in determining what exactly went wrong and how to prevent it in future performance. How the teacher reacts to weak student performances is critical in building this self-esteem and confidence. A poor performance needs to be seen as a temporary setback, not a lasting condition.

In those moments backstage immediately following a performance and in subsequent discussions regarding playing evaluation, teachers must be honest and supportive in their commentary. Too often I hear bland comments from teachers to students that either laud all students in the same way regardless of performance quality or point focused criticism at small details in a performance without a logical evaluation of the entirety of playing. As many performances are *first and only* opportunities, teachers need to remind students of this in their commentary. We need to stress that performing is a process that improves with each repeat experience. The teacher, for many students, is the only completely honest feedback they might have. Family, friends, and colleagues too often *sugarcoat* their feedback because it is difficult to point to inadequacies in the brief feedback time experienced without risking relationships. Oddly, when students have a truly successful performance, these voices still sound the same as when playing was unsuccessful, and so it is difficult for the student performer to process this feedback. It will end up being the totally honest teacher who convinces students of their progress and gives them the tools to develop better self-awareness of their playing and how to chart its improvement.

Exercises

- Take the time to record your student repeating short passages that you perform on your instrument. Play back the audio, and allow the student to evaluate the differences in your two performances. Steer them toward focused comments that will offer a path for them to alter their playing for better results.
- Find some recordings of you playing at the same exact age as your current students. Play them for students, and be sure not to skip over places where there were mistakes or breakdowns in your playing. In addition to identifying the weaknesses, allow students to identify the positive attributes of the performance. Finally, be sure to share with them the concept that, though you played much like them when you were their age, you still found a career path as a successful player. This contextual information will be important in countering tendencies to be too hard on themselves as players.

20

CONDUCTING BRASS PLAYERS

"Okay brass section, now let's do that again and this time,
take the edge off it!"

Donald Hunsberger
Director, Eastman Wind Ensemble

For most students, the early years of learning how to play a brass instrument are influenced heavily by their time in ensembles. The organization of these rehearsals and performances and the approaches of their conductors figure prominently in the development of quality brass players. Most band and orchestral directors are not brass players, so it is vital that they understand the unique physical demands of these instruments, especially as young players are developing. Awareness of these challenges in advance can maximize rehearsal time and minimize playing situations that lead to bad habits and block development. Conducting style, modeling through singing, and the ability to describe techniques to young players all can lead to enriching experiences that stimulate continued interest and successful participation.

Intonation Hierarchy

One of the biggest obstacles to brass tone production, endurance, flexibility, and power in an ensemble is intonation. When brass players find themselves in poor pitch environments, they often respond by engaging secondary methods of physical pitch manipulation as they struggle to find their place in group tuning. Because lipping and excessive pressure require increased physical exertion, endurance, accuracy, and strength of sound are all reduced when there is not a good center of pitch in an ensemble. Pitch, of course, is really about individual matching and listening rather than a group effort to all attain an ideal measurable on a needle or dial. The reason that professional players rarely tune carefully yet almost always exhibit good ensemble tuning is because they have established a *hierarchy of tuning* that determines who listens to whom in all playing circumstances. Although tuning your ensemble to a prescribed set pitch to start a rehearsal is fine, it is really the establishment of a system of listening to and matching others that will lead to an in-tune performance and allow for the most efficient brass playing in your ensemble.

In many groups, players tune to a set pitch from a tuner, oboist, clarinetist, or tuba player to start a rehearsal or performance. With the availability of tuners, it is really not significant who sets this initial tuning note; it is what happens later that is more important. In the brass section, although the tuba and bass trombone generally have the roots of chords, these instruments are also harder to hear in terms of pitch clarity and have a wide latitude for placing the pitch high or low of the center without cracking or missing the note. For these reasons, they should not be the leaders of pitch in the brass section, even if they may be involved in the initial tuning process. The first trumpet is the logical choice to lead pitch in the brass section for many reasons. First, it is usually the highest-sounding voice, so it is easiest to hear and match. Second, it presents the melody most often when all of the brasses are playing together. Third, the trumpet in the high register, like the horn, has the narrowest pitch latitude, and players are therefore prone to cracking and missing notes when they have to make surprise adjustments. And finally, trumpet players are the first to tire in the group and therefore need to do the least physical manipulation to match the pitch to increase their playing time.

When setting up a pitch system in your brass section, start by tuning the first trumpet and the lowest voice, normally the tuba. If these boundary voices are in tune, then the rest of the group will have an easier time finding their place in the tuning hierarchy. Spend time adding first horn, trombone, and euphonium to this process to get all the principal players to find pitch prior to adding the rest of the section players. Once the principals understand how to listen and match the first trumpet, then add the section players with the charge that their job is to listen to their section principal and concentrate on matching that pitch level. The same holds true for a jazz ensemble with lead players in the wind section. The only difference in jazz groups is the presence of the fixed-pitch piano. Here the lead trumpet needs to match pitch with the piano and then with the bass to establish the basic pitch construct. When the instrumentation changes, the highest voice should become the model pitch to match among lead players, with section players always focused on matching them. Setting up this system will do wonders for pitch and balance in your ensemble and can begin early in the development of your students.

It becomes obvious when establishing this hierarchy that to match your principal or the first trumpet, you must be playing at a volume that allows you to hear them. This realization also should happen early in the ensemble experience as overplaying is a frequent problem encountered, especially in young players. Within the section as well, the principal must be heard easily throughout the section to facilitate tuning. In most cases, this requires the principal to play stronger than others, and it means that section players who overplay the volume of the principal will disrupt not only the balance but also the intonation and consistency for that section. I find that it is instructive to explain these roles to students as soon as possible and to reinforce them frequently. The development of tuning leadership in principals should be an extension of their overall responsibility for the sound of their section, including fixing problems on their own. Of course there are also moments when a section player is placed in the role of principal. When this occurs, they must recognize the role change and play out to lead the section in the same manner.

Even when sections are in unison, the principal player needs to be a bit stronger than other players to set the exact pitch level. Equal voices actually lead to competition for pitch preeminence, and the result is a weaker presentation of the melody. In the overall ensemble sound, you should strive for intonation first as it is more important than dynamic level. If the group really plays well in tune together, the result will be greater clarity and greater power out in the room. If there are pitch and balance discrepancies, even with strong loud playing, the result is less power and less clarity.

If you encounter pitch problems that require focused attention in addition to the aforementioned balance and listening hierarchy, be ready to isolate a few chords and explore each player's role in tuning the chord. Always start with octaves involving the root of the chord when they exist. Migrate to open fifths, and then add thirds, sevenths, and other color notes and dissonances. Generally, you will find that most students will automatically lower the third after they hear the root and fifth of the chord well tuned. These small adjustments can be refined over time as students learn more about pitch demands and the capabilities of their instruments to meet them. Remember to reinforce the priority of mechanical pitch manipulation over physical manipulation when meeting intonation demands. Physical intonation fixes like lipping and excessive mouthpiece pressure yield a less vibrant sound and also will tax endurance heavily, so encourage players to use these methods only as a last resort.

Once your ensemble has established a listening hierarchy, solving problems becomes a more logical process. If you try to work outside this system, you can confuse students and weaken their ownership of the tuning process. For example, if you try to isolate individual players and ask them to tune too often to a tuner or fixed pitch outside the ensemble environment, you are not giving them the best tools to find pitch while the group is playing. It is better to remind them who they are matching and reinforce that relationship in the rehearsal. Within the hierarchy, principal and lead players should expect to be called out when their sections are out of tune, and you should spend quality time teaching them how to diplomatically assert their leadership in these matters. Sectionals with teachers and then with the students alone, led by the principal, are great for developing these relationships, so be sure to find time for these opportunities.

Releases Tell It All

It is important to treat releases in your brass section with the same scrutiny as attacks. After all, they are heard in much the same manner in the audience. A clean release in classical style on brass instruments should involve a vowel release that maximizes room ring and also continues the group pitch and balance after the cutoff. Abrupt accent with a tongue cutoff or closing of the throat actually creates a dissonance in the room, and this results in a more ragged ensemble sound. Try an experiment with your group when you are in a room that offers some ring in the sound. Have them play the ends of sections, and then cut them off with special attention to the sound that continues in the room following the end of playing. You can hear the consonance in the chord if they have all released well, allowing their true pitch to continue ringing. If they close their throats or cut off with their tongues, it will present itself as instant dissonance in the ringing sound. Many great brass chamber ensembles use this technique often to work on pitch through release style with a special focus on the ring of the sound in the performance space.

Notes in more extreme registers and dynamics offer a greater challenge to this vowel release, so it is important to spend time with your group isolating releases for listening and evaluation. Once students are aware of the need for controlled releases, they are more likely to work on them in their individual practice. It is also important from a conducting standpoint that your hand movements mimic vowel releases with their gestures and that, on occasion, you explain the clarity of a cutoff gesture in relationship to the style of release you are seeking. In fact, even the term *cutoff* is an unfortunate descriptor for a sound that we would like to ring in the hall.

Edge in the Sound

In ensemble playing it is important to strive for a wide variety of sound colors within the scope of control. Edgy or brilliant sounds are produced when the metal of the instrument is brought into vibration rather than just the air column within the internal dimensions of the instrument. When the metal of the instrument itself truly begins to vibrate, it emphasizes the higher frequencies and reduces lower ones. The result is a brighter sound. The thinner the metal of an instrument, the sooner a player meets this threshold when increasing intensity of airflow. Beginning model instruments have thinner metal and reach this brightness threshold easily. As the players are young, this allows for more security in the sound with less power needed from the air. The downside is that the volume possibilities are more limited for sounds below the brightness threshold.

Differences in the physical qualities of players as well as mouthpiece depth and size also impact when players reach the edge threshold. More experienced brass players naturally gravitate toward larger mouthpieces and heavier instruments to allow for a bigger, darker sound at higher volumes. Brightness is still a component of playing, but these instruments allow for more colors prior to the shrillness created at the boundary of good-quality sound.

Instrument choice becomes important when trying to balance the brilliance in the sound of your brass section, especially in the marching and jazz bands. With the popularity of drum corps has come new instruments that are constructed using thinner metals and also smaller bore sizes, which are favored by these ensembles. Due to these construction choices, these instruments achieve the edge threshold faster, creating excitement in the sound, but they also sacrifice some of the middle volumes and colors found in orchestral instruments. The uniform sound that drum corps achieve is due to the commonality of their instruments in construction, and it is one of the reasons they supply the instruments for their players. In the marching band, however, it is more likely to find a mix of instruments ranging from beginning level to more advanced orchestral instruments. This, of course, can create a sound balance problem within these types of groups.

For example, many marching bands have moved to shoulder-held drum corps–style tubas and mellophones rather than horns. These instruments are small bore and lightweight, allowing them to reach the edge threshold quickly. If you have these instruments in a brass section along with heavier trumpets and trombones, like the popular professional Bach instruments, you already have a color problem. I have witnessed many rehearsals where band directors are screaming at their trumpets and trombones to *blow louder* to match the brilliant color of these lightweight tubas and mellophones. Although sometimes there is truly a volume issue, many times it is the difference in the mellower, darker sounds of the orchestral instruments trying to match the brighter, lighter drum corps–style instruments. To achieve comparable brightness, the players of these heavier instruments need much more vigorous air, and many young players do not have the stamina to produce such sounds without developing poor habits. In these situations, I recommend that trumpet and trombone players instead opt for beginning-level instruments with thinner metals and also smaller mouthpieces to achieve a better color balance. In addition to tone color problems, the mismatch of instruments also can encourage orchestral instrument players to overblow constantly and damage their ability to play in other types of ensembles, especially at softer volumes and with darker, more resonant sounds.

Similarly in the jazz ensemble, we can see balance problems due to instrument selection and the style of music. Lead trumpet and trombone have unusual demands in terms of high register and brightness in these ensembles. Most professionals meet this demand with smaller, shallower mouthpieces and lightweight instruments. When these equipment changes are not available or understood, there can be problems meeting the demands of the ensemble in terms of endurance, projection, and tone color. Too often I hear lead trombone players, for example, trying to use a very large-bore, very heavy symphonic trombone to play lead in the jazz band. The resulting sound, even if they can play all the notes, is not lively enough or bright enough to lead the section and balance the trumpets and saxophones around them. There are many combinations of wind sounds possible in the jazz band, and it is vital that teachers develop this concept with players by choosing mouthpieces and instruments throughout the ensemble to facilitate a unified sound in all dynamic levels.

Soft Attacks

Brass players are as challenged with soft playing as are all wind instrumentalists. The demands to play loud and big are constant in a quality group but so is the need to play very softly with control. I often tell players that the only reason we can understand what loud sounds like is because we also can hear what soft really is. The ability to create contrast in music requires that we constantly pay attention to both ends of the dynamics spectrum. Soft playing is seen by many in the profession as the truest test of control and sophistication and must be practiced in earnest to be successful.

All brass players are the sum of their daily playing. In many cases, ensemble playing emphasizes louder volumes and might not demand soft, controlled playing. This is especially true in marching band and jazz groups but also in concert wind groups. In a nod to the development of drum corps and the expansion of the percussion section in wind ensemble and concert bands, composers have responded with works for the stage that utilize all those percussionists. Wind players in these groups have witnessed an escalation in volume due in large part to this influence of percussion and also compositional efforts to feature them. Many newer compositions for concert groups yield textures, melodies, and especially volumes that used to be heard only from marching bands. A common way of treating the brasses by modern composers is to have them sustain chords, while the rhythmic and melodic subdivisions are created in the percussion section. Often those sustained chords last for a long period of time and at loud volumes, serving as a pedal point against which composers feature more complex instrumentation and detail in the percussion section. It seems that in many concerts, works that require soft, controlled interplay in brass instruments, or even the woodwinds, are becoming less common.

If brass players spend the great majority of their time playing at volumes of mezzo forte and louder, it is logical that their ability to control their sound softer than mezzo forte will be impaired. Often, I encounter players who cannot even create a true piano dynamic on their instruments. All the loud playing, in essence, reinforces an embouchure around a larger aperture as a result of continually playing at louder volumes. To be able to play softly, players need to bring the balance between soft and loud playing into more equitable proportions. I tell players to think in terms of percentages. If a great percentage of time in ensembles requires loud playing, then practice time must feature an equally large percentage of soft playing. There is no fast solution to an imbalance, and many conductors need to keep this in mind as they consider how they spend their time with their ensembles.

The soft attack is a superb effect in brass playing and also a great test of tone control. To help players develop this ability, it is important to understand the relationship of the lips, tongue, and airflow in making such an attack. The lips provide compression that offers resistance to the moving air. Lesser resistance, paired with less vigorous air, creates a smaller aperture or vibrating space in the lips. The aperture is not formed in advance but rather is the result of the movement of the air against this resistance in the lips. The lips always should start together rather than attempting to form the hole or aperture prior to commencing a tone. When the airflow becomes more vigorous, the aperture formed is larger, as it is with lower and louder notes. Stronger lip resistance with fast air but less air volume results in higher and softer notes. The aperture created for loud, low notes is the largest, while that for soft high notes is smallest. When players do too much large-aperture playing, they lose the ability to match the controlled lip resistance for soft playing when the airflow becomes less vigorous. When this problem exists you can hear the air passing through the embouchure without being set into vibration, especially at the point of attack. Sometimes this leads to an airy tone and also might be evident in hearing only air prior to the tone being produced. As mentioned earlier, soft playing with *pu* attacks is a great therapy for this condition.

The best way to achieve a better balance in playing dynamics in your ensembles is to program works regularly that require soft and sensitive playing. Exposed soft solos and tuttis may be a bit intimidating to players at first, but with regular attention, you can improve this part of their playing and reinforce it as vital to their development. Ballads in the jazz ensemble also should be part of every program to challenge these players to play the softer range of dynamics and create warmer colors in the group.

Share Your Musical Ideas Early With Your Ensemble

Successful ensembles play in a unified manner that reflects a common concept of interpretation. This interpretation starts with the conductor but needs to involve each player as well. As we have discussed earlier, technique is striving to make the sounds in our imagination come alive on an instrument. The same is true for conductors because the ensemble is *their instrument*. When they begin to develop an interpretation, conductors need to do the same work we described for individual players regarding their knowledge of the music. They need to study the score, its structure, tonality, and other musical features because this awareness is essential to create a musical map for expression. They need to do this prior to the first rehearsal, so they can relate these ideas through their stick technique and face and body expression to the players from the very beginning.

I have had the misfortune to observe many conductors that I would label as *reactionary conductors*. This label I give them refers to their lack of score knowledge and musical intention while leading their ensemble. As they do not truly know what they want the work to sound like in a focused way, they simply react to the sounds that come out of the ensemble during the rehearsal. Many young conductors encounter this situation as they transition from playing an instrument to leading an ensemble.

When first crossing over from playing to conducting, there is sometimes a false sense of relief. Compared to the steady and consistent practice it takes to play an instrument, waving a baton seems quite *easy* in comparison. Keeping a steady beat with appropriate beat patterns actually is quite easy compared to playing a brass instrument, and sometimes students, when transitioning from playing their instruments to conducting, lose their dedication to practice. In actuality, you must spend more time practicing conducting and working through your musical ideas if you intend to be successful on the podium.

If you do not know what you want from the players in your ensemble, it is immediately obvious to them regardless of their level of experience. Maximize your rehearsal time by coming prepared to share your musical goals through your conducting and in your verbal commentary with them. Begin by setting the musical image early, even before the first reading. Help them gain an understanding for the best kind of sound, ultimate volume, and where the peaks and valleys of expression are. Why waste time allowing them to accidentally construct interpretations that guide their technical development in the wrong direction? When ensembles read music repeatedly without proper musical direction, whatever comes out of the group then *becomes* the interpretation. Each time you allow players to play it *any way they choose*, you allow them to establish an interpretation in their minds that will be harder to change as you finally get around to sharing your images in a clear and confident manner. Help them set goals that will direct their preparation toward a unified image of the music by doing your homework early. My favorite quote for this is: *Get the score in your head, and you won't need to have your head in the score!*

Modeling for Your Ensemble

Singing is a vital skill for a conductor, especially one who works with younger players. A verbal description of the sound is never as adequate as a rendition of a melodic line with your singing voice. Make sure you can sing musically to them and that your conducting matches the musicality in your voice. Quality conductors also can illicit musical responses from their ensembles with appropriate hand gestures, body leaning, and facial expressions. It is these triggers that must be practiced and refined prior to leading them in your plan for the music. I can remember a conducting assignment at the University of North Texas that required us to sing at pitch and conduct the famous flute solo from the *Daphnis and Chloe Suite No. 2* by Maurice Ravel. It was the first time that conducting practice felt very similar to trumpet practice to me. Conductors should be able to sing and appropriately conduct all melodies in their works. Singing these lines or playing them on an instrument is needed to clarify them in your mind, so you can reimagine them with your ensemble.

Conductors also need to be prepared for ensemble members who sometimes prefer to express their personal interpretations instead of the wishes of the conductor. I

172

remember playing second trumpet in the Grand Teton Seminar Festival Orchestra on the *Concerto for Orchestra* by Bela Bartok, one of my favorite compositions. In the last movement, the second trumpet begins a famous duet with the principal trumpet with a solo melody. I couldn't wait to play it as I had worn out my Chicago Symphony recording and loved their style of trumpet playing. I began to play, and I was very pleased with how I was sounding; it was just as I wanted it. The conductor stopped us. "No, trumpet, you must play very short," and he sang my solo in an interpretation that I totally did not like. Reluctantly, I followed his advice and played it in that style from that point on, though I still felt that it was poor musicianship. It was not until I heard the recording of the concert that I fully understood his interpretive ideas on full display. In that hearing, I appreciated how the short style of trumpet playing complemented his interpretation in other parts in the movement, resulting in a very unified presentation.

Always remember that the brass player perspective at the rear of the room is very different from what the conductor hears up front. As that conductor, you must be persuasive and confident with your players to follow your musical ideas, so their parts will contribute appropriately to the unified product. Many players will revel in their loudest and biggest playing, even if it creates balance issues in the ensemble. Some of these players follow the mantra, *the rehearsal belongs to him or her (the conductor), but the concert belongs to us*, in response to instructions to play lighter or softer. Of course, this philosophy does not lead to unified musicality, so such notions need to be dismissed early and often.

Understanding Brass Endurance

Most band and orchestra directors come to understand that trumpet and horn players are the first to tire in their ensembles. Especially for those who are not brass players, however, it is important to stress how the organization of rehearsals and selection of literature can impact not just the sound of their group but the future growth and development of these brass players as well as others in this section.

High brass players can play consistently for a maximum of about two or three hours in any given day, not including their warmup session. Depending on the demands of the compositions and the conditioning of the players, this playing time can be reduced or elongated. When comparing band music to orchestral music, it is clear that the time spent playing for them is much greater when in a band. With the movement away from larger concert bands and many players on a part to the wind ensemble with a one-on-a-part setup, the amount of playing time for brass players increases because of the absence of multiple players per part and less opportunity for individuals to rest. When you combine this development with trends in band composition toward higher and more daring brass parts, you can understand fully the challenges that bands can pose for developing brass players.

With the one-on-a-part philosophy and the increased demands on the high brass in today's bands, it often feels much like orchestral playing during loud, tutti sections but more often and for longer periods of time. In orchestras, there are long periods of rest during which composers feature the string and woodwind instruments. Also, orchestral compositions tend to be longer due to more complex thematic development, use of soloists within the ensemble, and combinations of small groups of wind instruments. Brass playing, like in percussion sections, in most orchestras involves much more resting and much less playing as a result. A loud brass passage in orchestral writing often is viewed as a *strong spice* that should only be used sparingly to highlight peaks and high levels of emotion.

Modern band works are shorter and rely more on big gestures for their expression. These big gestures almost always involve the brass and percussion. Brass instruments, of course, fill two roles in the band compared to the orchestra. They are the traditional strong spice as in the orchestra but also often present the melody in the absence of string players. Due to these differences, brass players in bands play more often with less resting. Although the pieces are shorter, concerts usually consist of several similar pieces with only a few moments of rest in between them.

Unfortunately, this environment, while it can be very helpful in developing strong players, also can create bad habits that inhibit further development in brass playing. You can limit the possibility of negative impact from band participation with a few commonsense choices. First, there needs to be soft, lyrical playing in every concert. It is sometimes tempting to sidestep this kind of playing as it can reveal weak individual playing because of its special focus on pitch and tone quality. There certainly is safety in sticking with loud and busy pieces, especially in competitive performance, but you should work hard to work on soft and expressive playing consistently. The soloistic nature of softer works will provide more rest for the brass section and also help members of this section balance their loud and soft playing.

You also should look at your works to gauge the percentage of brass playing to resting, especially for your trumpet and horn sections. Ideally it should be somewhere in the ratio of no more than two-thirds of the time playing with one-third resting. You also should do this for the entire program. Plan for assistant players on the highest and most demanding principal parts to ensure quality band sounds and more options in combining resting and playing. These extra players can double the principal part if the music warrants it, but the real benefit is to allow for staggered rest during each piece. If the Chicago Symphony and Eastman Wind Ensemble, with their amazing brass players, use this method of sharing the burdens of playing, certainly it is warranted for younger players who are still developing their skills.

Brass performance planning, like preparing for athletic events, should carefully choreograph combinations of playing and resting. Hard practice, even when playing efficiently, tears down muscle tissue that must rebuild during rest periods. In brass playing this means playing lightly or even choosing to rest instead of playing. As conductors plan for their concerts and competitions, there is usually an increase in the length and frequency of rehearsals as they get closer to a performance. This is helpful for gaining knowledge of the music and familiarity of those techniques it takes to play it. It is important to remember that although extra rehearsals in the day before and day of performances might enhance string, woodwind, and percussion playing, it also can *diminish* brass playing. Work to ensure that your brass players know their parts in advance of the other players. They will need to reduce playing right before a big concert rather than the opposite. Allow them to rest at times when running through the program if they can already play their parts. Although repetition is critical to a polished performance, tired brass players will make many more mistakes due only to their physical disposition.

One golden rule for repeating a section of a work when conducting is that you always should let the group know why you are asking them to play a section again. If there is something you want changed, you need to clarify that before playing again. Ensemble members, of all ages, do not appreciate just simply playing it over again, especially if they can hear mistakes and problems that need to be addressed. With brass players, remember that repetitions are physical in nature, and problems in accuracy and tuning make them more so. I can remember many repetitions of loud and high sections that killed our brass players because percussion players didn't understand when to play their parts. When this happens, spend some time with them alone, sing the brass parts, and give your brass players a rest! Engage with your players, and ask for their input during and after rehearsals. In this way many ensemble issues can be identified and remedied without involving the entire ensemble playing, so make use of alternate strategies to avoid needlessly tiring the brass section.

Finally, conductors too often, in my view, rely on rehearsal time to practice their own conducting. As the big concert or contest gets closer, they realize that they are not as prepared as they need to be, and they overuse the ensemble (their instrument) to cram at the last minute. I refer to many of the late dress rehearsals that I have observed as *panic rehearsals*. This is especially prevalent in rehearsals that are done right before a performance. Although this might be possible with a very short program, as is often the case in high school contest concerts, when planning longer programs, last-minute rehearsals can be devastating to brass players. In the professional ranks we even caution the conductor with "do you want it now or on the concert?" The panic that leads to last-minute rehearsing often is caused not by the lack of effort from the players but rather from the lack of planning and effort of the conductor. Be proactive and over-prepared earlier, and you will reach a higher level of music making. You always should consider how to save your brass players' valuable chop time from unnecessary repetitions that tire them needlessly, while you figure out how you want to conduct!

Exercises

- Take a section of your ensemble music when all the members of the brass section are playing. Start with only the first trumpet playing alone. Add the tuba and then the principals of each section. Pay special attention to balance and that all players can easily hear the first trumpet. Add section players, asking them to listen to the principals in their sections and not play louder than that voice. In the end, you can establish tuning and balance properties that players can apply to other situations as well.

- Encourage your principal trumpet and horn to learn their parts early, so they can determine their ability to play through the program and where they tire. Teach them how to use assistant players to create a shared plan for ensuring a consistent and exciting performance of the works in order. This can avoid those moments at the end of the program when everyone is tired and excitement suffers.

- Before introducing a work to your band, practice singing lines from the score at the correct pitch. Use the piano and your transposition skills to assure your accuracy. After you can deliver accurate renditions, be sure to use expression in your singing and conducting as you *practice* this method of performance from the podium.

21

CREATIVITY AND STUDENT OWNERSHIP

"Music is your own experience, your own thoughts, your wisdom. If you don't live it, it won't come out of your horn. They teach you there's a boundary line to music. But, man, there's no boundary line to art."

Charlie Parker
Jazz Saxophonist, Composer

The process of teaching and learning music, like all subjects, involves a delicate balance between organized, systematic progression and the freedom to depart from these systems when needed by the individual. This ability to depart is related directly to the concept of individual creativity, an essential element in musical decision making. From the first teaching a young student encounters, how this balance is struck impacts his or her creative thinking and approach to music. It is important to recall the cautionary concept of how teaching and learning, once organized into a systematic approach, are immediately limiting, so adherence to rigid constructs of thinking, by their very nature, restrict the ability to be creative in the broadest sense.

In music education, we have developed amazingly defined systems for learning music theory, music history, and performance. In my first freshman music theory class at Florida State, I was amazed at all the rules presented for writing music in four parts. It became clear that the class was presenting a historical manner of writing music, omitting much of the freedom and creativity involved in composition. What we really were learning was an *ideal* of music in theory, and our grades suffered if we departed from rigid rules. Even as a freshman I wondered why we spent so much time and effort on this type of study when I was already aware that many famous compositions in the past three centuries often departed from these rules. Although knowledge of historical composition styles is certainly valuable, I was struck by how we present them as *rules* that if broken, result in the punishment of lower grades and reputation with teachers. It seemed that the class should describe fully to students the antiquated and restrictive nature of this system to help them understand that music, in its truest definition, is *organized sound* and not bound by such rules. I also still cannot believe that basic music theory does not regularly teach the chord symbols used in jazz and popular music along with traditional Roman numeral analysis. By presenting both systems, it better prepares students for their musical careers and also instills a better understanding that what they are learning is one or two of many systems of writing and analyzing music.

The belief that creativity is essential to higher-level thinking has become an important part of the current national discussion as we contemplate the skills students will need to be successful in the future. Federal studies like the President's Committee on the Arts and the Humanities in their 2011 report, *Reinvesting in Arts Education: Winning America's Future Through Creative Schools*, and business organizations alike stress that problem solving through creative thinking is vital to the future of our next generation and the forward development of our society.[1]

As musicians, we use the term *creativity* everywhere as justification for our presence alongside subjects like math, science, and English. But sometimes, even we forget the flexible, individual approach creative thinking demands when we start to teach music in the classroom or in the private studio.

Currently there are ample educational strategies that promote systematic music learning with a wealth of supportive materials. With such models of teaching and learning, it is not surprising that many in our profession are attracted to a particular system in teaching and employ it to deliver music education to their students. It can be a favored band method book, tiered etude books, or even a prepackaged online learning system; all of these pre-organized systems offer a starting point for great learning. Unfortunately, such systematic approaches can also severely limit creativity in the learning environment if the teacher loses sight of the individuality that is essential in student learning.

As a studio teacher, I often am asked about which etude books I use, which warm-up is best, and which solos are the most important. If I am in my office, I usually open a very large drawer filled with etude books and tell them, "These are all fine." Of course, they do not like the answer, but then I continue with an explanation. It is not only what is in the books that is important. All of these books have exercises and etudes that can be used to develop technical mastery. It is how these materials are used that is vital to students and their learning experiences. I believe the same is true for band books and many other learning aids. They are more alike than different. What is truly important is the mind-set of the teacher and how he or she uses these aids, along with other strategies, to motivate students.

One of my predecessors ran all trumpet lessons in the same manner for all students. They played scales first, then etudes, and finally solos. If these exercises were technically acceptable, they were *checked off*, and more were assigned. When I heard these students upon my arrival in the program the next year, I was surprised to hear obvious playing weaknesses despite the fact that they had checked off many etudes in earlier semesters. They were not pleased when, during our first lessons together, I would listen to only part of an etude and attempt to engage them in critical listening and a deeper understanding of how they could improve their sound, articulation, or other facets of playing. It became clear to me, and eventually them, that earlier lessons did not demand the highest standards of playing, and even worse, students were not actively involved in substantial interpretation of their progress. In essence, they could have been learning how to lay bricks or make a martini. They followed a system of instructions, produced a generically correct rendition of the music, and then moved on to the next exercise in the sequence. They were missing out on the whole process of interpretation and expression through critical thinking.

Many students, of course, prefer to leave the evaluation of their work to others. It is an approach that requires less concentration, less awareness, and less discomfort. If the teacher passes off the etude, then it is deemed good. If they receive an A on the paper, then it *must* be good enough. It is too rare that students develop a more introspective approach to their education, especially at a young age. When students are invited to be active participants in their own learning, however, the limits on quality become limitless, and growth can be astounding. Why don't teachers tap into this process more often and more deeply? Perhaps it is because new thinking, new ways of playing, and new ways of measuring growth will challenge the system they employ in their teaching. Approaching students as unique individuals and contemplating their ideas for playing require much more time and focus from the teacher compared to plugging them into a systematic program.

When counseling students on careers, I usually draw a distinction between the two approaches to work that I mentioned earlier in this book. The *laborer* prefers to be told what to do, when they are finished, and the value of the work produced. When finished with these tasks, there is no more worrying about them or how to make them better. The *professional* is responsible for deciding what needs to be done, how much time to spend on it, and when it is finished. Because of the ownership of their work, they continue to consider how to make it better, even after the *workday*. How could a music student possibly imagine that the mind-set of a laborer could be successful in the field of music? Well, it is likely due to past experiences in music learning environments. The systems employed by ensemble directors and private teachers and how they balanced these with opportunities for creativity shape students and their understanding of what it means to be a *musician*. Student leadership in high school band programs can offer some great examples of the different approaches to student input in their musical development. Are students given responsibility for any aspect of the group, like chair placement, evaluation of music preparation, music selection for concerts and contests, or participation in musical festivals or events? You can find unbelievable variance in the manner in which band directors involve students in planning, decision making, and evaluation. In my high school experience, our director developed a system of student leadership that involved all of these activities. As a band officer, I was responsible for warming up the band, sight-reading new marches and overtures, and many other facets of the program. As a result, I felt some degree of ownership and responsibility for the program and thought about how to improve what we were doing outside of rehearsal or class time. I believe that these early experiences that offered opportunities for creative suggestions were vital to my later success in our profession.

In many schools, though, band directors do not develop leadership or ownership in their students. Perhaps it is seen as an unwise risk to empower students, or perhaps they do not feel that they have the time it takes to provide leadership opportunities. It is also possible that the system that these directors already use yields enough success in concerts and contests to make them question whether student leadership might take away from these achievements. The question I would ask is this: what about the education of the students? Is the goal simply a 1 rating at a contest? Who does that serve more: the future of the students or the future of the director? Are these directors missing out on an essential component of teaching? How do students develop critical thinking and problem solving if they are not asked to engage in these processes? For these students, their roles in music making are introduced too often as that of the laborer. They did what they were told when they were told and felt complete when they were told they were done. It should not be surprising that they would bring this mind-set into college even as a music major.

In the applied lesson, similar relationships can develop. Do students simply play what they are assigned in the manner directed? Will they have any choice in what etudes or music they will study? Will they be allowed to try new interpretations or ideas regarding performance? Will they learn how to truly evaluate their work and the work of others, or will the teacher always supply this evaluation?

Although younger students certainly need structure and discipline in teaching, it is also important to begin the process of ownership early. This can be done by offering opportunities for them to evaluate their playing by listening to recordings of themselves and also reacting while they are playing. It also can involve the evaluation of other students by placing them in the role of the teacher, even for a brief time. Mentoring of younger students by older students is also a great means to foster ownership as older students learn more about the role of the teacher and younger students see their older colleagues making decisions and value judgments.

Adopting a system for teaching and then applying it evenly to all students is a very simplistic way of approaching our profession. It is, of course, the easiest method of doing your job, and so many teachers, like laborers, go about their jobs doing what the principal, superintendent, department chair, or dean demand of them and then go home feeling complete when they are told they are done. These teachers are usually the ones asking their supervisors how much they are required to do and also complaining about the amount of work, regardless of how much time it takes. How many students, how many hours outside of class, how many concerts, how many competitions, and how much additional professional development are decided by others, and usually, that determines the focus of their planning.

Even when a music teacher fully expects that their students will arrive, eventually, at the same interpretation, evaluation, or conclusion as the teacher, it is worth the time to engage them in this process of self-awareness by independent thought. In doing so, you will help them gain confidence to learn on their own and eventually help others to learn in this manner as well. The benefit of having many fully engaged students learning together can unlock an enormous wealth of potential compared to what one teacher can offer by him- or herself. I often tell my university students that I consider them colleagues from the moment they walk in the door. The only difference between them and me is that I have more years of experience than they do. I also ask them if they think they are already good players and musicians. The usual response reveals that they are waiting for this affirmation from others. I then tell them, "Okay, you are a good player right now." If they are willing to accept this determination, then they will be more likely to accept the responsibilities required of a good player. They will strive to know when their playing is not ready and what to do to get it ready. They will also understand that good brass players prize individuality in how they interpret music, so they must be fearless in finding their own voice for the music they play.

Of course, many students shy away from this determination. It is easier to avoid responsibility and let others shoulder it and be liable for success or failure in music. They are surrounded by these messages from politicians, media figures, and many others, so it is not surprising that they embrace this concept. If you take control over your work and give the best possible effort, then you also must own the failures that might come along as well as the successes. The sooner students can confront this and learn to be self-motivated enough to overcome those low points that we all experience, the sooner they will be ready to soar as players and teachers.

Exercises

- Create levels of musical achievement for your high school band that correspond to officer positions, lettering in band, and qualification for other opportunities. Consider participation in solo/ensembles, composing, conducting, and the evaluation of fellow students and the band as you develop your levels.
- Bring several of your applied students together in a solo class, and have individual performances coached by other students. Let each student take a turn at being the *studio teacher* in this process. Simply by experiencing this, students will gain a better insight into becoming their own teachers, and it will help them gain more independence and ownership as music makers.

Note

1 President's Committee on the Arts and the Humanities, *Reinvesting in Arts Education: Winning America's Future Through Creative Schools*, Washington, DC, May 20.

BIBLIOGRAPHY

Agrell, Jeffrey. *Improvisation Games for Classical Musicians: A Collection of Musical Games with Suggestions for Use.* Chicago, IL: GIA Publications, 2007.

Baines, Anthony. *Brass Instruments: Their History and Development.* Minneola, NY: The Dover Press, 1993.

Barenboim, Daniel. *Music Quickens Time.* New York, NY: Verso Books, 2008.

Bernstein, Leonard. *The Unanswered Question: Six Talks at Harvard (The Charles Eliot Norton Lectures).* Cambridge, MA: Harvard University Press, 1976.

Copland, Aaron. *Music and Imagination.* Cambridge, MA: Harvard University Press, 1953.

Elliott, David J. "Musical Understanding, Musical Works, and Emotional Expression: Implications for Education." *Educational Philosophy and Theory* 31, no. 1 (February 2005): 93–103.

Farkas, Philip. *The Art of Brass Playing.* Bloomington, IN: Brass Publications, 1962.

Farkas, Philip. *The Art of French Horn Playing.* Van Nuys, CA: Alfred Music, 1956.

Fox, Fred. *Essentials for Brass Playing.* Van Nuys, CA: Alfred Publishing Co., 1982.

Frederiksen, Brian and John Taylor, *Arnold Jacobs: Song and Wind.* Gurnee, IL: Windsong Press, 1996.

Gabrielsson, Alf. "Emotional Expression in Music Performance: Between the Performer's Intention and the Listener's Experience." *Psychology of Music* 24, no. 1 (April 1996): 69–91.

Goff, Bryan. *Bryan Goff's Trumpet Pages.* http://www.bgoff.org.

Graham, David. "Teaching for Creativity in Music Performance." *Music Educators Journal* 84, no. 5 (March 1998): 24–28.

Green, Barry with Timothy Gallwey. *The Inner Game of Music.* New York, NY: Doubleday, 1986.

Haynie, John. *Inside John Haynie's Studio: A Master Teacher's Lessons on Trumpet and Life.* Denton, TX: University of North Texas Press, 2007.

Hunsberger, Donald and Roy E. Ernst. *The Art of Conducting.* New York, NY: McGraw-Hill Education, 1991.

Hunt, Norman. *Guide to Brass Playing.* Dubuque, IA: W.C. Brown, 1978.

Johnson, Keith. *Brass Performance and Pedagogy.* New York, NY: Pearson Education, 2002.

Kohut, Daniel L. *Musical Performance: Learning Theory and Pedagogy.* Engelwood Cliffs, NJ: Prentice Hall, 1985.

Lakin, James. "Basic Respiration for Wind Instrument Playing." *The Instrumentalist* 23, no. 9 (September 1969): 47–51.

Laudermilch, Kenneth. *An Understandable Approach to Musical Expression*. Galesburg, MD: Meredith Music Publications, 2000.

Lewis, Lucinda. *Broken Embouchures: An Embouchure Handbook and Repair Guide for Brass Players Suffering From Embouchure Problems Caused by Overuse, Injury, Medical/Dental Conditions, or Damaged Mechanics*. New York, NY: Oscar's House Press, 2002.

Little, Don. "A Young Tubist's Guide to the Breath." *TUBA Journal* (Winter 1981): 2–7.

Martin, Chris. "Six Months in Chicago," *Jay Friedman, Principal Trombonist, Chicago Symphony Orchestra*. 2006. http://www.jayfriedman.net/articles/six_months_in_chicago.

McAllister, Lesley Sisterhen. *The Balanced Musician: Integrating Mind and Body for Peak Performance*. Lanham, MD: Scarecrow Press, 2013.

McGill, David. *Sound in Motion: A Performer's Guide to Greater Musical Expression*. Bloomington, IN: Indiana University Press, 2007.

President's Committee on the Arts and the Humanities. *Reinvesting in Arts Education: Winning America's Future Through Creative Schools*. Washington, DC, May 20.

Ristad, Eloise. *A Soprano on Her Head: Right-Side-Up Reflections on Life and Other Performances*. Moab, UT: Real People, 1982.

Roth, Larry. "Mouthpiece Meditations." *Online Trombone Journal*. http://trombone.org/articles/library/mouthpiecemed1.asp.

Smithers, Donald. "Playing the Baroque Trumpet: Research Into the History and Physics of This Largely Forgotten Instrument Is Revealing Its Secrets, Enabling Modern Trumpeters to Play It as the Musicians of the 17th and 18th Centuries Did." *Scientific American* 254, no. 4 (April 1986): 108–115.

Stamp, James. *Warm-Ups and Studies for Trumpet*. Bulle, Switzerland: Editions BIM, 1978.

Trusheim, William H. *Mental Imagery and Musical Performance: An Inquiry Into Imagery Use by Eminent Orchestral Brass Players in the United States*. New Brunswick, NJ: Rutgers, the State University of New Jersey, 1987.

Weast, Robert D. *Brass Performance*. New York: McGinnis and Marx, 1961.

Whitener, Scott. *A Complete Guide to Brass: Instruments and Technique*. Boston, MA: Cengage Learning, 2007.

INDEX